CW01480927

RISK A

by

Professor Gordon C A Dickson

**Vice Principal and Pro Vice Chancellor
Glasgow Caledonian University**

OTHER BOOKS IN THE SERIES

Business Finance for Risk Management
Business Organisation and Finance
Corporate Risk Management
Insurance, Non Marine – An Introduction
Liability Exposures
Liability Risk and the Law
Local Government a Text for Risk Managers
Risk Control
Risk and the Business Environment
Risk Financing
Risk Management in Healthcare
Treasury Risk Management

British Library Cataloguing in Publication Data
Dickson, Professor Gordon C A
Risk Analysis – 3rd Ed.
1 Title
ISBN 1 85609 260 7

Notice of Terms of Use

The Institute of Risk Management
6, Lloyd's Avenue
London EC3N 3AX
www.theirm.org
Tel No: 020 7709 9808

RISK ANALYSIS

Third Edition

by

Professor Gordon C A Dickson

All rights reserved
Witherby & Co. Ltd.
32-36 Aylesbury Street,
London EC1R 0ET

1st Edition 1987
2nd Edition 1991
3rd Edition 2003

WITHERBYS
PUBLISHING

Professor Gordon C A Dickson

2003

ISBN 1 85609 260 7

Printed and Published by
WITHERBY & CO. LTD
32-36 Aylesbury Street
London EC1R 0ET
Tel No: 020 7251 5341   Fax No: 020 7251 1296
International Tel No: +44 20 7251 5341
International Fax No: +44 20 7251 1296
E-mail: books@witherbys.co.uk
www: witherbys.com

INTRODUCTION TO THIRD EDITION

It is sixteen years since the first edition of Risk Analysis appeared and ten since the last up-date. A very great deal has happened in the world of risk and risk management since then. We have seen the growth of global terrorism, some spectacular corporate collapses and the much greater emphasis on corporate governance on the running of organisations in the public and private sectors. We have also seen the growth in risk management as a discipline in its own right and the further embedding of risk management principles in many spheres of life.

Much of this text is almost independent of time as it covers general methodologies and approaches that can be applied no matter the nature of the risk itself or the changing environment in which risks occur. However, no text in the business world can stand completely unaltered over time and so this new edition up-dates the book throughout and adds a new chapter on certain risk analysis techniques that have merged over recent years.

I specifically acknowledge the assistance of Alistair Bulloch, Division of Risk, Caledonian Business School, Glasgow Caledonian University, in writing Chapter five.

I hope that you find this third edition to be of practical value and, if possible, even enjoyable!

Professor Gordon C A Dickson
Vice Principal and Pro Vice Chancellor
Glasgow Caledonian University
August 2003

INTRODUCTION TO SECOND EDITION

Three years ago, the introduction to the first edition of Risk Analysis began with a listing of major disasters. Since 1987, this list can be added to by such events as the King's Cross tube fire, Piper Alpha, Clapham rail crash, Lockerbie, Hillsborough and many others. All of those are in addition to the less dramatic catalogue of losses by fire, theft, accident, injury and disease.

The terrible toll of risk shows no sign of reducing and it is ever more important that organisations take steps to respond to risk in appropriate ways.

The first step in any risk management programme is the identification of risk. Nothing can be done by way of control and management unless risks are identified. The focus of this text remains the identification and analysis of risk.

Prof GCA Dickson
Glasgow December 1990

INTRODUCTION TO FIRST EDITION

Events such as those at Flixborough, Three Mile Island, Mexico City and Zeebrugge have impressed upon the public the importance of risk and of being able to identify it. In a much less dramatic way we are all exposed to risk both in our private and business life. The toll of risk in financial and human terms continues to increase each year and if risk is to be managed then the first step is to ensure that we have adequate mechanisms for identification and analysis. There can be little doubt that as business becomes more and more complex there will be ever increasing demands on those whose task it is to identify risk.

This book looks at the whole question of risk analysis. It starts with individual people and examines their attitude to risk and then moves on to the more objective ground of identification methodologies and statistical risk analysis. It concludes, as it started, with people and the communication of the results of risk analysis by means of reports.

Those who are new to the business of risk analysis will find that they are unfamiliar with many of the concepts in this book. They are however concepts which are widely used in industry. It is worthwhile remembering that the techniques of risk identification and analysis are practical and not theoretical tools. They had their origin in solving practical problems and so while you may not use all of them they nevertheless have their part to play. It is not possible to cover every industry type and so readers will have to take the basic theory and apply it to their own industry as best they can. However, risk analysis is important in its own right quite apart from any particular form of risk or individual industry.

Finally, I have benefited from discussions with very many risk managers over the years and I hope that this is reflected in the text. While it may be possible to measure the part other risk managers have played, the contribution of ones own family is beyond measure and their continued support is acknowledged now.

Dr GCA Dickson
Glasgow, October 1987

Contents

1

RISK ANALYSIS

1.1   INTRODUCTION

No course in Risk Management would be complete without the inclusion of a major component on risk analysis. Risk analysis acts as a kind of hub, around which many other practical aspects of risk management rotate.

This book concentrates on risk analysis and later in this chapter we will outline the scope of the book. In the meantime let us be clear what we mean by risk analysis. Collins *New English Dictionary* defines analysis as 'the division of a physical or abstract whole into its constituent parts to examine or determine their relationship'. There is also now a risk management standard and it sets out a definition of risk analysis, to which we will return in Section 1.3.

This is a good way to begin to think about the task of risk analysis. We are going to divide risk into its constituent parts. Viewed this way, risk analysis is more than just the identification of risks or the measurement of risk. It is a far broader task which will incorporate these two specific functions and others.

The diagram in Fig 1.1 shows the various stages of risk analysis.

Fig 1.1

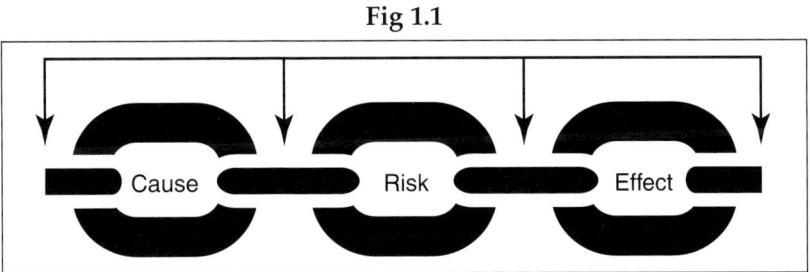

Various Stages of Risk Analysis

Every risk is caused by some factor or factors and results in some effect or effects. It can be viewed rather like a chain. The cause is linked to the nature of the risk and the risk itself is linked to the effect. Risk analysis is necessary at each stage in the chain.

There is need for the analysis of causes not yet known. We must look, in other words, for potential causes of risk. For example we must be vigilant in monitoring the use of new chemicals or other hazardous substances. New processes or methods of construction must be looked at carefully. Risk analysis is not limited to identifying those things which we know can cause loss.

The second link is between known causes and risk. We must apply careful and rigorous analysis to ensure that all known causes of risk are high-lighted.

Thirdly we must evaluate the impact of risk on an organisation, this is the third link, and at the fourth and last link we must ensure that all effects are identified, not just ones which have previously occurred.

1.2　THE NATURE OF RISK ANALYSIS

So far we have not said exactly what we mean by risk analysis. We have decided that it is a comprehensive task involving the risk manager and his department in a great deal of work, but what does that work entail?

For the purposes of this text book, we have divided risk analysis into three broad areas. Those areas are not necessarily of any operational importance but they should help us to build up a picture of all that is involved in the analysis of risk.

1.2.1　Risk and Human Behaviour

The first of our three aspects of risk analysis looks at the psychology of risk. It is important that those who will carry out risk analysis understand how others view risk and how they behave in the face of risk. If we understand a little better how people respond to risk then we may be able to frame our proposals and suggestions to them in different ways.

It is also important that we understand how people behave in groups as this is such an important aspect of business life. Many decisions are taken by groups or committees and the risk manager will often find himself having to report to or convince a committee on some point or other.

Chapter two looks at this whole area and attempts to provide a practical insight into risk and human behaviour. Towards the end of the book we also look at the general issue of communicating risk information and the particular task of writing reports.

1.2.2   Risk Analysis Methodology

The risk manager is not without practical assistance when beginning the task of risk analysis. The manager can call on an armoury of techniques designed to aid the task. It is unlikely that one technique will solve all problems or indeed that one technique alone is suitable for all industry types. There is a range of techniques, some of which are quantitative in nature and some qualitative, on which a manager can call.

These techniques have all been developed in the industrial setting, normally in response to some practical business problem, and they include physical inspections, organisational charts, check lists, flow charts, fault trees, hazard and operability studies and hazard indices.

Chapters three and four concentrate on these techniques and make use of a practical business problem which is followed through the chapters. Over recent years a number of new techniques have emerged and these are outlined in Chapter five.

1.2.3   Statistical Analysis

There is no doubt that we are living in an era when the use of numbers is becoming more and more important. The inexpensive desk-top micro computer means that many computational processes can now be carried out with ease and with the minimum of expertise.

In the field of risk management where data should be readily available then it is essential that the modern risk manager be aware of the uses to which statistical analysis can be put.

Chapters six, seven and eight introduce readers to the basic concepts of statistics and probability. The theory has been kept to a minimum and the emphasis is very much on practical application.

As we said earlier, these three aspects of risk analysis should not be looked upon as discrete components of the one discipline. They are split in this way only for the purposes of learning and in the real world there is a large measure of transferability among the three.

1.3   THE RISK MANAGEMENT STANDARD

In the introductory section of this chapter we made reference to the Risk Management Standard produced by IRM, AIRMIC and ALARM in 2002. This Standard is a step forward and resulted from a major piece of work involving these three bodies and others with an interest in risk. The Standard sets out to offer an agreed view on terminology, process, structure and objectives in relation to risk management. It is important therefore that we pause to reflect a little on what the Standard has to say about Risk Analysis, the subject of this text. The Standard is published by the three bodies mentioned above and copies can be obtained from them. The kind permission of IRM, AIRMIC and ALARM to use extracts from the Standard is recorded here.

Let us start with a definition. We have already used a common dictionary definition to help us disaggregate the components of risk analysis, but what does the Standard say? The Standard uses, as far as possible, the terminology for risk set out in the International Organisation for Standardisation (ISO) document, *"ISO/IEC Guide 73 Risk Management – Vocabulary – Guidelines for use in standards"*. In that Guide, risk analysis is defined as, *"the systematic use of information to identify sources and to estimate the risk"*. This is picked up by the Standard and Risk Analysis is then displayed as a three-fold process involving risk identification, risk description and risk estimation.

The following text is extracted from the Standard. It defines what the three parts of the risk analysis process are and ends with a reference to risk analysis methods and risk profiles.

An extract from "A Risk Management Standard"

Risk Identification

Risk identification sets out to identify an organisation's exposure to uncertainty. This requires an intimate knowledge of the organisation, the market in which it operates, the legal, social, political and cultural environment in which it exists, as well as the development of a sound understanding of its strategic and operational objectives, including factors critical to its success and the threats and opportunities related to the achievement of these objectives.

Risk identification should be approached in a methodical way to ensure that all significant activities within the organisation have been identified and all the risks flowing from these activities defined. All associated volatility related to these activities should be identified and categorised.

Business activities and decisions can be classified in a range of ways, examples of which include:

- Strategic – These concern the long-term strategic objectives of the organisation. They can be affected by such areas as capital availability, sovereign and political risks, legal and regulatory changes, reputation and changes in the physical environment.

- Operational – These concern the day-to-day issues that the organisation is confronted with as it strives to deliver its strategic objectives.

- Financial – These concern the effective management and control of the finances of the organisation and the effects of external factors such as availability of credit, foreign exchange rates, interest rate movement and other market exposures.

- Knowledge Management – These concern the effective management and control of the knowledge resources, the production, protection and communication thereof. External factors might include the unauthorised use or abuse of intellectual property, area power failures, and competitive technology. Internal factors might be system malfunction or loss of key staff.

- Compliance – These concern such issues as health & safety, environmental, trade descriptions, consumer protection, data protection, employment practices and regulatory issues.

Whilst risk identification can be carried out by outside consultants, an in-house approach with well communicated, consistent and co-ordinated processes and tools is likely to be more effective. In-house 'ownership' of the risk management process is essential.

Risk Description

The objective of risk description is to display the identified risks in a structured format, for example, by using a table. The risk description table can be used to facilitate the description and assessment of risks. The use of a well designed structure is necessary to ensure a comprehensive risk identification, description and assessment process. By considering the consequence and probability of each of the risks set out in the table, it should be possible to prioritise the key risks that need to be analysed in more detail. Identification of the risks associated with business activities and decision making may be categorised as strategic, project/tactical, operational. It is important to incorporate risk management at the conceptual stage of projects as well as throughout the life of a specific project.

Table 1.1 Risk Description

1	Name of Risk	
2	Scope of Risk	Qualitative description of the events, their size, type, number and dependencies
3	Nature of Risk	E.g. Strategic, operational, financial, knowledge or compliance
4	Stakeholders	Stakeholders and their expectations
5	Quantification of Risk	Significance and Probability
6	Risk Tolerance/Appetite	Loss potential and financial impact of risk. Value at risk. Probability and size of potential losses/gains. Objective(s) for control of the risk and desired level of performance
7	Risk Treatment and Control Mechanisms	Primary means by which the risk is currently managed. Levels of confidence in existing control. Identification of protocols for monitoring and review
8	Potential Action for Improvement	Recommendations to reduce risk
9	Strategy and Policy Developments	Identification of function responsible for developing strategy and policy

Risk Estimation

Risk estimation can be quantitative, semi-quantitative or qualitative in terms of the probability of occurrence and the possible consequence.

For example, consequences both in terms of threats (downside risks) and opportunities (upside risks) may be high, medium or low. Probability may be high, medium or low but requires different definitions in respect of threats and opportunities.

Examples are given in the tables that follow. Different organisations will find that different measures of consequence and probability will suit their needs best.

For example, many organisations find that assessing consequence and probability as high, medium or low is quite adequate for their needs and can be presented as a 3x3 matrix.

Other organisations find that assessing consequence and probability using a 5x5 matrix gives them a better evaluation.

Table 1.2 Consequences – Both Threats and Opportunities

High	Financial impact on the organisation is likely to exceed £X. Significant impact on the organisation's strategy or operational activities. Significant stakeholder concern.
Medium	Financial impact on the organisation likely to be between £X and £Y. Moderate impact on the organisation's strategy or operational activities. Moderate stakeholder concern.
Low	Financial impact on the organisation likely to be less than £Y. Low impact on the organisation's strategy or operational activities. Low stakeholder concern.

Table 1.3 Probability of Occurrence – Threats

Estimation	Description	Indicators
High (Probable)	Likely to occur each year or more than 25% chance of occurrence.	Potential of it occurring several times within the time period (for example – ten years). Has occurred recently.
Medium (Possible)	Likely to occur in a ten year time period or less than 25% chance of occurrence.	Could occur more than once within the time period (for example – ten years). Could be difficult to control due to some external influences. Is there a history of occurrence?
Low (Remote)	Not likely to occur in a ten year period or less than 2% chance of occurrence.	Has not occurred. Unlikely to occur.

Table 1.4 Probability of Occurrence – Opportunities

Estimation	Description	Indicators
High (Probable)	Favourable outcome is likely to be achieved in one year or better than 75% chance of occurrence.	Clear opportunity which can be relied on with reasonable certainty, to be achieved in the short term based on current management processes.
Medium (Possible)	Reasonable prospects of favourable results in one year of 25% to 75% chance of occurrence.	Opportunities which may be achievable but which require careful management. Opportunities which may arise over and above the plan.
Low (Remote)	Some chance of favourable outcome in the medium term or less than 25% chance of occurrence.	Possible opportunity which has yet to be fully investigated by management. Opportunity for which the likelihood of success is low on the basis of management resources currently being applied.

Risk Analysis Methods and Techniques

A range of techniques can be used to analyse risks. These can be specific to upside or downside risk or be capable of dealing with both.

Risk Profile

The result of the risk analysis process can be used to produce a risk profile which gives a significant rating to each risk and provides a tool for prioritising risk treatment efforts. This ranks each identified risk so as to give a view of the relative importance.

This process allows the risk to be mapped to the business area affected, describes the primary control procedures in place and indicates areas where the level of risk control investment might be increased, decreased or re-apportioned.

Accountability helps to ensure that 'ownership' of the risk is recognised and the appropriate management resource allocated.

In this text, the three areas of identification, description and estimation feature prominently. Specific chapters are devoted to the methodological approach to risk identification advocated in the Standard, as we said in 1.2.2, and in addition time is spent on understanding the techniques for estimating risk, mentioned in 1.2.3. As you read through the book, you will see the practical relevance of the Standard.

1.4   THE COST OF RISK

Before moving on to look at these practical aspects of risk analysis we shall take time here to place risk in perspective and to consider its cost.

Historical events at Flixborough, Seveso, Bhopal and Chernobyl all served to concentrate the mind of many on the catastrophic cost of certain risks. More recently we have seen major acts of global terror and a number of corporate collapses of a quite spectacular nature. Fortunately these large scale incidents are relatively infrequent and the day-to-day work of the risk manager revolves around much smaller incidents. They may be smaller but the personal suffering and financial effect may be just as acute.

1.4.1   The Costs to Individuals

For individuals the cost of risk can be measured in a number of ways. There are those risks which involve a personal injury, a loss of personal effects, damage to property and so on. There will be few people in the country who have not suffered at the hands of some risk or know someone who has.

The following Table illustrates some broad, United Kingdom-based figures for different forms of risk that cover the period 2000 or 2001.

The Reality of Risk

Type	Number	
Road Casualties[1]	– Deaths	3,450
	– Death or Serious Injury	41,200
	– All Severities	313,000
Accidents at Work[1]	– Fatal Work Injuries	252
	– Major Injuries	28,154
	– Over three days off	134,820
Insurance Claims[2]	– Fire Claims	£855m
	– Theft Claims	£740m
	– Motor Vehicle Claims	£7,078m

[1] *Annual Abstract of Statistics* (ISBN 92 64 09795-3)
[2] *ABI Insurance Trends 2002* (ISSN 13540734)

The purpose is simply to provide some perspective to the often abstract debate about risk. These incidents are everyday occurrences and put risk in perspective as far as individuals are concerned. What these figures show is that, for example, there are more than 36 road casualties every hour of every day throughout the year, over three people suffer a major injury at work during the time it takes us to watch an hour's television programme and about £225 every second of every day is spent on motor claims.

1.4.2   The Costs to the Country

Measuring the impact of risk on the country as a whole is a much more difficult task. We can fairly easily ask individuals how much they lost, for example in a fire, and what the personal trauma was like. It is not so easy to ask a large company and it is almost impossible to gauge the impact of, say, the fire risk on a country.

What we can do is look at some of the available figures.

The cost of fire claims met by members of the Association of British Insurers in 2000 was £855m. This means that, on average, £27 went up in flames every single second of that year. Put another way it means that if this loss was to be borne by everyone who was in employment that year then such people would have to have paid about £34 each.

It is important to make one point in relation to the cost of fire claims. It is that the claims figure does not include the full economic cost of the disruption caused by the fire. This means that all business interruption losses, i.e. loss of profits, increase in cost of working etc, together with all the spin-off effects of fires are not included. It is impossible to measure accurately what multiplier should be applied to the fire claims figure in order to arrive at the total economic cost but some industrial economists have suggested that it could be as high as eight. Whatever multiplier we use, we end up with an extremely large figure and in terms of the cost to the country, fire makes a considerable impact.

We looked earlier at the number of injuries at work. Whenever there is a serious injury at work then there will be lost production time, with all the consequences of that, there may be the need for re-training, cleaning or repair of machinery, time off for attendance at court or inquests. Again, a multiplier would be required to arrive at the full impact on the country.

So far we have only mentioned fire and accidents at work, but in 2000 insurance companies paid £740m for theft related claims, and we need to add to that list product liability claims, fraud, weather, marine and aviation claims, etc, etc, in order to get a fuller picture.

All of these losses are a cost to the country and must be paid for in some way. There may be insurance in force but in the end the cost of that insurance, and indeed the cost of losses where there is no insurance, is simply passed on to the consumer. In exactly the same way, the cost to the country of individual personal losses is also a drain on the economy as money has to be directed towards it rather than to some other, more productive use.

The whole role of risk analysis is one of national importance. Risks have to be identified and their impact measured. Private individuals and organisations of all kinds must venture on in the face of risk and the role of the risk manager, in relation to his organisation, is to ensure that he has adequately analysed the risks to which his company is exposed.

1.5   THE COST OF RISK ANALYSIS

So far we have tried to place risk itself in perspective. We will conclude this chapter by looking at the cost of risk analysis and try to place these costs in perspective.

Two points are worth making. The first is the obvious point that you cannot spend a ridiculous amount on risk analysis. There would be no point in going to elaborate steps to mount risk analysis for a risk which even in the worst case could not cost as much as the analysis. Students of risk analysis often miss this point in their enthusiasm. Faced with a question or problem they will apply elaborate and sophisticated risk analysis tools when the risk was not worthy of that level of attention.

The second point is that the company may not want to spend a lot of money on analysis of a particular risk. There may be some risk which is well known by the company and accepted as a necessary trading cost. It has been looked at carefully over the years and so there is little need to spend more time on it.

Having made these two preliminary points we could go on to say that we must always look for some benefit from the cost of risk analysis. We hope that the risk analysis will highlight risks which have not been identified before and will then allow us to take controlling action, thus reducing losses and consequently loss costs. However the benefit from our analysis may not be apparent immediately and may not even be apparent in the short to medium term.

Consequently, it is very difficult to decide when you are no longer getting benefit from the analysis. There will come a point when each additional pound spent on risk analysis is in fact losing money for the company rather than saving it.

The drawing in Fig 1.2 tries to illustrate this point. We can see that as the costs of risk analysis increase, so the return changes from positive to negative. The risk manager must always have a picture like this in his mind so that he continues to work within reasonable financial parameters.

Fig 1.2

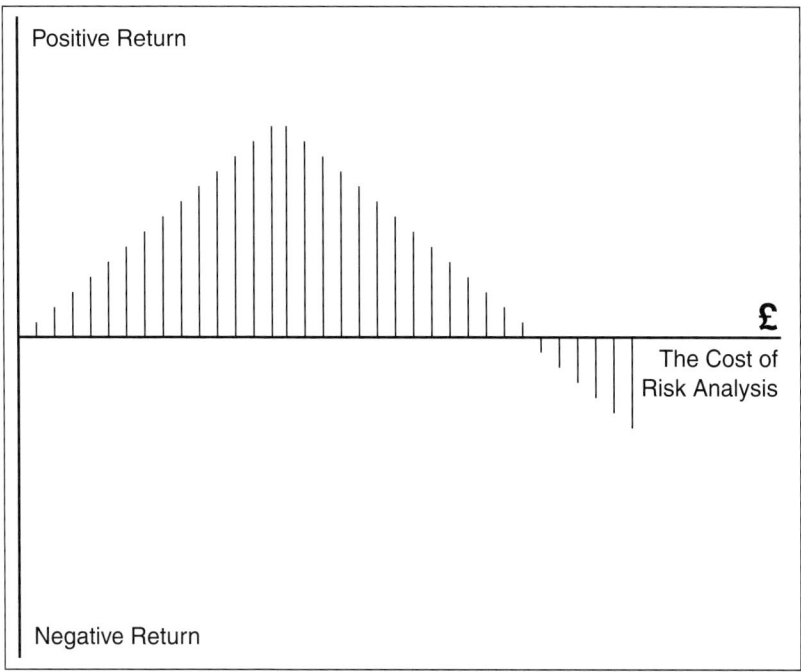

Positive and Negative Return

1.6   CONCLUSION

Having made all these introductory remarks concerning risk analysis we can now move on to the technicalities of the process itself. As we have said already, the remainder of this text concentrates on the different aspects of risk analysis. It is structured around the following chapters.

Chapter 2 – Risk and Human Behaviour
Chapter 3 – Identifying Risk 1
Chapter 4 – Identifying Risk 2
Chapter 5 – Identifying Risk 3
Chapter 6 – Statistical Analysis of Risk 1
Chapter 7 – Statistical Analysis of Risk 2
Chapter 8 – Probability
Chapter 9 – Communicating Risk

2

RISK AND HUMAN BEHAVIOUR

2.1 INTRODUCTION

In any book or course of study concerned with risk management a great proportion of space and time must be devoted to the practical aspects of risk identification, measurement and control. Often, however, in the rush to introduce those ideas, comparatively little attention is given to the nature of risk itself.

In Chapter one we tried to bring risk into perspective and in this present chapter we endeavour to place risk in a human perspective. We do this not in an attempt to dwell needlessly on theory but in an effort to enhance our total understanding of risk and its management. The whole area of risk and human behaviour could well occupy an entire text but in the context of a book on Risk Analysis we can confine ourselves to particular aspects.

The chapter is roughly in two parts. The first part concentrates on attitudes to risk and how such attitudes can be measured. The second part is concerned with the role that risk plays in the decision making process, a process with which the risk manager is not unfamiliar!

2.2 RISK AND HUMAN BEHAVIOUR

The picture painted in the previous chapter is one which emphasises the pervasive nature of risk. Risk enters into all aspects of life, it is as one person put it, "the sugar and salt of life". In the face of this omnipresent risk each one of us must make our choices as to how we will behave.

When we look around we see wide variations in response to risk. There are those who voluntarily assume risk by, for example, participating in some dangerous sport, those who select a hazardous occupation and others who gamble regularly. On the other hand some people rarely venture out of their armchair, prefer sedentary jobs and insure everything in sight. In short we are all different. There is no one 'correct' behavioural response to risky situations.

If this is the case for private individuals then it is equally accurate for business. Some banks lend money on far riskier ventures than others, some oil companies seem to exhibit more risky behaviour in their drilling decisions than others, certain exporters transact business with countries where the risk element is high while others avoid such countries.

This phenomenon exists and is easy to observe in the real world. When we turn our attention to risk management then the whole question of behaviour in risky situations is brought into sharp focus. In risk management we see individual behaviour combining with corporate behaviour. From the individual's point of view we see him or her faced with the risk of, for example, personal injury and having to decide whether or not to use the machine guard, the 'hard hat', the safety shield or the barrier cream. From the standpoint of the company we see it responding to exactly the same risks but for different reasons. It is not only concerned with the personal injury of the employees but must also consider the overall costs to the company of any risk materializing.

In situations like this it would clearly be advantageous for the behaviour of the individual to match the needs of the organisation, for example, by the person responding positively to safety advice. In order, however, to maximize the likelihood of this it would be useful to understand, to a certain extent, the nature of human behaviour in risky situations. If we can move towards some understanding of this, then such knowledge would not be limited to applications in the field of safety and accident prevention. An understanding of behaviour in risky situations could be applied to the whole range of risk management including, as we will see later, the important function of decision making.

In the meantime let us comment briefly on the relationship between attitudes and behaviour. So far we have concentrated only on behaviour. This is understandable as it is how people behave which is important, but what influence does attitude have? The extent to which attitudes determine behaviour represents a vast area of literature, and one which is full of competing views. For our purposes we might follow a model provided by the psychologist Kurt Lewin in the 1930s. He suggested that behaviour was a function of the interaction of a person's inner determinants, including attitudes, and environmental features as perceived by the individual.

This may seem rather theoretical but in operational terms it does make sense. You may have a very strong attitude against cigarette smoking, and if you were sitting in a restaurant and smoke began to drift in front of you, your reaction might be to object. When you look round and see that the person responsible is a six and a half feet 'all-in' wrestler you may allow this 'environmental' factor to modify your attitude.

In terms of risk management we can imagine circumstances where less extreme modifications of attitude may result. For example, a person may wish to avoid the risk of injury from a machine but may only use the guard when his 'mates' are not looking, just in case they think he is less of a man; a risk manager may have a very risk averse attitude and may want to spend money on some risk control mechanism but may have to modify his plans in the light of budget targets set by his finance manager.

Behaviour, then, is the result of your attitude reacting with the environment, as you see it. When the environment matches what we want to do then our attitude is a good predictor of behaviour but in other cases the person's perception of the environment may lead to some different form of behaviour than that predicted solely by attitude.

Whatever happens we all respond in some way and it might be useful to be able to predetermine what kind of attitude people have to risk. If we could do this then we might avoid placing people who may take risks into dangerous situations. In the same way we might avoid placing people who avoid risk into situations where some element of risk taking may be required. In other words the company knows the kind of people it would like in given situations and could use the knowledge gained of attitudes towards risk in the placing of individuals and their matching to specific tasks.

A knowledge of what a workforce feel about risk could also be useful in terms of how the company should promote safety training and education. If we have some idea of how the workforce perceive risks within the workplace then this could give positive guidance to the risk manager for his overall approach to safety education.

2.3   MEASURING ATTITUDES TOWARDS RISK

From the vast literature on measuring attitudes towards risk we can detect, at least, two broad methods emerging. It is important to say at this stage that it is extremely difficult, verging on impossible, to state that one person is a risk seeker and another a risk avoider. The best that can be achieved by most tests is a differentiation among people so that we can then say that one person is more of a risk seeker than another.

The first method is based around a concept known as the 'Standard Gamble' and is concerned with measuring attitude to risk in a financial setting. The second category of measurement techniques does not rely on judgement in a financial setting. It is more concerned with measuring 'how' individuals perceive risk. This latter category of methods is probably more important to risk management but in view of its importance, in the overall study of attitudes to risk, let us mention briefly the meaning of the standard gamble.

2.3.1   The Standard Gamble

Let us say that you were offered a gamble where you stood to win £40 on the toss of a coin. If the coin lands heads up you win £40, if tails up you win £0. This is a straightforward 50/50 bet, there is a 50% chance of winning £40 and a 50% chance of gaining nothing. Put this gamble on one side and now assume that you have been offered a certain amount of money, rather than a gamble. In other words you can play the gamble or have a sure amount of money. The question is, what is the least amount you would accept, for sure, rather than play the gamble?

For each one of us there is a unique amount of money at which, if we were offered it for sure, we would be indifferent between accepting it and playing the gamble. This is shown in a diagrammatic form in Fig 2.1.

The sure amount of £Z is really the equivalent, in certain money, to the gamble. It is often referred to as the certainty equivalent. In our example A would be £40 and B £0 and the probabilities of achieving either is 50/50. The figure of Z would be decided upon by the individual. A person may, for example, decide that he would be indifferent between accepting £10 for sure and the gamble where he could win £40 or nothing at all at a probability of 0.5 (in a scale where certainty = 1.0).

Fig 2.1

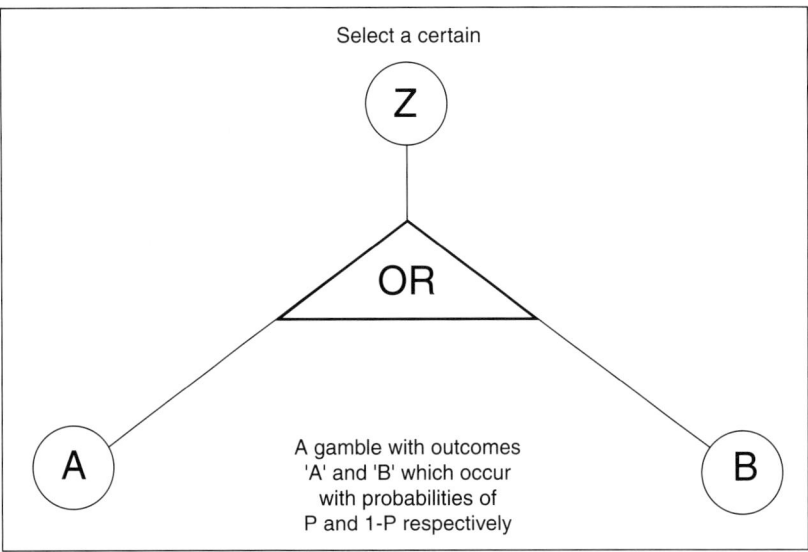

The Differences Between Accepting and Playing the Standard Gamble if given a Unique Amount of Money

With a large number of people answering the same question we could then rank them according to how much or how little their certainty equivalents were. Apart from that we can measure the extent to which each person deviated from the 'mathematically rational' answer. This mathematical or objectively rational answer is based on the fact that the 'expected value' of the gamble is £20, i.e. half the time you win £40 and half the time you gain nothing, therefore, in the long run you should 'expect' £20. If a person would accept less than the expected value then he has a preference for certainty while the person who would require more than the expected value could be classed as a risk taker.

This can be illustrated by taking the two extremes. If he was indifferent between accepting £1 for sure and taking the gamble then we would say he was extremely risk averse. On the other hand if the least amount a person would accept before giving up his right to gamble was £39 then we would say he had an extreme liking for risk.

There were several variations on the basic theme of the standard gamble but in essence they attempt to elicit some point or figure at which a person is indifferent between recovering, or paying, some certain amount and taking a chance.

One final example may illustrate the standard gamble in the context of risk management. Assume that an employee or third party has raised an action for damages against your company. The writ shows that they are suing for £10,000. As is very common, you know that the individual would accept an 'out of court' figure rather than take the trouble and risk associated with pursuing his claim through the court. From the company's position it must decide how much it would be prepared to pay in order to settle the claim. In short, it must decide the point or figure at which it would be indifferent between giving that amount as an out of court settlement and taking the chances associated with the case, of possibly being awarded £10,000 or nothing or some figure in between. This is the basic structure of the standard gamble. Let us say that counsel's opinion is that the plaintiff stands a 50/50 chance of success; referring back to our earlier example, we can judge how risk seeking or risk averse the company is in relation to the 'expected' payout of £5,000 (£10,000 − fifty percent of the time).

A company which is basically risk averse − avoids risks − would be willing to pay over £5,000 to settle. A company or individual risk manager may however be a little more risk seeking and not willing to go more than say £3,000.

Interestingly this same problem can be viewed from the individual plaintiff's point of view. He must decide how much he would accept − this time the minimum he would accept − before preferring to take the case to court with the chances of being awarded £10,000.

2.3.2 Perception of Risks

As we said earlier, the standard gamble has perhaps only limited application in the field of risk management. What we move on to now are techniques which have a more practical outlet.

A number of techniques have been developed which measure

a person's view or perception of risk by asking how likely an individual considers certain events to be. For example, a number of causes of death could be given to people and they are to suggest how many died from these causes. In this way we would see not only which causes were inaccurately assessed but also which people were not accurate in their assessment.

In risk management terms we could mention two techniques of this type and we will illustrate each one with a brief example.

Let us say that in a particular factory the risk manager has detected an unwillingness, among the workforce, to use machine guards. This unwillingness has been accompanied by a deterioration in the accident experience. The risk manager has a feeling that the workforce do not consider the machines they use to be as potentially dangerous as they are in fact. He/she gathers information on the seven types of machines in the factory and finds the number of accidents on each one during the last year to be:

Machines	Accidents
A	15
B	10
C	21
D	4
E	7
F	18
G	17

He/she prepares a brief form which asks the machine operators how many accidents they consider happened on each of the machines last year. There will have to be some careful definition of 'accident' and what is meant by 'last year'. Assuming these points can be overcome then the questions could be put to the employees. It may be useful to provide them with some 'anchoring' figure and so he could give them one of the actual figures. The form may look like that shown in Fig 2.2. The machines would not, of course, be described as A, B, C, etc, but by the name most familiar to the employees. This may or may not be the makers' name but it must clearly define the machine, in the eyes of the employees.

Fig 2.2

What is your estimate of the number of accidents that happened on each of the following machines during the last twelve months?

As a guide to you, the actual number of accidents on machine "E" has been put in.

Machine	Your Estimates of No. of Accidents
A	. . .
B	. . .
C	. . .
D	. . .
E	7
F	. . .
G	. . .

Thanks for you help in completing this form!

A Perception of Risk Questionnaire

To avoid any possibility of collusion it is probably best to give each person a form and wait for it to be completed. Once all the forms are returned the risk manager can calculate the average response for each machine. Let us say when this has been done we find, for the two hundred and fifty employees involved, that the average responses are:

Machine	Average estimate of No of accidents
A	13
B	16
C	25
D	3
E	7
F	15
G	16

We can tell at once that of the six estimates, four have been underestimated and two overestimated. This can be illustrated by a simple graph as in Fig 2.3. If the estimated number of accidents had matched the actual number exactly, then we would have ended up with a straight line which would cut the graph at an angle of 45°. What the risk manager found was that in the case of two machines the workforce overestimated the number of accidents, these are the two above the line. The number of accidents was underestimated for four machines, these falling below the line. The actual figure was provided for machine 'E' and so this falls on the line exactly.

Fig 2.3

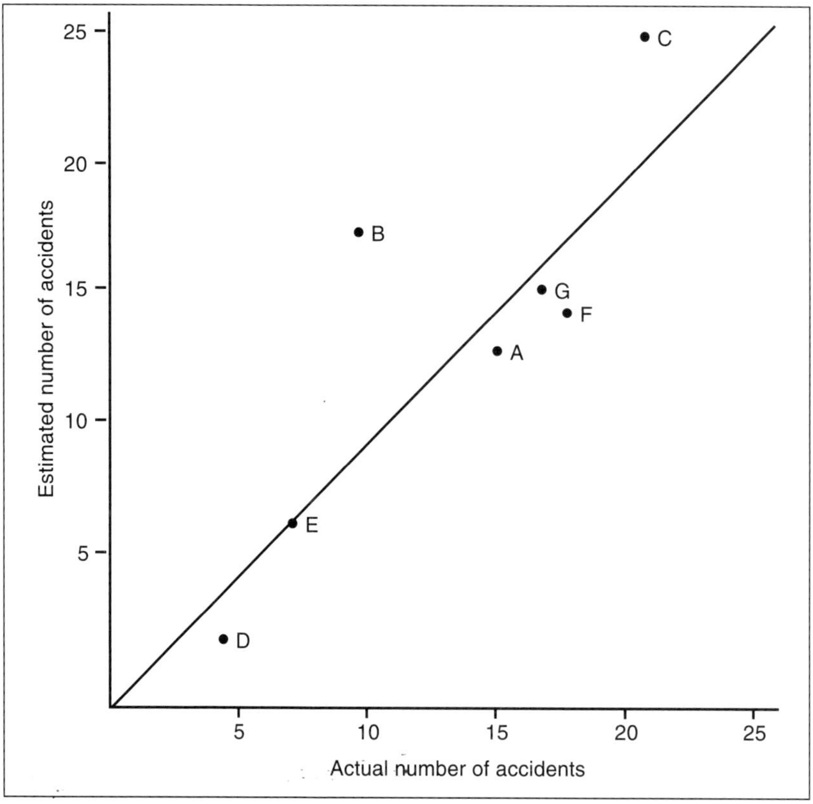

A Graph of Estimated Versus Actual Number of Accidents

The risk manager now has some idea of how the employees perceive the risk of injury from these machines. On the whole they do seem to underestimate the risks involved. In the case of one machine, however, machine 'B', the risk of injury was dramatically over-estimated. It can be seen from the graph that machines 'B' and 'G' were viewed by people as having the same number of accidents whereas, in fact, machine 'B' had seven accidents less than 'G'.

This knowledge may now be of some use to the risk manager in efforts to encourage the use of machine guards. There is some information on how the workforce perceive the risk of injury from the machines they use and the risk manager may perhaps decide to concentrate, as a start, on the machines where accident potential was underestimated.

The second technique we will illustrate, under the general heading of perception of risk, is one concerning the ranking of risks. In the above illustration people were asked to estimate the actual number representing their perception of risk. In this next technique the task is made simpler by only requiring that each person 'ranks' various things.

Let us say that the risk manager of a large construction company is looking into the whole question of employers' liability claims. She has extracted information from her records of all such incidents over the past few years.

In order to have some national comparison she categorises the various incidents according to the classifications used by the Health and Safety Executive. She finds the following number of incidents under each heading.

Fall or trip on level ground	180
Struck by an object	101
Fall from a height	97
Over-exertion, strenuous, awkward, movements	45
Caught under or between an object	20
Striking against an object	11
Rubbed, or abrased by an object	5
Electrical current	2

Rather than ask the workforce to estimate the number of accidents they feel are generated within these categories, an alternative strategy is adopted. This time the employees are asked to rank the eight different types of incident in order of likelihood. Therefore if a person believed that the most likely type of accident was that involving over-exertion then he would assign it the rank of '1'. The cause which he considered least likely would then be ranked number '8'.

The risk manager knows the correct ranking for her company, as she has the figures which we illustrated above. When the rankings are worked out for the workforce it will give some clue as to how the people, most closely involved, perceive the risk of accident.

A simple question form is shown in Fig 2.4.

Fig 2.4

A number of different causes of accident are shown on this form. You are in the best position to say how important each of these causes is.

Would you decide which cause produces most accidents and put the number 1 against it. Put the 2 against the cause which in your view produces the next highest number of accidents and so on until you place an 8 against the cause which you think produces the least number of accidents.

Type of Incident

Rubbed or abrased by an object	. . . .
Struck by an object	. . . .
Electrical current	. . . .
Striking against an object	. . . .
Caught under, between an object	. . . .
Over-exertion, strenuous, awkward movements	. . . .
Fall from a height	. . . .
Fall or trip on level ground	. . . .

A Sample Form for Ranking Risks

When all the forms have been completed by, say, the 500 employees, the risk manager can then calculate the average rank for each incident. From these average rankings it is then possible to rank the incidents according to the average rankings. Let us say this has been done with the following results:

Incident	Rank
Fall from a height	1
Over-exertion, strenuous, awkward movements	2
Striking against an object	3
Struck by an object	4
Electrical current	5
Fall or trip on level ground	6
Caught under, between an object	7
Rubbed or abrased by an object	8

On average the 500 employees in this form considered the most likely source of accident to be falling from a height and the least likely to be rubbing or abrasions by an object. What the risk manager can now do is to examine the extent to which this perception of risk matches reality.

One way in which she can do this is to construct a table showing the actual rankings for the company, the perceived rankings as measured by the risk manager and, if available, the rank order for these incidents on an industry-wide basis. Such a table is shown below.

Incident	Firm's Rank	Employees Rank	Industry* Wide Rank
Fall or trip on level ground	1	6	4
Struck by an object	2	4	1
Fall from height	3	1	3
Over-exertion, strenuous, awkward movements	4	2	2
Caught under, between an object	5	7	6
Striking against an object	6	3	5
Rubbed or abrased by an object	7	8	7
Electrical current	8	5	8

*Source: Health & Safety Executive – Health – Safety – Statistics – 1980

The risk manager can tell from this form of table that the most prevalent cause of accident, in her firm, is falling or tripping but yet that was not perceived by the workforce to be the most likely source. There does seem to be some mismatch between the employees' perception of risks and the actual incidence of accidents. This may then shape the direction of any safety or accident prevention campaign.

One other interesting comparison is that between the firm's experience and the industry-wide experience. This comparison does reveal some similarities but may point up any differences and perhaps suggest lines of enquiry which she could follow.

2.3.3   Value of Measuring Attitudes Towards Risk

As we said earlier, there is an extensive literature on the whole area of measuring risk attitudes. What we have done so far in this chapter has been to concentrate on individual attitudes towards risk and the means by which these can be measured. Prior to moving on to look at risk in a decision making context, let us itemise the value we feel can be derived from a knowledge of individual attitudes towards risk:

- firstly, we would have to say that the whole nature of risk management revolves around the concept of risk. Risk itself must be fully understood by risk managers and this includes all facets of the subject. Human attitudes to, and behaviour in the face of, risk is an important aspect of risk and as such merits careful attention from the risk manager.

- secondly, a knowledge of how to measure attitudes towards risk, even in a basic way, will give a valuable insight into how employees perceive risks. The risk manager may be alerted to activities, causes of injury or processes which are not viewed realistically by employees. As a result he or she may be able to take action which could raise levels of perception of risk from certain causes. If it is possible to raise perception then it may also be possible to introduce measures aimed at reducing the incidence of loss producing events.

- analysis of how people perceive certain risks may also be useful in a job selection sense. There could be jobs where a highly developed awareness of risk may be required. Should this be the case then some form of risk perception enquiry could be made as one part of an overall selection process.

- finally, risk managers may also gain a valuable insight into how they themselves view risks. Whatever decisions or actions risk managers may take will, in part, be a function of their own attitude towards risk. Some appreciation of this attitude should be beneficial in the long run.

2.4 RISK IN DECISION MAKING

The remainder of this chapter concentrates on one aspect of the risk management process in which risk plays a dominant role: decision making. In only a very few cases are decisions ever taken in a certain environment and in risk management problems there is usually some inherent risk. A range of possible outcomes may be known, but which one will actually occur is not known. Nevertheless a decision has to be taken or a case for a decision, supported.

The remainder of this book is involved with the practical aspects of risk identification and measurement, other books are concerned with equally important and practical features of risk management. However, once all our techniques have been applied to a problem it is usually necessary to make some decision. We may be faced with decisions such as: will we install sprinklers? should the system of work be altered? are existing theft prevention measures adequate? what insurance covers should be purchased? how much of a risk should be retained? should a captive be formed? and so on.

Decision making is an extremely important aspect of risk management. Peter Drucker in his book *The Practice of Management* emphasised the importance of decision making when he wrote, "whatever a manager does he does through decision making. These decisions may be made as a matter of routine, indeed he may not even realise that he is making them ... but management is always a decision making process".

Already we have mentioned the words 'decision making' several times. The use of these words as opposed to decision 'taking' has been quite intentional. We will look upon decision 'making' in the sense of 'building' or 'construction' rather than the final step of selection which is implied by the words 'decision taking'. Decision making is so important in itself that the process by which we make decisions assumes an importance quite distinct from the detail of any one problem.

For our purpose we can say that the decision process is as outlined in the diagram in Fig 2.5.

Fig 2.5

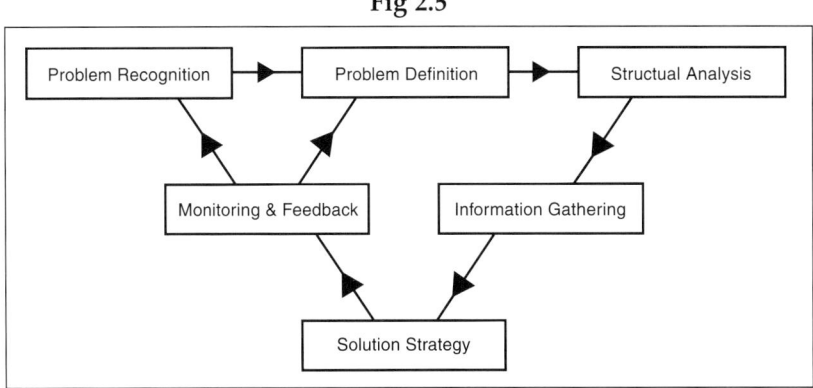

Outlining the Decision Making Process

We can recognise three main phases in the process. Firstly there is the recognition and definition of the decision problem and its structural analysis. Secondly there is the gathering of information necessary to lead on to the third phase of actually selecting one course of action. The continuing monitoring and feeding back of information has been slotted in at the second phase.

These phases in the process of making decisions are best illustrated by means of a practical study, during which we can also look at where risk and attitudes to risk play their part.

2.4.1   The Decision Making Process

Let us say that the risk manager of a large departmental retail store group has been studying the figures relating to 'shrinkage'. For this manager's company 'shrinkage' is looked upon as the aggregate of shoplifting and staff pilfering. He realises that the level of shrinkage has fluctuated over past years but does, in any one year, represent a substantial financial loss. He decides that something must be done.

2.4.2   Problem Recognition

Here then we have the first part of the process. In this example the recognition of the problem was generated by the risk manager's own review of his records. Some external stimulus could equally well have been important: a report from the finance director; an annual report from the chief accounting officer. The obvious uncertainty here is that problems go unrecognised. The risk manager must therefore be alert, in a practical way, to the need to spend time reviewing his own data and analysing information which may come to him from outside his own department.

2.4.3   Problem Definition

Having recognised that a problem exists he must now be careful to define it in a precise manner. The eventual solution will only be as good as the definition of the problem allows. The risk here is that the problem is inadequately defined. This may arise in a number of ways, at least two of which are important for the risk manager.

The first risk he runs in defining his problem is to think in terms of symptoms rather than causes. For example, a risk manager may have recognised a large and increasing number of back injuries. The problem is not, however, the number of back injuries, this is simply the symptom of the real problem. The problem may be the method of work, equipment used, layout of the plant, etc. In our example the symptom of a problem is the level of shrinkage. The problem itself is that there may be inadequate protection, the absence of staff security checks, unwillingness by the company to prosecute thieves, etc.

Secondly, the manager must try to avoid defining the problem in terms of implied solutions. A risk manager faced with one particular employee on one process, who is persistently involved in minor accidents, may define the problem as being how to make the process safer. This implies the solution before he has had the opportunity of properly structuring the decision. This disguised solution will then make it difficult for him to turn his mind to a wider range of solutions such as re-training the employee or moving him to another process.

In our decision the problem definition should not, for example, be limited to how better to protect the goods being stolen. This definition then excludes other possible solutions such as prosecuting all persons found stealing, introducing random staff security checks, etc.

2.4.4   Structure of Decisions

Having looked at the nature of the decision problem we must now turn our attention to the structure of the decision itself.

We will identify three components of this structure, starting with the alternative courses of action. It is, in part, the existence of more than one possible course of action which places us in the dilemma of having to make a choice. The list of alternatives must be as comprehensive as possible. It is obvious, but nevertheless worthwhile, to state that the best decision will not be taken if the appropriate alternative is missing.

The risk, then, is that valid alternative courses of action are omitted. There are a number of factors which may limit the selection of all possible alternatives. Some of these limiting factors may be quite appropriate and outside the control of the risk manager, for example the law, social pressure and company policy. Other alternatives, however, may not appear among the list of alternatives for less obvious reasons and it is in this area that the risk manager must be on his guard. The particular risks, in this respect, should be recognised. The first is the possibility of being 'company blind'. This is the story of the entrepreneur who has sold a product at £9.99 for years and fails to recognise the potential of a product which sells at, say, £20. He has placed a constraint on his own thinking. This risk has to be identified and avoided. In our shrinkage example it could well be that the risk manager does not consider, as an alternative course of action, the introduction of random staff checks. He fails to consider this, not because he dislikes such an idea, but simply because the company has never in the past done this kind of thing.

The second risk connected with not ascertaining all possible courses of action is associated with the previous experience of the risk manager. In the cases where a person has met and resolved a problem in the past, there is a strong tendency to rely on that previous solution. In our example it may have been that this particular risk manager solved shrinkage in another company, by installing glass shelving on top of all open display counters. It is easy to see how this alternative may be given priority in his thinking in relation to this problem. The risk is that an alternative leading to a more optimal decision has been left out.

These same considerations apply to the next component of the decision, states of nature. States of nature is the phrase used to describe the uncertain environment in which the decision has to be taken. A simple example is the decision to invest money. Let us say there are three options open to us: shares, the building society, index linked bonds. The eventual return on the investment, whichever option is selected, will only be known when the interest rate for the year has been fixed. This interest rate could end up being the same as it is at the moment, higher or lower.

It was thought by many that this situation is similar to a game where nature is some mechanism which generates events in the real world. In the investment example, nature may produce high, low, or similar interest rates. We do not know at the outset which event will occur but must nevertheless make our decision.

In the shrinkage example the risk manager will have to consider what events, or states of nature, may play upon the problem over the time period with which he is concerned. Similar comments to those mentioned for alternatives apply to the generation of states of nature and the ways in which all possible states may not be considered.

In the end what the manager has before him is a decision matrix. Down one side he can list all the alternatives he wishes to consider and along the top all the relevant states of nature. Such a matrix is shown below in Fig 2.6 and from it we can see that this risk manager is contemplating three alternative courses of action and has in mind three states of nature.

Fig 2.6

	Rate of Shrinkage Increases	Rate of Shrinkage Unaltered	Rate of Shrinkage Decreases
Store Detectives and Random Staff Checks	14	12	10
Re-design of the Counter Layout	20	14	9
TV Scanners and Random Staff Checks	18	16	8

The Decision Matrix

For the sake of this illustration we have limited the decision matrix to three alternatives and three states of nature. In the real world there would be many more.

The last of the three components of the structure of the decision is the payoff or outcome. In our example we will have nine payoffs, one corresponding to each alternative and state of nature combination. These have been included in the matrix shown in Fig 2.6. The payoff is the financial result of selecting an alternative and finding that a particular state of nature occurred. In our matrix the payoffs have been measured in terms of net loss savings, i.e. the savings in losses which are expected, less the cost of carrying out the alternative.

We can see from this matrix that if the rate of shrinkage increases then re-designing the counter layout is the optimal choice. Should the rate of shrinkage go down then it would be better to employ the store detective, while an unchanged shrinkage rate would lead you to install the TV scanners.

This is the pattern of decisions where risk and uncertainty exist. We do not know what state of nature will apply but must nevertheless take our decision now. It is not the purpose of this chapter to concentrate on how the decision would, could or should be taken but suffice to say that a substantial body of information including many practical aids now exist to help in the eventual choice of an alternative.

To conclude this chapter we will turn to one important aspect of attitudes to risk which applies both within and outside the realm of decision making, the question of working with others.

2.5 GROUPS AND RISK TAKING

A great deal of the time the risk manager works together with others either in departmental groupings, local management committees, safety committees or in other ways. Equally so he is often in the position of having to persuade a group to take a certain course of action. In our shrinkage example he may well have had to sit on a store security committee. During this time he will have been exposed to a range of different views and attitudes to the problem of shrinkage. Following these deliberations he may well then have had to present his case to a financial management group or local board or meeting of store managers.

In short, much of the activity surrounding this decision and its implementation takes place within groups. In view of this it is as well that the risk manager has some knowledge of what takes place within groups.

Fig 2.7 illustrates in diagrammatic form the group process. A number of individuals come to the group with some notion or particular attitude towards a situation and after some group process there evolves a group view.

Fig 2.7

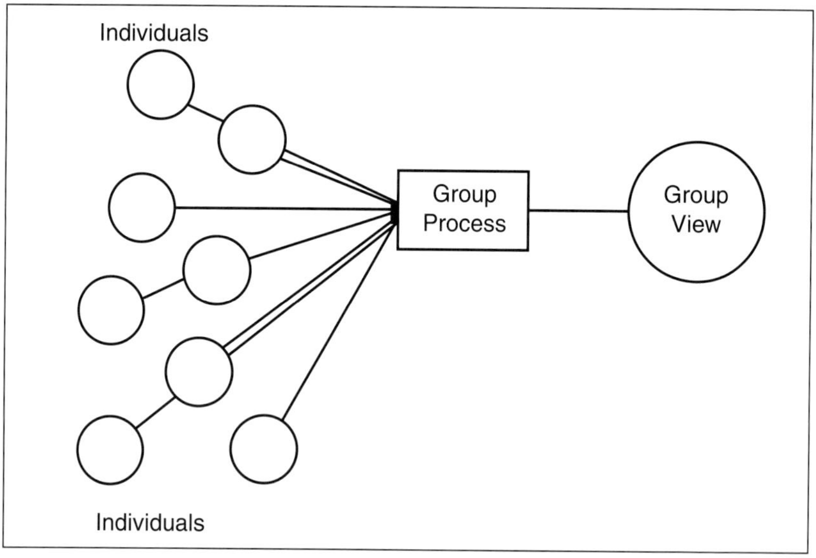

Illustration of the Group Process

In relation to risk and attitudes to risk, what this means is that individuals approach the group with some attitude and enter upon the group process. The question which must be asked is, do groups of individuals acting together exhibit the same attitude to risk as the individual members of the group held prior to the group process? The collective response of the group is a function of whatever happens during the group process but will there be any difference between the attitude put forward by the group?

Conventional wisdom might lead us to believe that the group process would result in a 'conservative' approach to any risky problem. We often have a view of groups or committees as being slow, cumbersome and rather reluctant to innovate, "...if you want something done don't give it to a committee". With this general impression in mind we might think that groups would be much less risk taking than the individual members.

2.5.1   Risky Shift

This popular wisdom was apparently shown to be inaccurate by the work of one J A F Stoner in 1961. In a *Master's Thesis* while studying at Massachusetts Institute of Technology he reported the results of research concerning groups and attitudes to risk. He tested a number of people for their attitude to risk and then assigned these people to groups of six. The groups then had to respond to a number of questions aimed at measuring their attitude to risk. He found that the group decision was riskier than that of the individuals, as previously measured. This was against what most people thought would be the case. There followed a large number of articles, many of which attempted to explain the phenomenon which by then had become known as 'Risky Shift'.

Four main points arose. Firstly, it was suggested that during the group process more information was produced about the particular decision. This is fairly obvious, that when acting with others and taking part in discussion there should be more information available to members than they had on their own. This extra information led to greater confidence and this increased confidence in turn led to a greater willingness to take risk.

The second explanation of risky shift was based on the nature of leadership within the group. Strong, dominant personalities are actually associated with the risk takers in society. On the other hand the quiet, less forceful individual is the image held by society of the cautious risk averse person. Given these views then the strong members of the group will dominate it and eventually influence the final decision. As they are prone to be risk takers, then the eventual decision will tend to be riskier than that of most of the individual members of the group.

When more than one person is responsible for the decision then it is likely that individuals will tend toward a more adventurous approach than would otherwise be the case. If the decision to cancel a particular form of protection lay with you alone then it is likely that you would also carry the responsibility to answer if the company was later involved in a large loss. When these thoughts run through your mind they may well result in your deciding to retain the cover. Where a similar decision is being taken by a group it is far easier for those in the group to be a little more risky as the responsibility for a 'wrong' decision has been spread.

The final explanation concerns the view that society, in general, has of the risk taker. In general terms it was argued that most people value the risk taker and look less favourably on the cautious risk averter. If this is the case then there may well be a tendency for some in the group to emulate the risk taker or at least assume some of the characteristics of the risk taker.

All of these explanations for the risky shift phenomenon are intuitively appealing but over the years the notion of risky shift has decreased in importance. It was found, on closer examination of the Stoner research, that much more was happening in the group process than simply a shift towards being more risky. In fact when the individual questions, put to the groups by Stoner, were examined there was evidence of a shift towards caution and a number of cases where no shift occurred at all.

2.5.2   Choice Shift

As a result of this, and other work, most people now prefer to talk in terms of a choice shift rather than risky shift. This choice shift can be looked at in two ways.

Firstly there is the possibility that during the group process there will be individual members who look for dominant values held by others. These are the people who need some guide to what they should themselves be thinking. If the dominant value turns out to be one of risk aversion then they will move that way. Similarly they would move towards risk taking if they perceived that to be the dominant value.

Fig 2.8

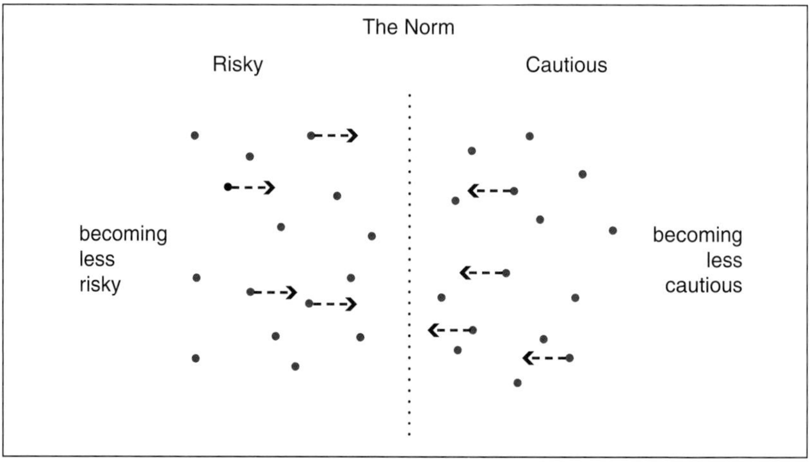

Acceptable Social Shift in Both Directions

This move towards dominance should not be confused with falling into line with some norm. The dominant value may be quite different from the norm as in the case of one strong, persistent influential voice, and a quiet majority which more accurately reflects the norm.

Secondly, choice shift may in fact be caused by social norm. Where some socially or corporately acceptable norm is recognised by members of the group then there can be a move towards that. People will not want to be too far from what they consider to be acceptable. This also involves shifts in both directions as is illustrated in Fig 2.8.

Some of those who start with a risky view move towards being more cautious while those who began as cautious may move the other way, all in an effort to line up with a perceived norm. There will be others who will stay where they were at the outset of the group process.

Risk and the problems which it brings will always be with us and indeed few of us would relish an environment where no risk or choice existed. This book now develops the analytical approach to the management of risk and it is good to build this upon the foundation of our knowledge of what risk is and how we behave in the face of it.

3

IDENTIFYING RISK 1

3.1 INTRODUCTION

The previous two chapters have served to set the scene for the much more practical aspects of risk analysis which occupy the remainder of this book. It has been useful to emphasise that the task of risk analysis must be carried out with realism and with a proper perspective, both of the risks themselves and the costs involved in analysis.

In this chapter and the next two, we will look at a number of different techniques which can be used for the analysis of risk. At this stage it is important to understand what we mean by 'analysis'. In the context of this book we will not enter into a debate about whether identification of risk is the same thing as analysis of risk or whether analysis has some distinct and separate characteristic. For our purposes such a discussion would be of little value and certainly at the end of the day it will not matter whether you *identified* or *analysed* a risk, provided it was economically controlled.

We shall look upon risk analysis as the entire task of identifying and measuring the potential impact of risk. In this chapter and the next two, we will concentrate on the techniques of identification and in subsequent chapters turn our attention to the problems of measurement.

The role of risk analysis is absolutely crucial in the whole risk management context. Risks can only be measured and controlled once they have been identified and so the process by which risks are identified assumes an importance that is quite distinct from any particular risk.

3.2 IMPORTANT FEATURES OF RISK IDENTIFICATION

While there are a number of different methods or techniques of risk identification there are also a number of common features of importance. Before embarking on a study of the techniques themselves it is valuable to remember the following:

It is unlikely that one particular method of identification will be sufficient to address all the problems of risk posed by any company. It would not be wise to latch onto one or two particular techniques and use them to the exclusion of all others. It is much more likely that a combination of methods will be required in order to ensure that the fullest possible job has been carried out. The risk manager should also be alert to changes in methods and advances in methods of risk identification which may be suitable for his industry. This is easy to say but of course much more difficult to put into practice. However time should be devoted on a semi-regular basis to scanning the relevant magazines for any developments which may be valuable.

It is also the case that certain methods are more useful in some industries than others. This in part reflects the fact that the various methods themselves had their origins in satisfying problems within an industry. A flow chart for example is an appropriate way of identifying risk in an industrial process which involves goods or materials moving through a number of different stages. We shall see this in chapter four. Where however flow is not the main activity as in the case of an office, then another form of identification tool would be better.

The task of matching the method to the risks which are thought to exist is important. It is not possible to lay down firm guidelines as to how this is to be done but it is aided if the risk manager has a firm understanding of his industry in general and of the company in particular.

The previous point mentioned the need to understand the industry and the company fully. This is greatly helped by consulting with as many people outside the risk management department as possible. Before embarking on the task of risk identification the risk manager should identify the people whom he considers could be of help in the task he has to perform. This will mean consulting with various line managers and others of the workforce who know the company and possibly also have their own firm views of the risks which exist. It may seem that you are not getting on with the job of actually identifying any risks but at the end of the day the analysis you eventually carry out will be all the better.

The fourth feature of risk identification is that it should not be a one-off exercise. Mounting a large scale risk identification exercise will probably reveal a number of risks but risks do not respect time and in a few weeks or months new risks will emerge. There must be an on-going programme of risk identification. Quite apart from keeping people on their toes it is essential that risks which have been identified are monitored and new risks highlighted. Having a programme of risk identification involves careful planning on the part of the risk manager.

Whatever you plan to do must be financially reasonable. Remember what was said in Chapter one, there is little point in spending £100 to identify a risk which you know can only ever result in a £10 loss. The task of risk identification is crucially important but it must be carried out with realism.

Accurate record keeping must accompany any risk identification. Well before the actual task of risk identification begins it is necessary to prepare the form of record keeping which will be used. Once the job has been done the relevant data must then be inserted on the forms or whatever type of record which is being kept. What is to be remembered is that in another year's time you are possibly going to visit that plant again and you will want to be able to recall, fairly easily, what you found the year before.

The final point to make about risk identification is that a certain element of imagination is required. This is something which does not come from reading books or even from passing examinations. Experience is probably the best teacher in this regard and all who are involved in practical risk analysis probably shudder when they look back at early reports of work they carried out. Be prepared to learn from your experiences, both the good ones and the bad ones.

3.3   TYPES OF TECHNIQUES

The methods we are going to study could be categorised in a number of ways. There are some which are predominantly desk based while others could not be completed without site visits. There are others which seem more appropriate to the post-loss situation than to the pre-loss position. Some involve the use of quantitative analyses while others are essentially qualitative in style.

These various dichotomies are interesting but not terribly valuable in a practical sense. As we said above, the main point is that risks are identified.

Whatever is said here concerning the various risk identification techniques will of necessity be of a general nature. It would be impossible to cover all industry types and all the different forms of risk which exist. What is hoped is that a general framework is put down on to which the individual reader can build his own particular applications.

As a means of assisting understanding of the techniques and in an effort to show their applicability in the real world, a hypothetical company has been created which will act as the base for all the methods we will look at. This company is not intended to represent any known company and any connections which readers may see are unintentional. The actual processes involved in the particular company have been simplified so as not to obscure the main function of the example, which is only to act as a common base for the techniques. Please do not get too involved in the actual technicalities of the industrial process; a broad awareness of what the company is trying to do is sufficient. With that disclaimer made, let us now describe the company.

The company is Imperial Rubber Company plc (IRC) and has been in existence for eighty-five years. It occupies a large sprawling site on the outskirts of Manchester, within easy reach of the airport and the national motorway network. Access to an international container terminal is also fairly easy.

The buildings are the original premises built at the turn of the century with a few additions over the years. The main addition in recent years has been a distribution facility added on to one gable end of the main factory unit. A rough plan of the site is shown in Fig 3.1.

The company imports raw rubber from three overseas countries and processes it for a number of particular purposes. In the main there are three outlets for the processed rubber. Firstly, the company will make products to order and does so on a large scale for the motor and aircraft industries. It also undertakes large scale contract work of an industrial nature where rubber linings or coatings are required. This contract work can either be carried out at their own premises or at the premises of customers.

Fig 3.1

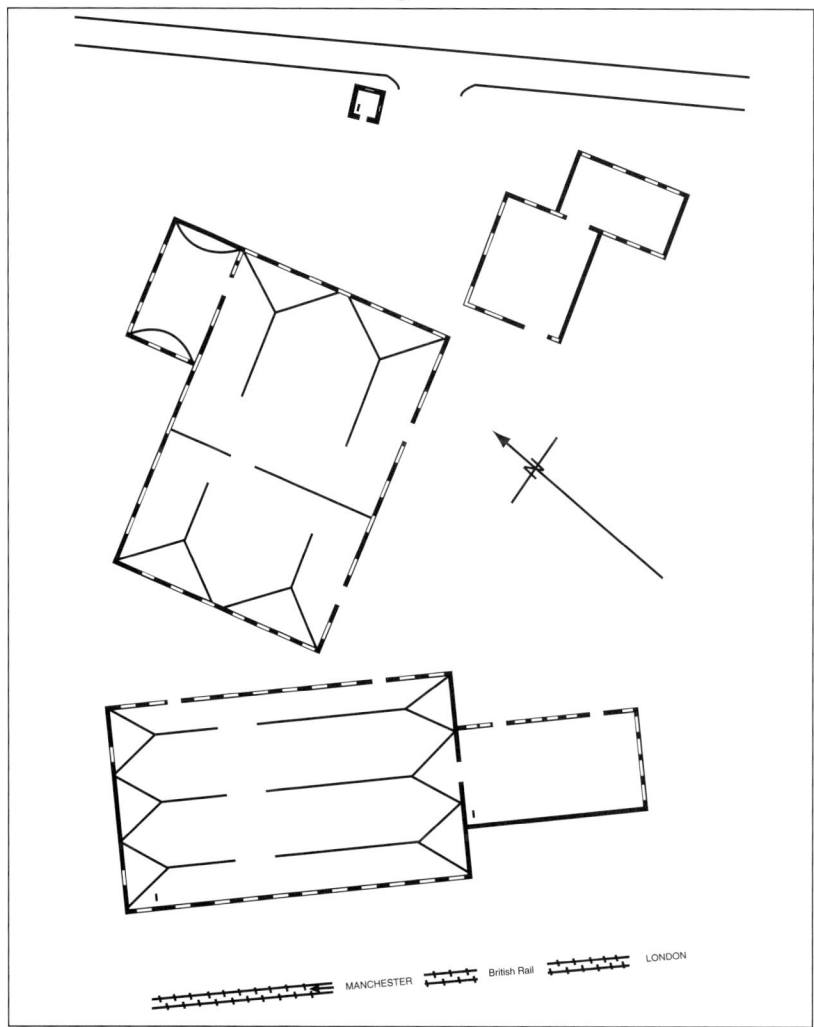

Imperial Rubber Company plc – Site Plan

The second outlet is directly into the retail market. The company manufactures a range of products both domestic and industrial which are sold to the public and industry through a number of retail outlets owned by IRC and trading under the name of National Bounce Company. NBC has recently begun moving its outlets to industrial trading estates as the bulk of its business is done with small to medium sized companies, many of which occupy premises on industrial estates.

The third outlet for the rubber is the supplying of two subsidiary companies, Imperial Rubber (Civil Engineering) plc and Imperial Pipes and Hoses plc. These two companies have been operating for many years and supply specialist industrial rubber products. These two concerns are supplied solely by IRC and operate from premises in Birmingham.

The actual process of converting the raw rubber into a marketable product is a complicated one and one which has changed over the years in response to advances in technology. In simple terms the raw rubber is received at the factory and undergoes a process of mastication, during which it is reduced to pulp by a system of grinding and crushing. After this various chemicals are added to the pulp before the mixture is vulcanised. During vulcanisation the rubber is treated with sulphur under heat and pressure in order to improve its elasticity and strength. On the completion of the process the product is then sent either for moulding and cutting prior to distribution to National Bounce or is sent to the fabrication area for the completion of orders. The new distribution centre is common to both National Bounce products and customers' orders awaiting dispatch.

The company employs 560 people, 420 of whom are men. There is a Risk and Insurance Manager who is responsible to the Finance Director for all matters of insurance, risk and safety. He happens to be male but references throughout this should certainly not be taken as implying that all risk managers are male. This is not the case and we would want to avoid this implication.

This is only a thumb-nail sketch of this hypothetical company and is not intended to represent an accurate account of how rubber products are made or sold. It is however fairly realistic and should serve our purpose of being a skeleton on which to hang our risk identification techniques.

3.4   PHYSICAL INSPECTIONS

The list of techniques which follows is not in any particular order but this first method of physical inspection is probably the best known and most often used technique for identifying risks. It is also extremely time consuming as apart altogether from the distance which may be involved in travel, there is also the time it would take to carry out an inspection of even a smallish plant such as Imperial Rubber. Before embarking on an inspection it is therefore essential that as much preparatory work as possible is done.

3.4.1   Preparation for the Inspection

- the first and probably most obvious point to get clear is the actual time that the proposed inspection will take. Visiting any plant will have to be programmed into all the other tasks which have to be performed. You will have to give serious thought to how long you anticipate the inspection taking and when in the year it would be best to do it.

- with that preliminary point over you can begin to give more detailed thought to the visit itself. You can imagine that a person just cannot arrive at a plant with no preparation. Even a fairly small plant like the one shown in Fig 3.1 involves a number of different areas and buildings, all of which could house potential risks. There must be some logical approach to the business of identifying risk, an approach which will minimise the chance that something important is overlooked. One way to approach the task is to have some sheet or report to complete as you go round. This could take the form of simply completing an entry for each item you see. An example would be:

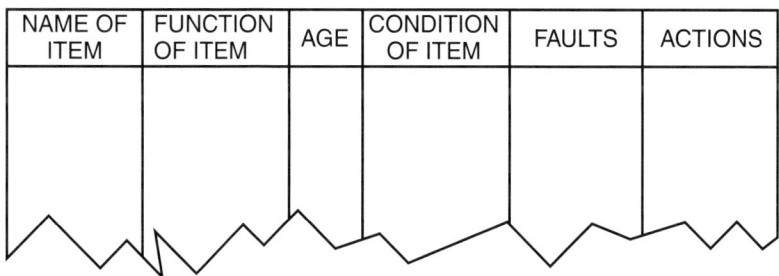

NAME OF ITEM	FUNCTION OF ITEM	AGE	CONDITION OF ITEM	FAULTS	ACTIONS

It would not be possible to complete an entry for each item you see on the inspection. An item could be a piece of machinery or a building or even a process. The actual headings to the various columns are less important than the reasons for having a pro-forma. It gives some structure to the visit and may cut down both the time it takes to complete the job and the risk that something important will be overlooked.

It is likely, however, that not all visits can be handled in this way and even where the form is used it may not be suitable for all parts of the plant. The main thing is that you are flexible enough to make use of an aid like this when it is useful and not use it when it could be counter-productive.

- the next thing you will want to do, if this is not the first time you have visited the plant, is to look back at the previous report and see if there are any matters which are still outstanding or any points which you would particularly like to look at again. This is when a pro-forma of the sort we discussed above is valuable. If you completed such a form on a previous visit you can simply turn to it now and recall what you felt was important after the last visit. Say for example you look back and see the following section of the report from last year:

NAME OF ITEM	FUNCTION OF ITEM	AGE	CONDITION OF ITEM	FAULTS	ACTION
Acme Press Company No 471	Rolling rubber during vulcan-isation.	14	Fair to poor in need of some work.	Automatic safety bar had broken and had not been attended to.	Write to the plant safety manager and send a copy to the plant manager.

- by looking back at this report you can see that a particular machine had a broken guard and that you had written to the Safety Manager and the Plant Manager about it. You can now check on that correspondence to see if anything was done. It is likely that some cross-referencing will have been made to avoid having to look up a separate file, but if this is not the case then an actual check of your files will show if the faulty safety bar had been repaired. You may also want to check on the general condition of the machine. It will now be 15 years old and was already in a poor state of repair last year.

- however there may have been no faults detected last year or this could be the first time you have visited the plant. In this case it may be advisable to prepare a list of those points you would especially want to inspect on the forthcoming visit. You may for example want to look at the heat process and check on the chemicals being used, the protection available to the workforce and the extent to which the available protections are used.

There has been a new distribution base built; we noted this above in the description of the company. You will probably have been involved in this at the planning stage but nevertheless you will want to carry out a full scale inspection of this new facility for the first time. (In an ideal world the risk manager will have been consulted during the planning and building of the new extension. However this is not an ideal world and it may be that the visit is the first time the risk manager sees the new extension. If this is the case it does raise a number of questions about the adequacy of the communication flow within the company and these questions cannot be ignored.)

- one final point to clear up before the visit is to ascertain the person to whom you are responsible at the plant. This may well be known beforehand but you should have a clear understanding of the management structure at the plant and the person who is responsible for matters related to risk and insurance.

There is little that can be said about the actual inspection itself. The art of inspecting plant is not one which is acquired by reading a text book. Experience is the great teacher and the more inspections which can be carried out the better. Imagination and flexibility are two words which we have used before and they are particularly appropriate to the task of physical inspections.

After the inspection has been made and you have returned to your office much of the real work of the visit begins. You must now implement all the actions you wrote down during the visit. In addition to any special actions, like the one from last year concerning the machine guard, you will also have a host of more routine matters which require attention. There will for example be all the insurance valuations which will have to be updated and any alterations to the premises or plant notified to insurers. You may well have a department which can handle all of this or more likely you will have to do it all yourself. The main thing is that you do ensure it is done within a reasonable time from the visit.

Finally the new report should be logged away for future reference and clearly marked to which year or month it refers.

What then are the advantages of carrying out these physical inspections and what are the disadvantages?

The great advantage is that you see the plant for yourself and do not have to rely on reports from others. In addition to seeing for yourself you are also seen by others and this is important. In trying to build up or maintain good links with those on the shop floor and those in charge of various plants, it is essential that you are seen and approachable. Visiting plants does bring you into contact with the people on whom you will rely for much of your information concerning risks and hazards on the shop floor.

The disadvantage is the time it takes to carry out inspections. We have commented on this earlier but despite all that you may do to streamline your activities, you will still have to invest a considerable amount of time in each inspection. This investment of time also means cost, and all of this will have to balance against the advantages you hope to gain from the inspection. Another disadvantage could possibly be that by visiting plants on a regular basis you may in fact discourage others from being vigilant themselves in the identification of risks. Against this is the equally valid point that local plant managers may in fact be more alert to risks knowing that you do visit regularly.

There are pros and cons for physical inspections and whether one is to be carried out or not can only be judged in the light of all the circumstances.

3.5 CHECK-LISTS

A possible alternative to the actual visit is the completion of a check-list or some other form of questionnaire. This is clearly not as good as going to see for yourself but it does have some advantages as we shall see later.

Once the check-list has been prepared the risk manager can either send it for completion by someone at the plant or, if he wishes, he can use it as a pro-forma to complete while he inspects the plant personally. The main use of check-lists however is in having them completed by someone on site. If this is to be the case then the form must be clear and unambiguous in every detail. If you are not there then the person completing the check-list must be in no doubt as to what you want filled in in answer to every question. This is very difficult to achieve and will probably take several drafts before a list emerges with which you are happy. An idea is to seek the assistance of some managers with whom you are on fairly good terms. They may be willing to look over drafts for you by way of a pilot study so that when you send the final version out you are sure it is comprehensible by those intended to complete it.

There are a number of different types of check-lists or styles which can be used. The choice of style is really arbitrary but it may be that one form is preferred for one kind of risk or indeed that one style is already used by the company in a check-list employed in connection with another purpose altogether. We shall look at three styles but you will see that they are not exhaustive of all possibilities.

The first form of check-list calls for a simple checking of facts. An example is shown in Fig 3.2.

You can see that this form really only prompts the memory as to what to look for. The appropriate person needs very little knowledge of risk and can simply enquire into each point raised. The problem is that no direction is given to the person completing the form and what he considers satisfactory may not satisfy you.

Fig 3.2

Security Check-list

Please ensure that all the items mentioned on this list have been checked. When you are satisfied that all the items are satisfactory then sign the form and have it counter-signed before returning it to the Risk Management Department.

Premises
– Alarm systems
– Testing of alarms
– Keyholders
– All locks/bolts
– Roofs
– External fencing and walls

Goods
– Raw materials store
– Stock checks
– Finished goods area
– Despatch building

Money
– Cash
– Money in transit
– Safes

Signed: . . . .

Plant Manager:
Date of Completion: . . . .

Counter Signature: . . . .

Accountant:

Imperial Rubber Company – Simple Checking of Facts

The form is signed, in this case by the plant manager, and the date of completion inserted. A counter-signature is valuable and in this case the accountant has been asked to sign.

An improvement on the simple listing of points to look at is to raise each point in the form of a question. In this way the person completing the form at least has to think about each item in your terms. It is possible to be much more direct in your approach and thus guide the appropriate manager as best you can. An example of this style is shown in Fig 3.3 and is concerned this time with the fire risk.

Fig 3.3

Fire Check-list

This check-list is to be completed by the plant manager and returned to the Risk Management Department by the end of this current month. If any problems are encountered in completing the form please telephone the Risk Management Department for assistance. Where a negative answer is given please insert in the 'action' column what action you are taking or which action you would suggest the Risk Management Department take.

Distribution Building	*Yes*	*No*	*Action*
Are all fire doors clear?			
Are all the emergency fire exit signs in working order?			
Is there at least 18ins from the sprinkler heads to the goods on the top rack?			
Are all goods stacked neatly?			
Is all heating equipment protected and in a safe place?			
Is all waste material removed regularly?			
Are all goods off the ground?			
Are all unused pallets stored in the yard outside?			
Is all combustible material stored in the brick built combustible store?			
Is there uninterrupted access to the extinguishers and hoses?			
Are all the extinguishers shown in the Fire Safety Manual in position?			

Distribution Building	Yes	No	Action
Are all the test cards on the extinguishers marked up to date?			
Are all the sand and water buckets full?			
Are all fire doors in working order?			
Is the sprinkler test card marked up to date?			
Is the fire alarm test card marked up to date?			
Have all fire drills been completed in accordance wth the Manual?			

Are there any other points you wish to raise which are not catered for by the standard form? Are there any alterations you would suggest should be made to the form as it stands?

Signed: . . . .

Plant Manager:

Date of Completion: . . . .

Counter Signature: . . . .

Accountant:

Imperial Rubber Company Fire Risk Check-list

The manager has to answer yes or no to each question raised and this has a useful psychological advantage over the previous method. This time the manager is actually stating that something is the case and where a negative answer is given he is also expected to say what he has done. This does seem to place the responsibility on him and is no bad thing in trying to encourage local plant managers to think that they have a part to play in the effective management of risk.

This check-list has been for the Distribution Area only and of course there would have to be a form for all areas of the plant. It may also be advisable to break down the form and have sub-sections dealing with different aspects of risk. This has only been a rough idea of what such a check-list should be like. In common with the example in Fig 3.2 it should be clear and free of ambiguity.

The third style we will look at is rather different from the previous two. This time descriptions of the condition of an activity or piece of property are given and the person completing the form must indicate which description is most appropriate. The form can describe a sub-standard set of circumstances, an above average set of circumstances and a normal position. Fig 3.4 is an example of this style.

Fig 3.4

Liability Check-list

Please read the descriptions provided for each of the following activities, events, etc, and indicate which description is most appropriate. The three descriptions are labelled 'A', 'B' and 'C'. If you think that description 'A' is most appropriate in a particular case then place the letter 'A' in the column headed 'Check here'. Should you have any problems in completing this form then please contact the Risk Management Department as soon as possible. Return the form to the Risk Management Department by the end of this month, having had it counter-signed.

Activity	Check here	A Sub Standard	B Average Standard	C High Standard
Use of machine guards		Guards are used only rarely and are often not even in working order	Guards are in use most of the time and are operational	Guards are always used and every guard is in excellent working order
Use of face masks and other breathing protection apparatus		The masks etc are rarely used and not kept in an easily accessible place	Masks etc are used in most cases and access is reasonable	All masks are issued to staff and are worn at all times
Safety notices and other accident prevention information		Few safety signs are visible and many are out of date	The usual safety signs are posted	In addition to the normal signs there are a number of notices specific to the plant

Imperial Rubber Company Liability Check-list

This example concentrates on the liability risk and provides the reader with a number of different descriptions. The person completing the form must then decide for himself which description most accurately describes the position at his factory. Comparisons with other plants in the group, if there are any, are therefore possible and could be quite revealing. Once the form has been returned to the risk manager he will want to take action where he considers that activities, machines or processes are generally below standard.

This is a much more difficult form to compile and you can see from the three activities in the example that it is not easy to write brief descriptions. The descriptions you eventually use could of course be based on findings from a previous site visit or a prior run of the form. Either way you must endeavour to derive descriptions which are seen to be relevant by those who are to complete the form.

This is really by way of an early warning system for the risk manager and he is given the opportunity to respond quickly to remedy any potential problems.

One difficulty in completing this kind of form is that the local manager does not want his plant to be shown up in a bad light and therefore understates the poorer aspects of the plant and avoids using the extreme descriptions. This is difficult if not impossible to avoid and arises also to a certain extent with the other methods. Before embarking on any project like this it is essential to 'take the local managers with you' in the sense that they are fully appraised of the objects of the exercise. If they can be made to see that the whole exercise of risk identification will in the end lead to a safer and hence more efficient plant, they may be more willing to complete the forms accurately. This may be rather idealistic but at least it is worth trying.

Before moving on to another technique let us just briefly comment on the principal advantages and disadvantages of check-lists:

- the main advantage must be that they are a reasonably inexpensive method of generating a great deal of information about risks within the company. They are inexpensive in time and money in comparison for example with the physical inspection.

- they are also very simple in essence and can be arranged quickly and implemented with not a great deal of fuss.

- they allow for a fairly rapid comparison with previous years and this makes for efficient monitoring of risks year by year.

- they are also adaptable and can be changed very simply to keep up with changes in the company or just to take account of improvement in the layout of the form itself.

Advantages are rarely gained without some price and there are some disadvantages to the use of check-lists:

- in most cases they are completed by someone other than the risk manager and as a result it is possible that inaccuracies creep in during their completion.

- it is inevitable, even with the best form, that there will be ambiguities and hence a measure of subjectivity when the forms are being completed. This may lead to a differing standard each year and also to differing standards being applied among different plants within the same group.

- in practical terms it may be difficult to have the forms completed on time and several reminders may be required. If this occurs then some doubt must be cast on the validity of the returns.

- a problem with all questionnaires is that it is not possible to say 'how' the form is completed. It is hoped that the form was given thought and that the answers are valid but there is no way of knowing this unless you actually go with the form and see it completed.

3.6   ORGANISATIONAL CHARTS

The check-list was a desk based method for the identification of risk. Another such method is the organisational chart. These charts are useful in illustrating different aspects of the company's activities and structure. The check-list and physical inspection attempted to identify actual risks, the organisational chart endeavours to pinpoint 'areas' of risk. This is a slightly different approach but nevertheless one which is valuable to the risk manager.

Fig 3.5

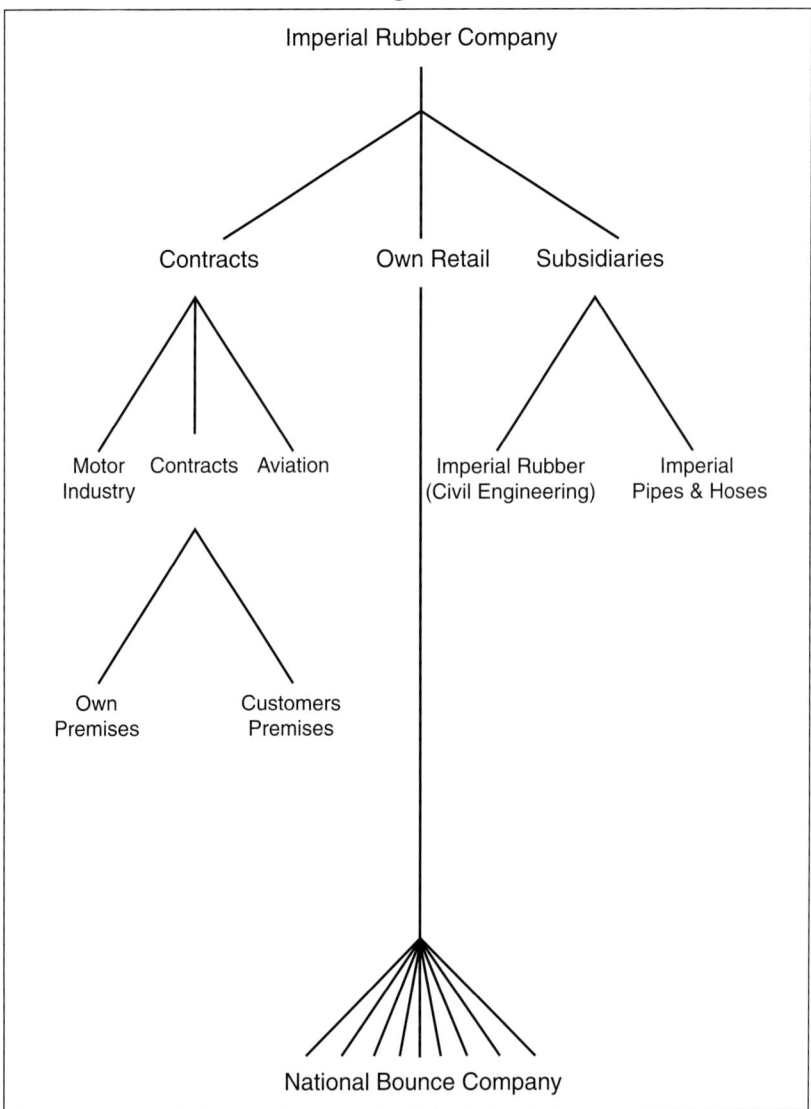

Imperial Rubber, the Structure as a Whole

The first step would be to draw a simple chart of the organisation of the group. By looking back at Section 3.3 we can build up a picture of the structure of the group as a whole. There is the main company, Imperial Rubber, and there are three subsidiary companies plus a contracts division. This could be represented in a chart such as the one shown in Fig 3.5.

This chart shows the three main aspects of the group's activities, contracts, retail and specialised subsidiaries. There are certainly other ways in which the chart could have been drawn but the main point is that all the areas of activity are shown somewhere. This chart is really an essential starting point for any understanding of the group's work and it is highly likely that a chart such as this would appear in company literature somewhere. If one does not already exist then the risk manager should set about drawing one. Apart altogether from any risk identification value which it may have, it is an excellent way of getting to know and understand the structure of a group, and nowadays these structures can be extremely complex.

The chart in Fig 3.5 was of the structure of the group as a whole; what the risk manager can now do is to construct a chart which is more tailored to the identification of risk. He could for example draw a chart which was company based and showed the management and administrative set up. Such a chart is shown in Fig 3.6.

Fig 3.6

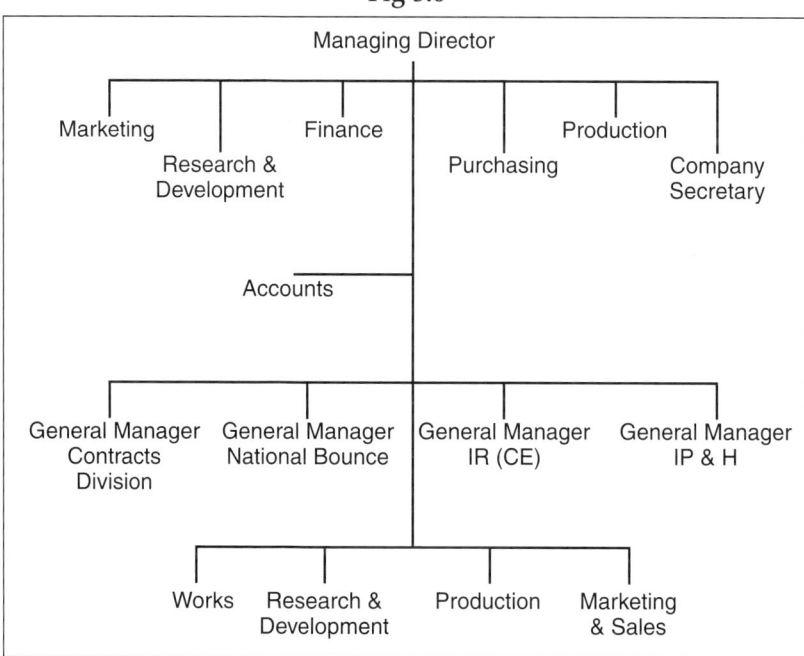

The Management and Administration of Imperial Rubber

This chart differs from the first one in that it concentrates on the companies which make up the group and on their management structure. The starting point is the same, the managing director of Imperial Rubber. Under him we can see the various functional managers including marketing, research and development, finance, purchasing production and the company secretary. There seems to be a central accounts function and this is displayed on the next level. Under this we have the individual units which make up the group. There is the contracts division, National Bounce and the two specialised subsidiaries, Imperial Rubber (Civil Engineering) and Imperial Pipes and Hoses. Each of these operating units has its own general manager and the chart shows that they also have their own works, research and development, production and marketing managers.

There are no rules about how these charts should be drawn and different companies will present different structures and hence suggest different charts. Where, for example, a company has a number of main products then it may be wise to draw a chart based on these products. In this way you could show all the products and their management teams rather than the subsidiary companies as we have done for Imperial Rubber. The first step is to get the basic structure down on paper and this may well dictate the shape of any other charts you have to draw.

We will look back at the charts we have drawn and see what they tell us about areas of risk within the group but there is one final chart we could draw first. We could take each of the divisions of the group and draw a chart for them. For example we could take Imperial Pipes and Hoses and draw a chart similar to the one in Fig 3.6 but this time only for the one subsidiary. We have done this and the chart is shown in Fig 3.7.

We already know from the chart in Fig 3.6 that there are works, research and development, production and marketing managers for Imperial Pipes and Hoses. The chart in Fig 3.7 can now extend this and show that there is an accounts function and a legal department for the two parts of the company, pipes and hoses. There are heads of these two divisions and then a number of account liaison supervisors. This could be done for all the divisions of the group and the various charts combined to produce an omnibus chart of the management and administrative structure of the entire group.

Fig 3.7

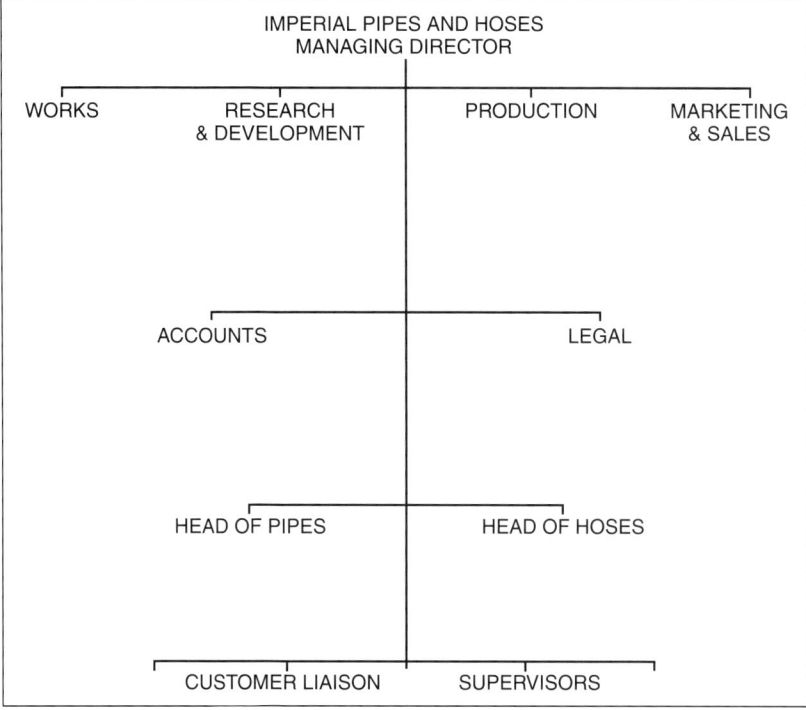

Charting the Subsidiaries

We said earlier that the organisational chart did not identify individual risks but rather it highlighted areas of risk. We can look back at the three charts we have drawn and see what areas of likely risk have been revealed if any.

These charts usually show up at least three forms of probable risk. They can highlight duplications, dependencies and concentrations. If we look at Fig 3.6 we can see that the research and development function is repeated four times as each of the four main divisions of the group has one. This may not in itself be a risk but the risk manager must satisfy himself that he has good communication links with all of these departments. The work which is carried out by these departments may well produce risks for the present or the future and he will want to make sure that he is up to date with all the work they are doing. Still with the chart in Fig 3.6 we can see that the marketing function is also repeated for each of the main divisions. Again, this level of devolution of tasks and responsibilities may not be a bad thing and may not increase the risk to which the group is exposed but it should put the risk manager on enquiry. He will want to ensure, for example, that all of the marketing departments are aware of any special instructions which the product liability insurers require to be given with products. Good communication links are once more important and the chart may show deficiencies which otherwise may not have been revealed.

Dependencies may also be uncovered by the chart. The chart in Fig 3.7 shows that the pipe and hose divisions both rely on the one production department. There may be nothing wrong with this in itself but once more the risk manager must satisfy himself that there is no increase in risk as a result of this dependency.

Fig 3.8

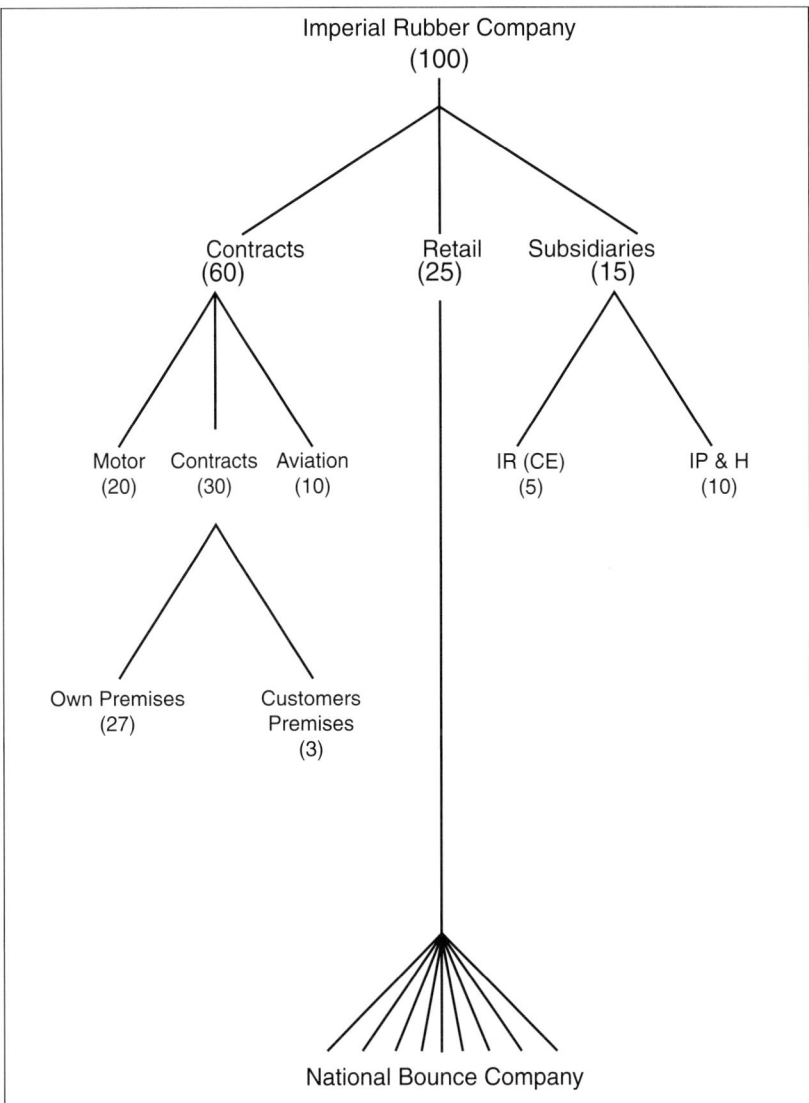

Imperial Rubber Company
(100)

Contracts (60) — Retail (25) — Subsidiaries (15)

Motor (20)   Contracts (30)   Aviation (10)   IR (CE) (5)   IP & H (10)

Own Premises (27)   Customers Premises (3)

National Bounce Company

Distribution of Revenue Generation

A possible concentration risk is revealed by the chart in Fig 3.6. It would seem from this chart that all the accounts records are kept in the one place for all the divisions of the group. This may have been a definite decision taken by management but the risk manager must once more ensure that no increase in risk is caused.

One final thing we could do with the charts is to add on some figures. We could for example add on the fact that the two specialised subsidiaries obtain 100% of their raw material from Imperial Rubber. This is clearly a risky situation and one which the risk manager may want to investigate further. There may be no other supplier capable of meeting their demand or it may be that the main company depends on the revenue from the subsidiaries. We could also add on the revenue or profit figures for each part of the group. By adding on the revenue figures to the chart in Fig 3.5 of the structure of the group as a whole we can see which divisions are responsible for the highest levels of revenue (Fig 3.8).

The contract work done at the premises of Imperial Rubber accounts for 27% of total revenue, the highest single percentage contribution of any division of the group. This is not to say that the work done on the premises for customers is the most profitable but it does produce the highest revenue.

Placing figures on these organisational charts can be of marginal assistance in the identification of risk but there is one technique which can make use of charts and figures and that is the flow chart.

3.7   FLOW CHARTS

The flow chart is not restricted to the organisational structure of the company. It can be used to describe any form of 'flow' within the company. In any organisation there will be many different aspects of flow. There will of course be a production flow, as raw materials are converted into a finished product. In a service company there will be a service flow as the company attempts to satisfy the demands of its customers. There will also be accounting flows, marketing flows, distribution flows and many others. For the risk manager the most important is probably the production flow. From such a flow chart the risk manager can see where the raw materials come from, how they are processed, the various stages of production and the final destination of the product.

At any one of these stages there can be risks and it will be the task of the risk manager, not simply to describe the flow but to interpret the chart in terms of potential risk.

The first step is to ascertain exactly what the various stages in the production process are. This will involve lengthy discussion with those most closely involved in production. It may be that some form of flow chart of production activities already exists but it is a useful exercise for the risk manager to ensure that he knows for himself all that is involved in manufacturing the product.

Once the details of the flow of goods through the plant have been ascertained, a rough chart can be drawn which illustrates the process. Let us take a very simple sub-set of the activities of Imperial Rubber to introduce the idea of the flow chart.

Raw material in the form of vulcanised rubber is moulded to make a particular product. This product is then sent to the finished goods store for eventual use in a further process, while the remainder is sent to the National Bounce Company outlets for sale to the public. Forty percent goes to National Bounce by rail with the remainder being stored by Imperial Rubber for future use. Of every moulding, ten percent of the raw bulk rubber is waste and returned to the raw material store for reprocessing. The moulding process is powered by gas and electricity both of which are drawn from the local town mains supply. With this description we can now begin to draw what we know in readiness for a full flow chart.

The drawing in Fig 3.9 illustrates what we know of the process. It is not essential to make an illustration like this as it is possible to proceed directly to the flow chart we will use for risk identification. However, such a chart has its uses and if time permits it may be valuable for future purposes to have one drawn. At least now the risk manager has on paper what he has determined is the process and can send this to the various line managers involved for their comments. It is much more likely that they will be able to follow this chart than the one we will eventually draw for risk purposes. By sending this chart out for comment and revision the risk manager can be fairly satisfied that he has a firm understanding of what is happening. With this drawing as a base he can then make any revisions as time passes and alternations are made, sure in the knowledge that at least the starting off point was accurate.

Fig 3.9

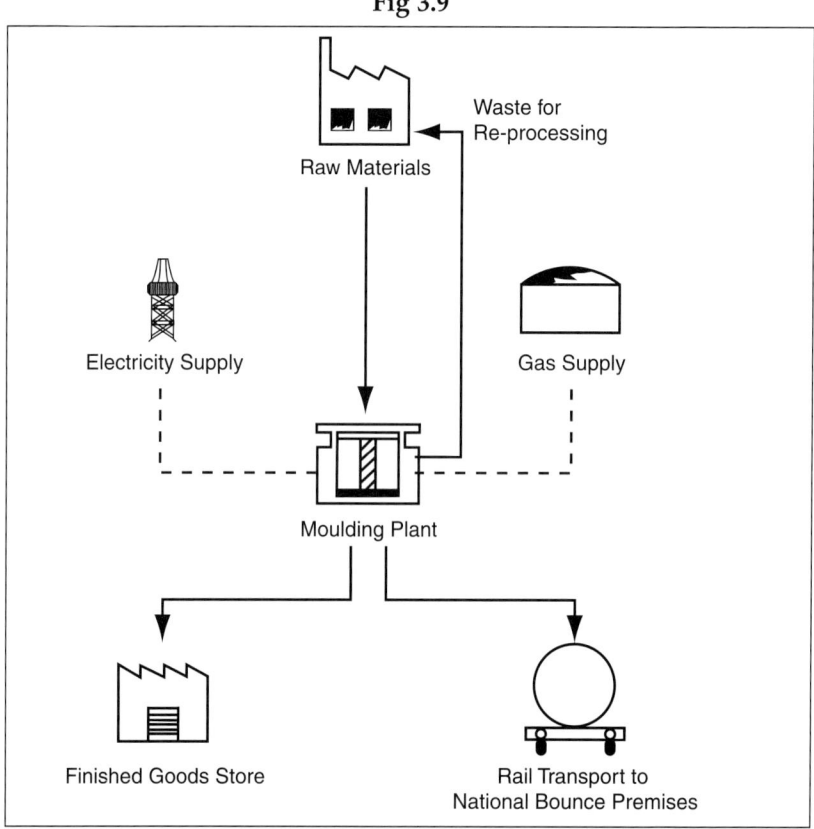

Raw Materials

Waste for
Re-processing

Electricity Supply

Gas Supply

Moulding Plant

Finished Goods Store

Rail Transport to
National Bounce Premises

An Illustration of the Production Process Key Stages

From the drawing in Fig 3.9 the risk manager can identify the key stages in the process and then set about drawing his own flow chart. In this simple example there is only one process but you can imagine that in a real case there will be a number of processes taking place at the same time and the possibility that a complex web of inter-relationships will exist. We will see something of this when we attempt a flow chart of the whole operation of Imperial Rubber ... but not until we have tried to master this simpler example.

There are no real conventions for the drawing of these flow charts in risk management and so the risk manager can draw according to what pleases him and produce a drawing with which he is perfectly happy. One simple rule would be to use a square symbol for the input stages of the process, such as the stores of raw materials, and to use a circle for process stages such as the moulding plant. A flow chart is shown in Fig 3.10; study this for a moment and try to see the connection between it and the drawing in Fig 3.9.

This flow chart shows that a quantity of raw rubber blocks was sent for moulding. This could be a quantity for a day, a run of the machine, a shift or any other time period which was thought appropriate. The quantities would relate of course to the time period and would be defined in a document which would have to accompany the chart. In this example the time period is one shift and the quantity is measured in pounds.

We can see that 300lbs of raw rubber is passed to the moulding press and during the process we produce 90% of the raw rubber in the form of the finished product. Out of the 270lbs of product produced, 60% is sent to the finished goods store and will be used by Imperial Rubber in some later process. 40% goes directly to National Bounce. The remaining 30lbs of raw material is in the form of waste and the flow chart shows that this is returned to the store for future use.

The materials involved in the flow are described by letters, and so 'R' is the raw material, 'P' the finished product and 'W' is the waste. The volume of the material which is flowing from stage to stage is shown against the line of flow and so we can see that 300R is passed from the raw material store to the moulding plant. In a larger flow chart there is the need to conserve space and the use of these abbreviations will be essential. It is necessary however to remember to include some form of key for your own use and the use of anyone else who may need to read the chart.

Drawing the flow is the simple part of the whole exercise. It is now that the risk manager must interpret what he has drawn. We have said already in this chapter that an imaginative and flexible mind is required for the task of risk identification and these qualities are required in great measure now, if the flow chart is to be made to reveal all the risks in the process.

The flow chart is not intended to identify the causes of loss such as fire, theft, liability, etc; what it does do is to highlight the effect of certain events. The risk manager can ask a number of 'what if' questions and use the chart to suggest the answers.

Fig 3.10

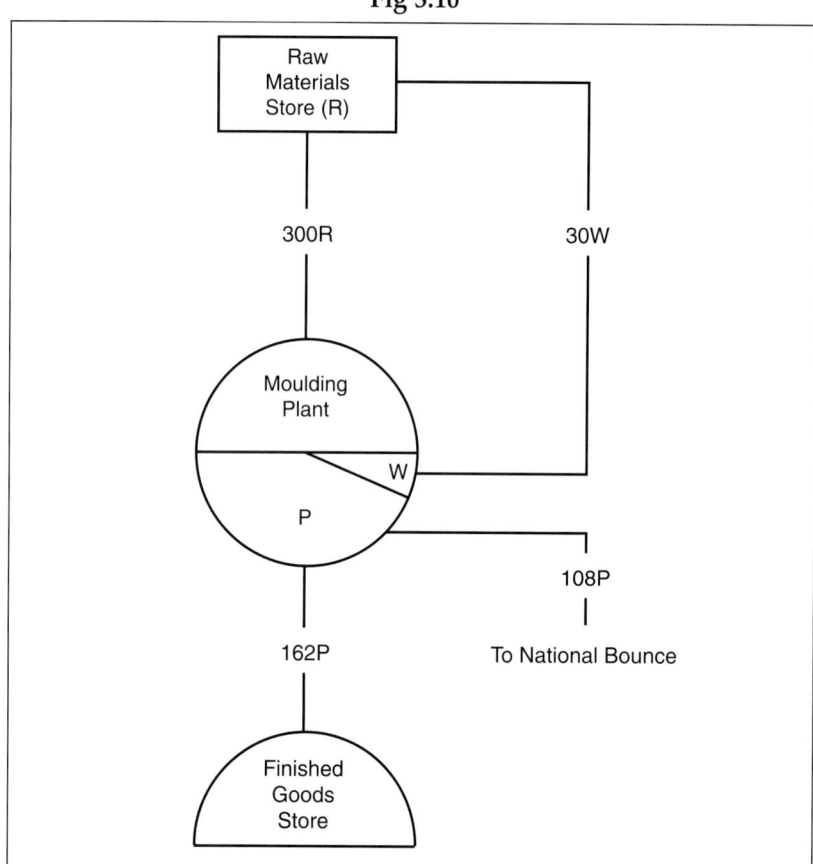

The Input Stages of Processing

For example in our simple chart we could ask what would happen if the electricity or gas supplies were cut off. We are not so much concerned at this stage with how we could lose the supply but more with what will happen if the supply is lost. This is the classic pattern of the 'what if' line of enquiry. If the source of power was interrupted we would lose the use of the moulding machine and hence all the production for the duration of the power loss. This would lead us to ask whether or not there was an alternative source of power. It could lead us into an enquiry of the total expected cost of any lost production and the comparable cost of having a secondary source of power available.

What if the moulding press broke down for some reason, what would be the effect of this? In essence the effect is exactly the same as if we had lost the power. The machine will not be able to produce the finished product. This will mean that the supply will have to stop and we will have to enquire as to the effect this will have on the company as a whole. It will be the case that the production schedule will take into account the demand made by the moulding machine. Now that this demand has ceased what effect will it have on their production? Does National Bounce have an alternative supplier? We know from our earlier description that it obtains all its stock from Imperial Rubber and so a stop in production will have serious consequences for its sales.

We could continue this line of enquiry until we felt that we had exhausted all possibilities. There is however a certain lack of structure to our approach and the chance is there that we miss something altogether, not because it was omitted from the chart but because we did not ask the right question.

One way to bring some structure to the interpretation of the flow chart is to produce a simple table for completion as you read the chart. For example your table could have four simple headings such as:

Stage	Likely Loss Producing Events	Likely Causes	Possible Consequences

We could now take each stage in turn and list all the events which are likely to cause a loss and then look at causes and consequences. If we do this for the moulding stage in our simple flow chart we could end up with the following:

Stage	Likely Loss Producing Events	Likely Causes	Possible Consequences
Moulding press	Moulding press out of action	– Fire – Explosion – No gas – No electricity – Industrial action	– Lost production – Over capacity in production of 'R' – Loss of revenue to National Bounce – Reduction in Imperial Rubber stock

If this had been a chart involving several different stages you can see how such a table could be of value in structuring the approach to risk identification. What we could add is a column for possible actions. Alternatively we could simply keep a note of what we intend to do in the light of the risks we have found.

Notice, once more, that what we have used the chart for is to identify broad areas of risk rather than individual perils. Approaching the problem of risk from this broad perspective will inevitably lead to consideration of individual perils but it is felt that casting the net as wide as possible in the early stages of analysis yields better results in the end.

We have said already that the flow chart in Fig 3.10 was fairly simple in comparison to what we may find in the real world. The flow chart in Fig 3.11 is a little more complicated but still much simpler than could be the case. This chart is for the entire operation of Imperial Rubber as we have described it.

The various materials are described by letters and the quantities by numbers. These quantities and numbers are shown alongside the lines which connect the different stages of the flow. Starting at the top of the chart we see that 1620A – this could be 1620lbs or 1620 tons of raw rubber – is sent in equal portions to plants 1 and 2. These plants are where the raw rubber is broken down and various chemicals are added. We see that three chemicals are added in different quantities. In total a volume of 180 is added which means that 180 plus the 1620, 1800ABCD, then flows on to the next stage which is plant 3. Plant 3 is simply a combining stage where the products of plants 1 and 2 are mixed together before being sent for the vulcanising process in plants 4 and 5. Notice that during this combining process there is a residue of property A left and this is sent back to the raw material bulk store of A and is used again in the process. At plant 3 the total quantity of ABCD which is passed on to the next stage is 1700 and 1000 is sent to plant 4 with the remainder going to plant 5. The output of plant 5 is therefore 700R. 400 is sent for rolling in plant 6 and is then despatched to the contracts division for use by Imperial Rubber in their contract work. The remaining 300R is transported to Birmingham for use by Imperial Rubber (Civil Engineering) and Imperial Pipes and Hoses. Plant 4 treats the other 1000ABCD which comes from plant 3. This 1000ABCD is split among plants 7, 8 and 9 in the quantities 400, 300 and 300 respectively. There is waste to the extent of ten percent at each of these plants and so in total 100W is produced. (This section of the flow chart is the sub-section we looked at in Figs 3.9 and 3.10; if you look back to these charts you will see the vulcanising process and then the moulding press with the ten percent waste.) Plants 7, 8 and 9 are moulding presses which produce products P1 and P2. P1 is for use by Imperial Rubber and P2 is for sale to the public through National Bounce outlets. You will see that plant 7 is exclusively devoted to products for Imperial Rubber, while plant 9 is devoted to National Bounce goods. Plant 8 is divided between the two. The waste from the three moulding presses is sent to plant 10 where there is a reprocessing machine capable of recovering 20 percent A out of the waste it receives. This 20A is returned to the bulk store and the 80W, which is looked upon as industrial waste, is then disposed of by an industrial waste contractor.

Fig 3.12 shows a rough drawing of the whole process and is the kind of drawing which could have preceded the actual flow chart itself. Fig 3.12 is the equivalent of Fig 3.9 in our simple example.

This has taken a little while to explain but is a small plant in comparison to many, and the complexities of the actual process have been reduced to the minimum, as anyone who knows anything about the production of rubber products will see. However, the main point of all of this is not to understand the rubber industry but to understand the use of the flow chart in the identification of risk. What we would do now is to draw up a chart so that we could go through each stage of the process and describe the likely loss producing events, likely causes and possible consequences. For the chart we have drawn this would take some considerable time and you are urged to look at the chart carefully and try to draw your own conclusions from it.

In the meantime let us take one stage and see what the chart could tell us about the risks faced by Imperial Rubber. We will look at plant 2, this is one of the two plants where the raw material is broken down and the chemicals added prior to the vulcanising process. The likely loss producing events at this stage include the loss of use of the plant either permanently or temporarily. The causes of such a stoppage could include fire or other perils, mechanical or electrical breakdown or industrial action. For the risk manager, who may already be quite well aware of most of the causes of loss at the site, the more important aspect of the chart will be to identify the likely consequences of the loss of use of the plant.

Fig 3.11

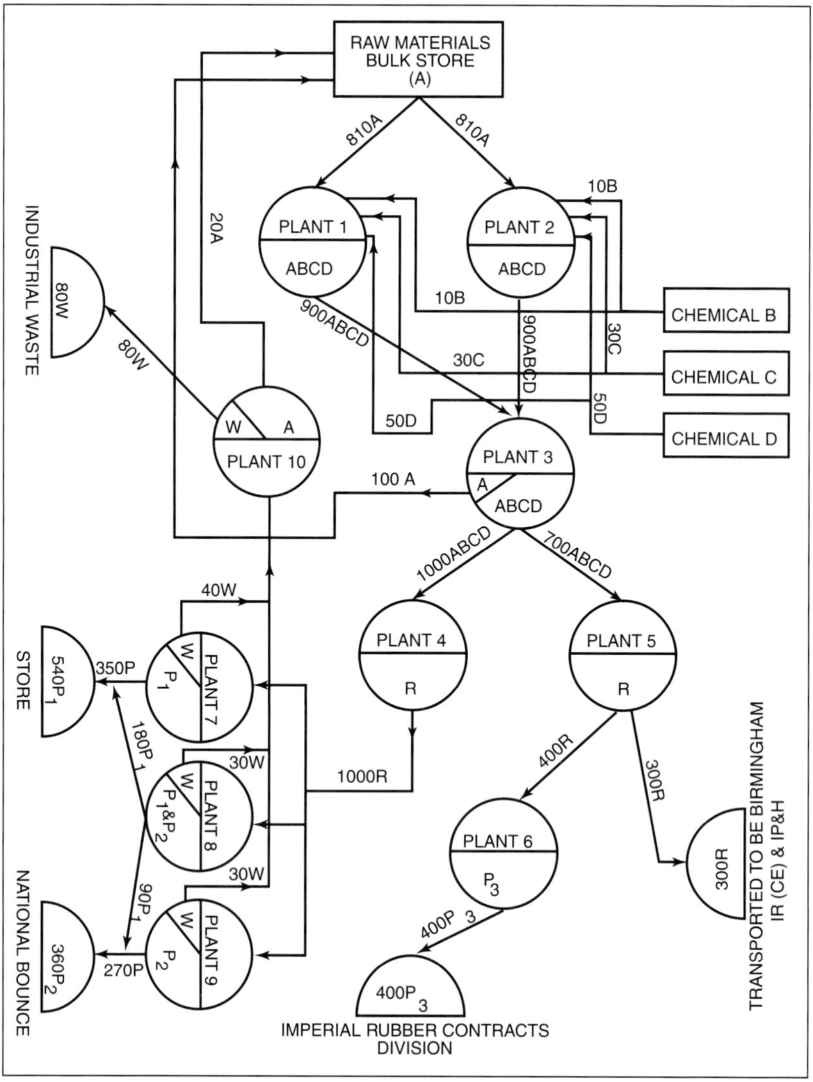

The Entire Operation of Imperial Rubber

These consequences will include:

- if plant 2 is out of action there will be a reduced demand for the chemicals B, C and D. Is the supplier of these chemicals in a position to reduce the supply at short notice or if not is it possible to store the chemicals until they are required? This raises a number of risk related questions for the risk manager to enquire into and follow up.

Fig 3.12

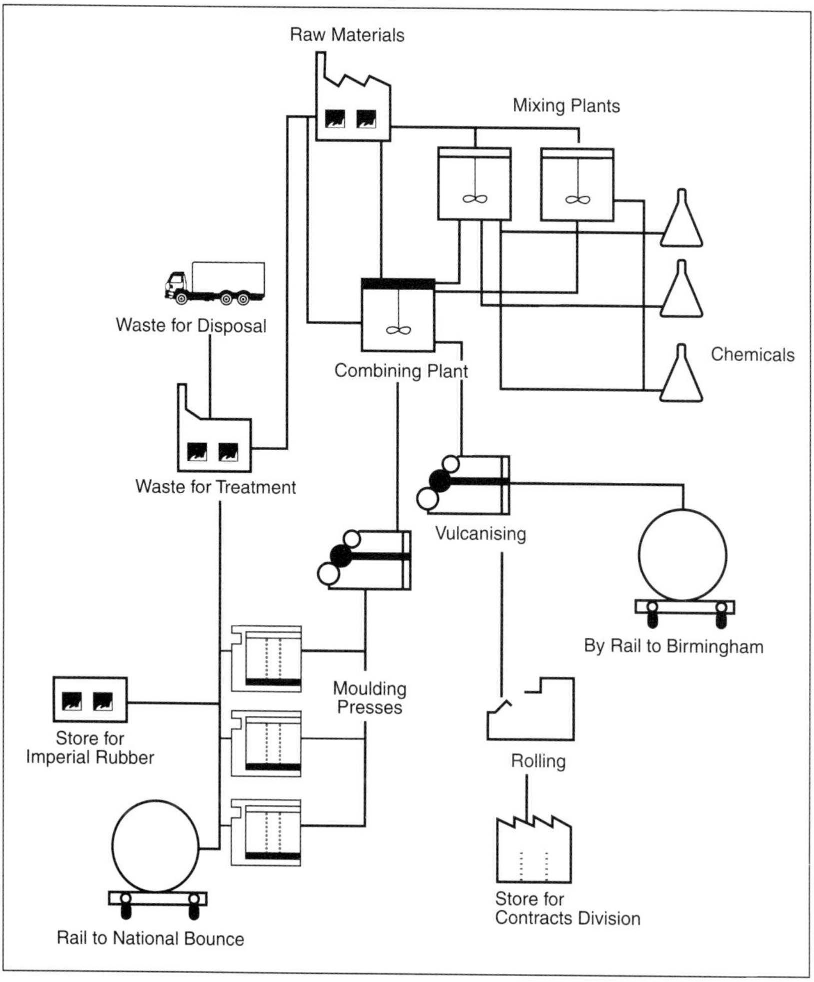

A Rough Drawing of the Whole Process

- plant 3 will not be able to work at its normal capacity if the production from plant 2 is lost. This may mean laying men off or short time working.

- there will now be only about 850ABCD produced instead of 1700 and this will mean of course that the amount going to Imperial Rubber (Civil Engineering), Imperial Pipes and Hoses, the contracts division and National Bounce will all have to be reduced. What will be the effect of doing this? Will the two specialist subsidiaries have contracts to fulfill?

Would it be better to shut down one of the plants, either plant 4 or 5, rather than run on short measure?

- depending on whether we shut down 4 or 5 we may have to close one or more of plants 7, 8 or 9. In any event the output will be reduced and plans will have to be made as to how best the shortfall is to be managed.

- the reprocessing plant, plant 10, will sustain a substantial reduction in the amount of waste it will receive and it may be better to shut this plant down until the stoppage in plant 2 is over. The waste could then either be stored or sent for disposal without trying to recover any raw material from it.

- some of the raw material which is used at the beginning of the process does in fact come from later parts of the process itself. On the flow chart we can see that 20A comes from plant 10 and 100A comes from plant 3. Some or all of this will be lost and therefore the amount of A going into the process at the start will be reduced. This may not be a problem as we will be looking for ways of reducing the throughput of material until the plant is fully operational but we will have to remember that reducing the input of A will result in a consequent fall in the store of A.

There are many other consequences which we could list and a great deal more detail we could have gone into, particularly in the effect on the main operating subsidiaries such as National Bounce, Pipes and Hoses, etc.

Having listed the possible consequences of the loss producing event the risk manager could be keeping a note of what actions he would take. This means that should the loss occur at some time in the future he will have at least a start in knowing what actions to take. He could for example consider the possibilities of doubling the output of plant 1 or having two shifts at plant 1. He may also institute enquiries to see if any raw material could be purchased at short notice from some other supplier. It is certainly best to make all these plans in the relative calm of the pre-loss situation rather than in the heat of the post-loss activity.

What we have looked at is only one stage in the whole process and the risk manager would have to move on now to another stage and another, until all important stages had been covered and all loss producing events identified and consequences plotted. You can see that this will be a lengthy process but one that will be rewarding both in terms of the insight gained into the operation of the firm and the risks which may be revealed.

Some may look back over the list of events, causes and consequences we have mapped out and wonder if they really are the province of the risk manager. It may well be that certain of the events we identified would be handled by some other member of the management team but that is not an excuse for the risk manager to ignore them. The history of large scale industrial incidents is chequered with managers assuming that someone else was doing the job of managing risk. The sole function of the risk manager is to manage risk and it will not be good enough, the day after a loss, for him to say that he thought someone else looked after a particular form of risk.

Before leaving the flow chart let us say what we believe the advantages and disadvantages are. On the plus side we could say that the use of flow charting is an excellent example of breaking a problem down into manageable proportions. It is a daunting task at the best of times to begin the job of risk identification but once a large problem is broken down into smaller sections then the work can at least begin.

The chart also has the advantage of letting the risk manager see the whole process in the one chart. For complex operations this may mean more than one chart but nevertheless the advantage remains that the manager can look at a chart and see the entire operational flow of the company. This is preferable to having to read a number of publications describing the processes.

The chart also allows for structured thinking about the problems of risk. It not only allows for structured thinking but almost demands it if the chart is to be used properly. This logical approach to risk identification is often what is missing but the chart guides the manager through the process of identifying risk.

The disadvantages of the flow chart certainly include the time it takes to complete a study. From understanding the processes involved to drawing the chart can take a considerable amount of time and then the real work of interpreting the chart begins.

It is also possible for some charts to be extremely complex and this can be a disadvantage. If the chart is so complex that it obscures the risks then it may well be that a flow chart is not the best technique to adopt.

The chart could also be said to be very general in nature. It covers the whole process in a general sense but does not concentrate on any one specific part of the process which itself may conceal all kinds of risks. This is a disadvantage associated with any form of risk identification which takes the broad brush approach adopted by the flow chart.

A final disadvantage is that the flow chart does not comment on the likelihood of events occurring. We mention likely loss producing events but we do not say whether we believe the events to be extremely likely or hardly likely at all. This absence of any measure of likelihood will be favoured by those who shy clear of using numbers but it is nevertheless a disadvantage which we should recognise.

The final two disadvantages, that of the general nature of the flow chart and the lack of measurement, are taken up in Chapter four, when we turn our attention to a number of techniques which are far more detailed in nature and make use of numbers in the quantification of likelihood.

4

IDENTIFYING RISK 2

4.1   INTRODUCTION

In the previous chapter we looked at a number of techniques for the identification of risk. They were all in the main concerned with highlighting broad risk areas. We looked at physical inspections, check lists, organisational charts and flow charts. Each of these methods adopts a kind of broad brush approach to risk and is not concerned with identifying individual sources of risk, no matter how small. When we listed the possible disadvantages of the flow chart we said that it was a very general technique and also lacked any quantification of likelihood.

In this current chapter we are going to turn our attention to certain techniques which overcome these disadvantages. The first is the hazard and operability study.

4.2   HAZARD AND OPERABILITY STUDIES

The hazard and operability study (HAZOP) is a qualitative approach to risk identification which can be employed at the planning stages of projects. It has had its origin in work done by ICI and is now used extensively in the chemical industry. In essence the HAZOP is a critical enquiry into the operation of a plant, from the hazard point of view. It follows the basic logic we have seen already that many problems are extremely complex and must be broken down into manageable parts. A plant is divided into a number of parts and each part is then examined extensively in order to identify all the hazards associated with it. A logical framework is laid down by which this identification is achieved.

There are four main questions with which the HAZOP study is concerned:

- the intention of the part examined
- the deviations from the declared intention
- the causes of the deviations
- the consequences of the deviations.

A particular section of the plant is selected and the intention of that section is defined. This is clearly a crucial stage as if the intention is not accurately stated then the deviations from it will also be suspect. The HAZOP is best carried out by a team and the team will jointly derive the intention of the section of the plant under enquiry. The study is not just on the one selected section as once the work on that part is done then another section and another will be chosen until the entire plant has been examined. It is important that the team, rather than an individual, describes the intention of the part as no one person on the site is likely to have a comprehensive knowledge of all that the particular section is intended to achieve. In addition different people will perceive the purpose of the section from their own perspective and this may not be the only, or correct, perspective.

Once the intention is declared then the deviations from the intention are to be listed. What we are interested in are all the possible departures from the declared intention. Here again the team approach is valuable in viewing the problem in the widest possible way. These deviations are obviously at the core of the HAZOP study and a great deal of time is required on them. Rather than leave the team to spot deviations in a non-structured way, the HAZOP method makes use of a number of guide words which are to be applied to each part or section being studied. These guide words are examined later when we look at our first example of a study.

A cause or list of causes for each deviation is then drawn up. Again the team is valuable in being able to bring their own area of expertise to play on the problem. All possible causes are to be listed, not just the ones which seem most likely or have already occurred in the past.

The results of the various deviations are then listed and these will give rise to a number of possible actions which the team may want implemented once the study is over. It is as well to note these actions down as the study is being carried out rather than at the end.

The approach we have described briefly is similar to the flow chart method we looked at in the last chapter; we approach the task with a pre-arranged method of enquiry and structure our thinking about how to identify possible risks.

Let us take a very simple example and try to illustrate the use of HAZOP in action. We will assume that Imperial Rubber has an underground petrol tank which it uses to store fuel for its fleet of motor vehicles. There is one hand pump and associated valves and displays of how much fuel is used. A rough drawing is shown in Fig 4.1, from which you can see that the petrol is stored underground and is drawn to the surface by means of a pump. The pump is activated when the hand-held nozzle is removed from its casing in the pump assembly. This is similar to the petrol pumps seen in many filling stations.

Fig 4.1

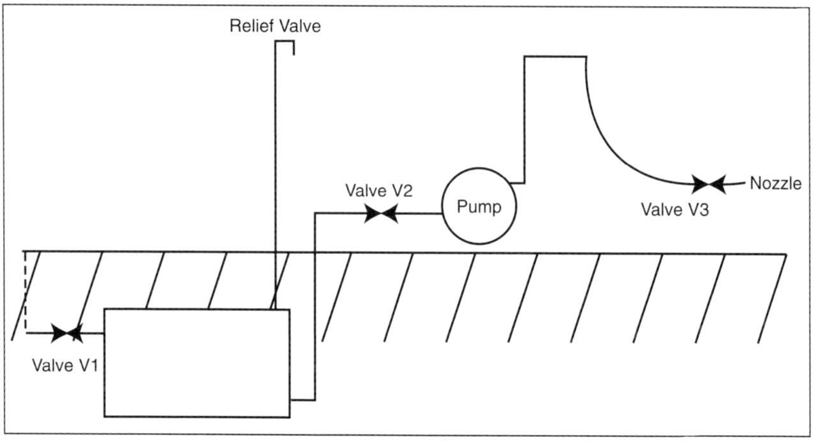

A Rough Drawing of Imperial Rubber's Petrol Pump

This could have been a small section of a large plant or process system and we could have selected it as the first section to study. We have however decided to look upon it as an entire system for the sake of illustrating the concept of hazard and operability studies.

The first thing to do is to decide what the intention of the system is. Let us say that the intention is to store petrol for motor vehicles. What we need now is a chart so that we can plot our way through the structure suggested by the HAZOP method of working. We will need columns for deviations, causes, consequences and actions plus a column for the guide word which will alert us to the deviations from the design intention of the system. We could head up a sheet of paper, or more probably several sheets, in Table 4.1:

Table 4.1

Guide	Deviation	Causes	Consequences	Actions

Before saying anything about the guide words we will have to decide what aspect of the system, or what property of the system, we are going to investigate. We know that the system in Fig 4.1 is the entire system but we must decide if it is the flow through the system with which we are interested or the pressure or some other property of it. In most plants and with most systems there will be a number of different properties which could be potentially hazardous and in need of investigation. Properties such as flow, volume, temperature, pressure are all properties which could, if they deviate from the norm, cause loss. Once the intention of the system or part of the system is decided then the team must list the important properties and begin their task.

In this case we will say that the property under investigation is that of flow – the flow of the petrol from the tank to the vehicle.

We now know the intention of the system, we know that it is the flow of petrol with which we are concerned, and so we can begin to apply the various guide words. These guide words are shown in Table 4.2 and are intended to 'guide' the user through the different possibilities. This is again similar to the 'what if' line of questioning we mentioned in the previous chapter.

We can now head up our paper with the columns shown in Table 4.1 and begin the actual analysis of the system.

We could continue at length thinking of all the possible deviations which could occur and all their associated causes and consequences but we will stop here. The general idea of the HAZOP study can be seen from this simple example. We have defined the intention of a small system and then set about determining all that could possibly go wrong with the system. Each cause has been numbered and the corresponding consequences and actions inserted with the appropriate number.

Table 4.2

Hazard and Operability – Guide Words		
Guide Words	*Meanings*	*Comments*
No or Not	This is the complete negation of the intention	No part of the intention is achieved, i.e. there is no flow or no heat or no pressure. Nothing else happens, there is simply no part of the intention achieved.
More or Less	There is an increase or a decrease in the quantity of the property	There could be more flow than was the intention or less flow. In the same way there could be more heat or less pressure, etc.
As well as	There is a qualitative increase in the property	The design intentions are achieved but an additional activity occurs, e.g. water gets into the system and flows into the petrol tank of a vehicle.
Part of	There is a qualitative decrease in the property	Only some of the intention is achieved and some is not. This is not a quantitative decrease that would be less than but is a decrease in the quality of the property.
Reverse	The logical opposite of the intention	An example of this could be where the flow is reversed or instead of boiling a liquid it is frozen.
Other than	The complete substitution of the intention	No part of the original intention is achieved and something entirely different takes place. For example some other liquid may be put in the tank and then flow down the pipe to the vehicle.

You can now see how this method is particularly suitable for the design stage of any process or plant. The design team, including the risk manager, can sit down and explore all possibilities long before any actual construction work starts. We must stress once more that imagination and flexibility of thought are of the essence in doing this kind of work. This is best achieved or at least aided by working with others and pooling the resources of several experts.

Table 4.3

Guide	Deviation	Causes	Consequences	Actions
No	No flow	1 Tank empty. 2 Inlet valve V1 is shut. 3 Pump not working. 4 Other two valves shut. 5 Hose blocked.	1-5 No petrol gets to vehicles. 4 Petrol seeps out of pipes. 5 Hose bursts.	1 Regular checking of tank. 2-4 Valves to be checked every day. 3 Regular maintenance on the pump.
More	More flow	1 Pump faulty.	1 Spillage.	1 Regular maintenance.
Less	Less flow	1 Pump faulty. 2 Valves not fully open. 3 Hose partly blocked.	1-3 Longer to fill tank in vehicle.	1-3 As for no flow.
As well as	Water as well as petrol	1 Water in storage tank.	1 Water gets into the tanks of vehicles.	1 Regular cleaning out of storage tank.

Now that we have introduced the concept with a simple example let us imagine a more complicated problem involving Imperial Rubber. Let us say that they are contemplating a new automated system for breaking down the rubber and mixing in the various chemical additives. The new system is still very much at the design stage and it has been decided to carry out a hazard and operability study. A team has been formed and the risk manager is to be a member.

The system under consideration is shown in Fig 4.2. In brief terms the raw rubber would be fed into the bunker at the top of the diagram and would be partly broken down. It then drops on to a conveyor belt which carries it to the next part of the system. Here the partly broken rubber is dropped into a further bin where it is broken down into finer particles, fed by suction into a tank into which the chemicals are added. There is a pressure relief valve on the tank. After the mixing process is complete the whole mixture is sucked into an outlet pipe and carried on to the next stage in the process.

This is only a proposed system and so you cannot go and see it working for yourself. You must therefore rely on the drawing to tell you all you need to know before conducting the HAZOP study. Let us say that the drawing in Fig 4.2 is the only one available at the moment and so you must work from it. The first thing to do is to draw up a sheet with the appropriate columns on it of:

- guide words
- deviations
- causes
- consequences
- actions

Once you have done this you can start with the first most appropriate guide word and work your way through them all. Remember that not all the guide words may apply to this particular problem but you will be working in a team and it is likely that the combined knowledge of everyone involved will produce the best list of guide words possible.

When the sheet with the columns has been headed up and the first guide word selected you are almost ready to start the task of identifying causes and consequences. Before doing that there are two things still to be done. The first is to work out the order in which you are going to work your way through the system. The earlier example we used was an entire system in itself and we simply carried out the HAZOP on it as a whole.

The drawing in Fig 4.2 shows a system with a number of different lines and tanks, etc. So that we do not miss anything important we should section the drawing off into small parts for the purposes of the HAZOP study.

The second preliminary step is to decide exactly which property of the system you are investigating. Remember that in any system you may have a number of quite different properties, as we mentioned above. In this example, we could have flow, pressure, suction and possibly others. We will concentrate on flow.

Let us assume that all these preliminary decisions have been taken and that we are now ready to carry out the analysis of the section of pipe leading from the bottom of the bin to the tank where the rubber is mixed with the chemicals. This section of pipe has one valve on it and the rubber particles are drawn through it by suction, as we were informed earlier.

Fig 4.2

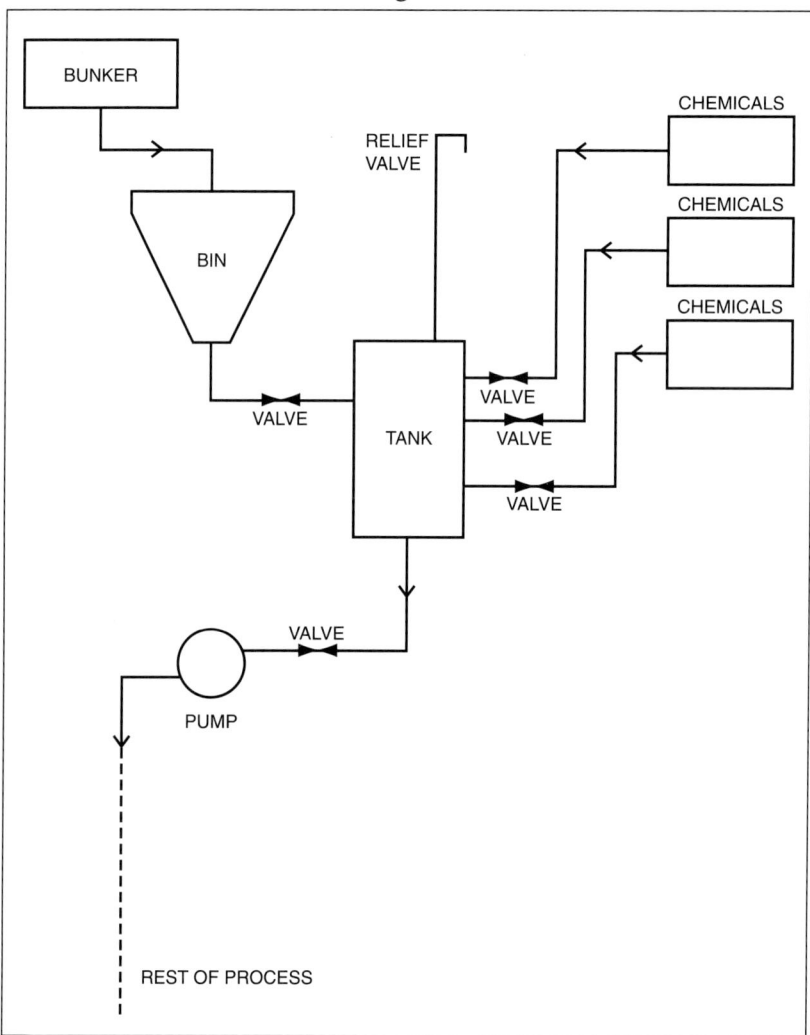

The Proposed System for Making Rubber

Table 4.4

Guide	Deviation	Causes	Consequences	Actions
No	No flow	1 Bunker empty 2 Bin empty 3 Conveyor broken 4 Valve shut 5 Outlet jammed 6 Suction fails 7 Industrial action	1-7 No raw rubber in tank 1-7 Excess of chemicals in tank 1-7 Possible explosive mixture 1-7 Lack of supply to the rest of the process	1-3 Visual check on bunker and checklist completed 3 Visual check and regular maintenance 4 As for 3 5 Test runs 6 Install a gauge to be read by by the operator
More	More flow	1 Excess of raw rubber 2 Suction is excessive 3 Conveyor too fast	1-3 Wrong ingredients in tank 1-3 Lost production 1-3 Contaminated goods 2 Suction system breaks down 3 Conveyor over-heats	1 Visual check on quantity 2 Install a gauge 3 Install a speed meter
Less	Less flow	1 Suction not working properly 2 Blockage in pipe 3 Valve partly shut 4 Tank already full 5 Less than usual amount being fed into the bunker 6 Conveyor too slow	1-6 Lost production 1-6 Wrong ingredients in tank 1-6 Contaminated goods 1-6 Excess of chemicals in the tank	1-6 Same as for more flow

Guide	Deviation	Causes	Consequences	Actions
As well as	As well as other material	1 Faulty loading of bunker 2 Dust or debris in bunker or bin 3 Wrong raw material delivered by supplier	1-3 Contaminated goods 1-3 Lost production	1 Manual check 2 Grids on bin and bunker 3 Spot check deliveries
Reverse	Suction reversed	1 Raw rubber drawn back 2 Possibility of chemicals being drawn into bin	1 Bin overfills 1 Loss of rubber or rubber 2 Possible explosive mixture in bin	1-2 Install a non-return
Other than	Something other than rubber flows	1 Wrong raw material in bunker	1 Lost production	1 Manual check on all the deliveries

We can now mark this particular line or pipe as having been examined and move on to the next section. You can see that an extensive list of causes and consequences can be derived. Remember that this is only for the one section of pipe, all the other sections have still to be done. At the end of the exercise there would be a comprehensive list of possible causes of loss, their consequences and the actions to be taken. We can begin to see the advantages of structuring our thinking about risk in this way. Not all of the causes, consequences or actions would be the direct responsibility of the risk manager but there is sufficient to concern him in the study as to justify his full involvement.

Now that the study has been started, the team will want to ensure that it does not accidentally leave out a part of the system. You can see how this could come about, especially in a complex system with many different vessels, tanks and pipe lines. It is useful to have a simple flow chart which can guide you through the work. Such a chart is shown in Fig 4.3.

The chart simply shows the various stages in the study and should minimise the chance that you overlook any section.

Fig 4.3

Prepare a drawing of the plant and section it off into smaller parts/lines or sections	1
Prepare a sheet with columns for guide words, deviations, causes, consequences and actions	2
Define the general intention of the whole plant and all the parts/lines/sections	3
Select the property for investigation e.g. flow, temperature, pressure	4
Select one part/line/section	5
Apply first guide word	6
List all deviations	7
List all causes	8
List all consequences	9
List all actions	10
Repeat 7-10 for all deviations	11
Repeat 6-11 for all guide words	12
Mark the part/line or section as completed	13
Repeat 5-13 for all parts/lines/sections	14
Repeat 5-14 for any other relevant property	15

A Simple Flow Chart of the Entire System

Once the entire process has been examined the drawing should show that all the sections have been examined and the sheets, containing all the comments made, can be filed away with the drawing for future reference. It will be necessary to diary ahead many of the actions so that you can keep a track on when they have been taken.

We will conclude this section on the HAZOP study by looking, briefly, at the main advantages and disadvantages. As far as advantages of the study are concerned we could say that the identification of possible risks is carried out in an extensive way. There is little likelihood that anything major will be omitted, assuming the study has been carried out properly. It also has the advantage of involving a team of people in the task of risk identification and this may well pay dividends in the future for the risk manager. The HAZOP also allows each part of a complicated system to be examined in detail and this is something which can be very hard to achieve in the absence of a structured approach.

The main disadvantage is the time involved in carrying out the HAZOP study. Not only will the risk manager be involved but there will be others on the team and the combined investment of time will be expensive. A further disadvantage is that it may be necessary to simplify a system in order to draw a diagram and then work your way through it. If this is done then there is the risk that some aspect which may be risky could be omitted.

Taking all the advantages and disadvantages together we must conclude that the HAZOP is an important technique for the identification of risk and one with which the risk manager should become familiar. It may well be that HAZOPs are being carried out in many firms without the involvement of the risk manager, but this may be due to his lack of knowledge of the technique rather than an unwillingness, on the part of others, to involve him. The risk manager should endeavour to keep up to date with modern risk identification methods and not be content with the traditional physical inspection or checklist as the sole or primary source of information.

4.3   FAULT TREES

At the end of Chapter three we said that the flow chart had two weaknesses, among others. We said that it dealt with risk in a broad way without concentrating on the detail of systems. The HAZOP study is certainly an answer to that disadvantage. The other weakness was that the flow chart did not make use of figures to quantify the likelihood of events occurring. We move on now to a method which can use numbers in the quantification of risk, the fault tree.

We say that the fault tree 'can' make use of quantitative analysis as it does not always do so. Fault trees are essentially quantitative in nature but they can certainly be used as a qualitative tool and indeed this is possibly the best way to introduce them.

Fault trees were probably first developed in the sixties by the Bell Telephone Laboratories in America when working on the

Minuteman space project. Since then there has been considerable development in the field and even now people are still working on refining the technique, particularly with the aid of computers. The fault tree is a diagrammatic representation of all the events which may give rise to some major event. It shows the way in which individual events can combine together to produce potentially dangerous situations and it forces us to consider all aspects of the problem, including quantification of likelihood.

We will start with a small example, as we have done with other new techniques, and then work our way up to a more complex illustration. Look back at the drawing in Fig 4.2. This is the drawing of the proposed new system for processing the raw rubber. Let us say that we are concerned that the pressure in the tank may reach such a level that an explosion could result. You will recall that when we were carrying out the HAZOP we did mention the risk of explosion on a few occasions. The raw rubber is sucked into the tank at one end and the chemicals enter at the other side. The mixture is then drawn from the tank by a pump. There is a pressure relief valve on the tank but we can still imagine circumstances where an explosion could occur. In simple terms there would be an explosion if the pressure in the tank rises and the relief valve does not operate. This is shown in Fig 4.4.

Fig 4.4

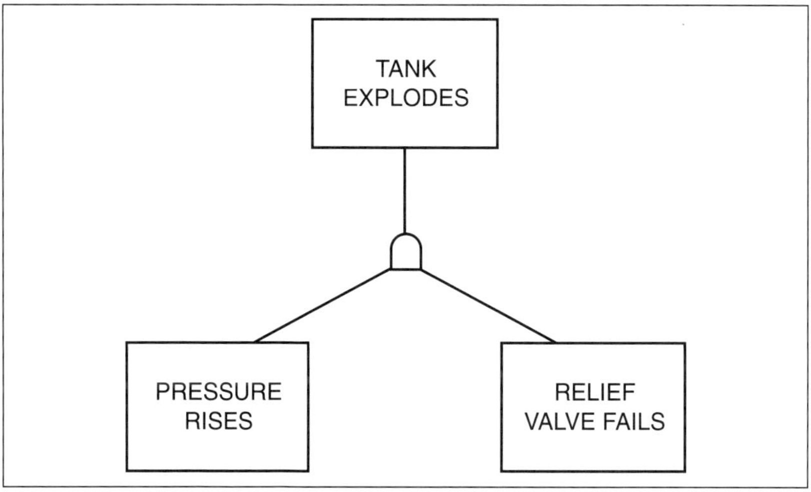

An Explosion will Occur if the Relief Valve Fails

The event that there is an explosion is at the top of the tree and the two events which may give rise to the explosion are shown as the branches of the tree. The two events are linked to the top event by an AND gate as both events must happen for there to be an explosion.

It is often the case that one or other of two or more events could cause another event and so there is the need for an OR gate in addition to the AND gate. Fig 4.5 shows a simple tree with an OR gate.

This time we are interested in the event that the pressure rises in the tank. This can come about, we have decided, in one of two ways: either the pump fails to operate and the rubber particles are not extracted from the tank, or there is an excessive amount of raw material fed into the tank at the top end. Either one of these two events could cause the pressure in the tank to rise; they both do not need to happen but of course they both could.

Fig 4.5

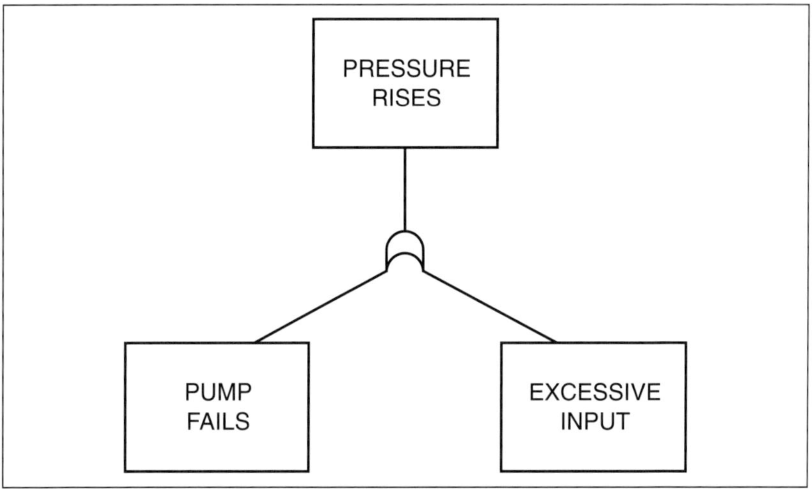

A Simple Tree with an OR Gate

Both of these simple examples use the same logic in their design:

- the event with which we are concerned is shown at the top of the tree. It is also possible to show the main event at the left or right of the tree but either way it is at the tip of the tree.

- in building the tree we work down from the main event. We do not start with all the causes we can imagine but begin with the event and then consider all the ways it may come about.

- the branches of the tree represent all the ways that events may come about and are linked by the use of gates.

- gates can only be AND gates or OR gates, there are no other possibilities. These are logical gates and must conform with 'common sense' in their interpretation.

What we have not shown so far is any mention of likelihood and we can now introduce this to the two simple examples in Figs 4.4 and 4.5. Two amended trees are shown in Fig 4.6.

Fig 4.6 (a)

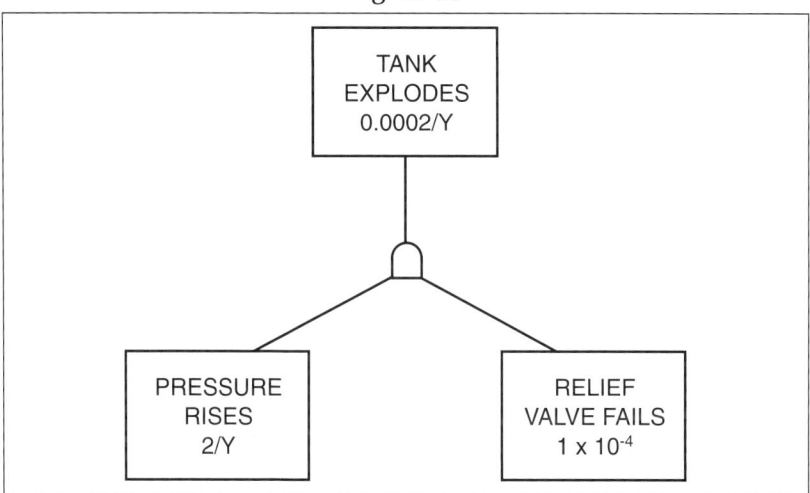

Fig 4.6 (b)

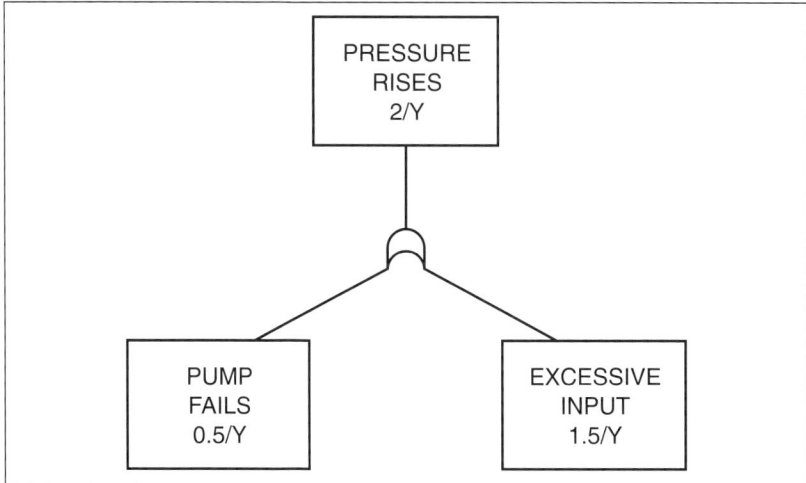

In Fig 4.6(a) we have inserted the likelihood that the pressure rises and that the valve fails to operate. Normally we would measure these events over the period of one year and so we can see that the pressure has risen twice. This is probably an average measurement and not simply taken from one year on its own. We may have gathered information on all the occasions when pressure has risen and on average this worked out at twice per annum. An explosion does not occur each time there is a pressure rise as the relief valve will operate to release the excess pressure. An explosion will follow when the relief valve fails to function during a time of high pressure. This is shown clearly on the tree as the two events are linked, in the logic of the tree, by an AND gate. Let us say that the probability of a valve failure is estimated at 1×10^{-4}. In other words there is a one in ten thousand chance that the valve will fail. The notation 10^{-4} is an example of a form of notation which is very common when referring to events where the probability is extremely low. There may be some who are unfamiliar with this style of expressing probabilities and so a brief explanation is given in the following paragraph. Those who feel quite confident with the notation can omit this paragraph and move straight on to page 91, where the text continues.

We know that probabilities measure the likelihood of events occurring. Probabilities can be any number between 0 and 1, where 1 equals certainty. We can express these probabilities as fractions or decimal fractions and so the probability of getting a head on the flip of a fair coin is ½ or 0.5. The more unlikely the event becomes, the less certain it is, then the smaller is the fraction. The chance of drawing the Queen of Hearts from a pack of playing cards is 1/52 or 0.0192307.

An event which occurs one time in a hundred would then have a probability of 1/100 or 0.01. One in a thousand would be 1/1000 or 0.001. One in ten thousand would be 1/10,000 or 0.0001, one in one hundred thousand would be 1/100,000 or 0.00001 and one in a million would be 1/1,000,000 or 0.000001. Including probabilities such as these in a fault tree or other calculation would be very cumbersome and so a shorthand means of saying the same thing is employed.

You will recall from your school algebra and arithmetic, or maybe you won't!, that we can express fractions by raising figures to negative powers. In this way we can say that 10^2 is 100 and that 10^{-2} is 1/100 or 0.01. For those who are interested in 'why' this is so then we must go back to the way in which 'exponents', the powers, are multiplied and divided.

10² multiplied by 10² is 100 x 100 or 10,000. We know that 10,000 is the same thing as 10⁴. And so we can say that $(10^2)(10^2) = 10^{(2+2)} = 10^4$. The exponents are added together when numbers carrying exponents are multiplied. When they are being divided the exponents are subtracted.

An example would be the case of dividing 10² by 10⁴. We know that this is 100/10,000 or 1/100 or 0.01. Remembering what we have said about subtracting the exponents then what we have is, $10^{(2-4)} = 10^{-2}$. And so 10⁻² is the same thing as one in a hundred, 1/100 or 0.01.

Raising numbers to negative powers simply produces fractions and so one in a hundred becomes 10⁻², one in a million is 10⁻⁶ and so on. These very small numbers are useful for extremely unlikely events that can often be seen in use when describing the risks associated with the nuclear industry. They are also used in comparing mortality statistics for different causes of death. In these cases the numbers of people dying from particular causes are often expressed as a rate per one hundred thousand or per million. If there were 170 deaths in an industry which employed, nationally, 85,000 people then the risk of death is 170/85,000. By dividing both parts of this fraction by 85 we get 2/1,000 which can be expressed as 2 x 10⁻³; there is a two in one thousand risk of death in this industry. We can now compare this with figures for any other industry simply by expressing all figures as deaths per 1,000.

This has possibly been a roundabout way of saying that 10⁻⁴ is a one in ten thousand risk or 0.0001. It is a form of notation which is common and one with which the risk manager should not be totally unfamiliar.

The two events, pressure rises and relief valve fails, are joined by an AND gate and so both must occur to cause the explosion. The risk that both will occur is found by multiplying the two together. This is an example of Boolean algebra but all we have to remember is that events linked by an AND gate are multiplied and events linked by an OR gate are added. The result of multiplying the frequency and the probability gives us the likelihood that pressure will rise and at the same time the valve will fail. The result is shown on the tree in Fig 4.6(a): there is a frequency of explosion of 0.0002 per year. This is extremely low, it is equal to one explosion every 5,000 years, but it is for the company to decide if the risk is acceptable or not.

Fig 4.6(b) illustrates the tree using the OR gate, this time with the relevant likelihood figures included. We can see that the pump fails, on average, once every two years or 0.5 times per year. The input of raw rubber has been found to be excessive, on average, once every eight months or at an annual rate of 1.5. Either a pump failure or an excessive volume of rubber will bring about the increase in pressure, and we can see this by the use of the OR gate on the tree. As we said above we must add these either/or frequencies to ascertain the likelihood of the pressure rising and when this is done we see that pressure will rise, on average, twice per year.

The trees we have used so far have involved either an AND gate or an OR gate; this is rather simplistic as clearly both kinds of gate could easily be in the one tree. Fig 4.7 shows a tree which is the two trees in Fig 4.6 combined. Here we have the main event, the tank exploding, still at the top of the tree and we can see that this event is contingent on both pressure rising and the relief valve failing to operate. Pressure will rise if either the pump fails or there is an excessive input of raw rubber. The frequencies have been included, as in Fig 4.6, and the main event is seen to have a frequency of 0.0002 occurrences in a year, which we earlier said was equivalent to an explosion once every 5,000 years.

This is still a simple tree in comparison to many and we will move on to elaborate on it but in the meantime let us make a note of what we consider the value of trees like this to be.

These trees have considerable practical value and are in use in many different areas of industry, and it is as well that the modern risk manager familiarises himself with them. We could say the same here as we said about the HAZOP study: the risk manager may not feel that he gets involved in studies using this technique but that may be because he himself is unfamiliar with it. The value of the fault tree method can be seen in the following ways:

- the fault tree is an excellent way of describing a complicated process or system. It provides the structure which may be required in order to fully understand how a particular process works. Drawing the tree is a discipline in itself and even if we went no further we should at least understand the system a little better.

Fig 4.7

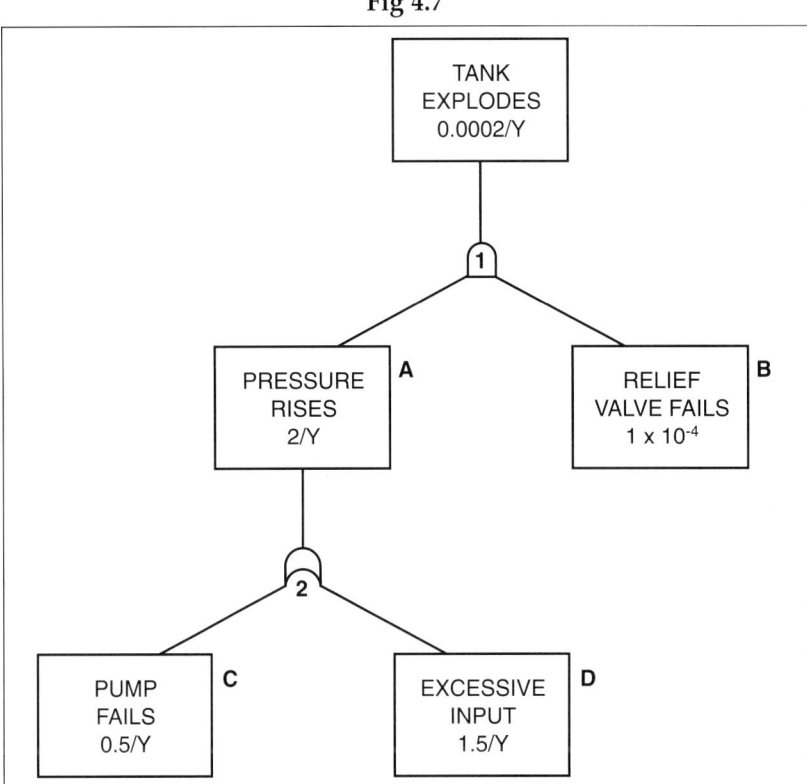

A Combination of the Two Trees in Fig 4.6

- the tree approach also allows for the identification of risk as the tree is being built. Building the tree involves not only an understanding of the process or system but also the risks which are inherent in it. In our simple example we had to work out all the events which could result in an explosion of the tank. Once these events had been identified they themselves had to be analysed to see all the ways by which they could come about.

- once the tree has been drawn it can be used to see how sensitive it is to changes in the system or to ascertain which parts of the system or process have the most impact in terms of risk. Let us say that a new valve is proposed which the manufacturers say has a failure rate of 1×10^{-6} rather than the existing rate of 1×10^{-4}. This means that the new valve has a one in a million chance of failing. If this is so then the risk of the tank exploding will be 0.000002 per year or once every 500,000 years. This compares to the existing rate of failure which is once in 5,000 years. This proposed change in the valve does seem to bring about a major reduction in the risk of explosion.

We could now compare this suggestion to a proposal to buy a new pump. Remember that the tank will only explode if the pressure rises and the valve fails at the same time. Replacing the valve is one way to bring about a change in the risk but another possibility is to minimise the chance of the pressure rising. This could be done by purchasing a pump which had a lower failure rate than the one you already have. Let us say that a pump with an estimated failure rate of 0.25 occurrences per annum is on offer. This compares to the current pump which has a failure rate of 0.5 per annum. If we bought this pump then the pressure would rise, on average, 1.75 times per year ($0.25/Y + 1.5Y$). The risk of the tank exploding would then be $(1.75/Y)(1 \times 10^{-4}) = 0.000175/Y$. This is a failure rate of once every 5,714 years on average, which compares to the existing rate of once every 5,000 years. The change, the reduction in risk, is not very great. You may however argue that the comparison is not very valid as the frequency of the pump failing has been halved from 0.5 to 0.25 occurrences per year but the probability of the valve failing dropped from one in ten thousand to one in a million.

To make the comparison absolutely fair we could make a comparison based on the same decrease in risk for the pump and the valve. The pump failure frequency is half the existing frequency; let us say then that the valve failure probability is also half the existing figure. This would give a failure rate of 0.5×10^{-4} instead of the 1×10^{-4}, a risk of one in twenty thousand rather than one in ten thousand. The risk of the tank exploding, given this new valve, would then be $(2/Y)(0.5 \times 10^{-4}) = 0.0001$ or once in ten thousand years. This compares directly to the figure of once in 5,714 years if we installed the new pump.

We can see now that the same reduction in the risk of different, subsidiary events occurring will not necessarily bring about the same change in the likelihood of the main event. You can see how the tree provides the mechanism for calculating the sensitivity of changes in the system.

Finally, the fault tree allows us to calculate all the ways in which a main event may come about and, more importantly, it lets us determine the minimum number of combinations of events which can bring about the main event. An industrial process or system could have several different aspects to it all producing a complicated tree diagram. The main event being considered could be dependent on a large number of subsidiary events, some of which could overlap or be duplicated elsewhere in the process and hence elsewhere in the tree. If we could work out the minimum number of ways in which the main event could come about then we could see which set of events is the most likely, which has the greatest impact on the main event and where changes in the system could be most effective.

In fault tree jargon the minimum number of ways a main event can occur is known as the 'set of minimum cut sets', and the cut set is the group of events or primary sources of failure which can bring about the main event. In the example shown in Fig 4.7 we can deduce the minimum cut set, the minimum number of ways the tank can explode, by looking at all the primary events in an algebraic way.

The main event is E and this comes about if both A and B occur:
$$E = A.B$$

The event A occurs if either C or D occur and so we can substitute this in the equation:
$$E = (C + D)B$$
$$E = CB + DB$$

When we insert the appropriate frequencies and probabilities we get:
$$E = (0.5/Y)(1 \times 10^{-4}) + (1.5/Y)(1 \times 10^{-4})$$
$$E = 0.00005/Y + 0.00015/Y$$
$$E = 0.0002/Y$$

The minimum number of ways that we could have an explosion is two, C and B or D and B. In words this does make sense as it says that the explosion can only occur if either the pump fails and the valve fails or there is excessive input of material and the valve fails. And so we can see now that the event DB is the more likely of the two sets of events and that changes in the design to minimise the risk of there being an excessive input of material is likely to be an effective way of reducing the risk of the tank exploding.

One final tree is shown in Fig 4.8. This is an extension of the trees we have already used and shows a number of additional events. Read this tree and make sure that you can understand how all the events contribute to the main event of the tank exploding. You will see that we have added on the way in which the pump could fail. We have said that the speed of the pump increases and the speed gauge did not register the correct speed. If the gauge had been in good working order then the operator would have switched the pump off or taken some other steps to prevent a total failure. You will also see that the excessive input of material can be caused either by the conveyor running too fast or some human error, not defined. Human error is also a possible cause of the valve failing, dirt in the valve being the other.

This tree differs from the others in that the primary or source events are enclosed in a circle rather than a box. This is the usual way of displaying these events and indicates that the event in the circle is a root cause and not one which has any subsidiary causes. We may simply believe that it is not worth enquiring any further.

The minimum cut set for this tree is a little more difficult to calculate. We could do it by the algebraic method we used above but there is clearly the need for some method by which we can deduce the minimum number of ways a main event can occur. There are indeed a number of such methods and we will look briefly at one proposed by a Mr Fussell.

This method arrives at the minimum cut set by working its way through all the gates. It starts first by completing Table 4.5 as follows:

Table 4.5

Gate	Type	Inputs	Input Numbers
1	and	2	2 3
2	or	2	4 5
3	or	2	E F
4	and	2	G H
5	or	2	I J

You can see that we have inserted the gate number and then the type of gate, the number of inputs into the gate and finally the numbers from the tree of the inputs to the gate. Gate 1 was an AND gate with two inputs, which were gates 2 and 3. Gate 3 was an OR gate with the inputs E and F.

Fig 4.8

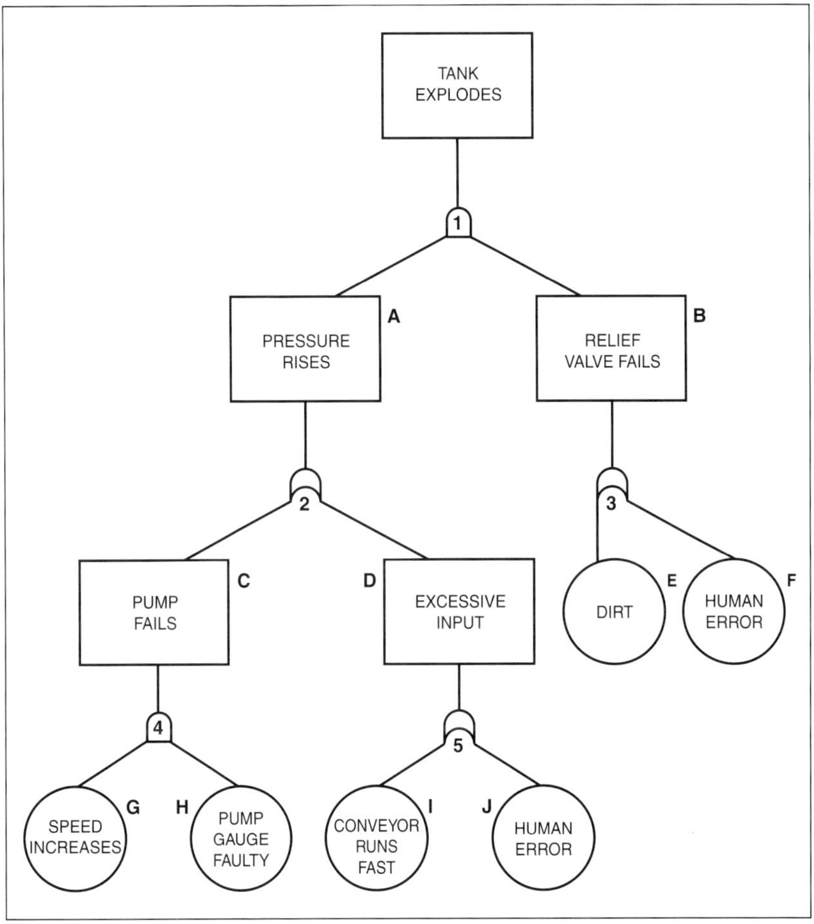

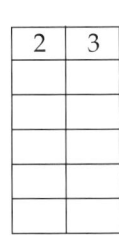

TANK
EXPLODES

1

PRESSURE
RISES — A

RELIEF
VALVE FAILS — B

2

3

PUMP
FAILS — C

EXCESSIVE
INPUT — D

DIRT — E

HUMAN
ERROR — F

4

5

SPEED
INCREASES — G

PUMP
GAUGE
FAULTY — H

CONVEYOR
RUNS
FAST — I

HUMAN
ERROR — J

An Extended Tree with Additional Events

Once the table has been drawn a series of matrix charts are compiled in the following way:

Chart 4.1

1	

2	3

4	3
5	3

4	E
4	F
5	E
5	F

G	H	E
G	H	F
	I	E
	J	E
	I	F
	J	F

The first gate is shown at the top left hand corner of the first matrix. In the second matrix this gate has been replaced by its inputs from the table, namely 2 and 3. These are shown across the matrix from left to right because gate 1 is an AND gate. In the third matrix the gate 2 has been replaced with its inputs of 4 and 5. This time the inputs are inserted down the way from top to bottom as gate 2 is an OR gate. Notice that when 4 and 5 are inserted we also associate input 3 with each one as 2 was linked to 3 by an AND gate. This is continued and in the fifth matrix we end up with the minimum number of independent ways that the main event can occur.

Let us conclude this section on the fault tree with some comment on the main advantages and disadvantages. The advantages have been referred to as we have gone along. They included the structured approach to risk identification, simpler analysis of complex systems, tracing of causes and their impact, etc.

The disadvantages include the time it takes to carry out a study using a fault tree and the time which may be involved in learning the appropriate techniques. These are disadvantages which are shared with many risk identification methodologies but are nevertheless important and real if you are the person implementing them.

One major problem with the fault tree which was not apparent with the other methods, so far, is the derivation of probabilities. We have to work out where the relevant probabilities are to come from as if they are not accurate then the rest of the calculations, particularly the measurement of the likelihood of the main event, will be suspect. There are a number of sources of which the following are a few:

- there may be some past experience at the plant or elsewhere within the company upon which frequencies can be based. Most firms will have records going back over a considerable time and these can often be used to get a good measure of likelihood.

- if company based figures are not available then there are possibly industry wide figures which could be used. Trade groups or professional bodies often keep records of relevant events and these figures may be useful.

- manufacturers may also be a source of figures especially on the failure rate of equipment. They may keep such information or may be prepared to put you in touch with a major user to get some measure of reliability from them.

- finally it is possible to extract subjective probabilities from your own company employees. Methods of deriving subjective probabilities are well established, but without going into them we can imagine presenting relevant people with our measure of how likely we believe an event to be and then asking them to refine our judgement. We could do this a number of times until we were confident in the assessment.

4.4 HAZARD INDICES

The third technique we will examine in this chapter is the hazard index. This is a technique which attempts to express the degree of hazard by using a number. There are a number of different ways in which this can be done but the method we will look at is one that was refined by the Dow Chemical Company. A number of other methods have also been developed by industrial concerns and risk management consultancies.

While we use the Dow Index for illustrative purposes, the basic philosophy of any index system remains the same, namely to measure the likelihood of loss and express the result as a number to which other numbers can then be compared and differences monitored.

We shall concentrate on the Dow Index and use it as an illustration of how a hazard index is constructed. A number of the technical features will be abbreviated as the index itself goes into considerable detail in order to arrive at the correct assessment of likelihood. We can summarise a number of these details without prejudicing our chances of understanding the concept.

The best way to see how the index is compiled is to follow each step, in its construction, in turn:

1. The starting off point is to decide which 'Process Units' would have the greatest impact on a fire or would contribute most to a fire or explosion. Once this Unit, or more than one if this is necessary, has been identified then the Material Factor must be calculated. This Material Factor

is a measure of the intensity of energy release from certain named chemicals or substances which you may have in the Process Unit. The Material Factor is an indication of the hazard which it is estimated is present when the particular chemical or substance is used. A comprehensive listing of chemicals and substances is provided with the documentation accompanying the Index. The person computing the Index would then check for all the relevant chemicals and substances in the Process Unit and calculate the Material Factor. The resultant figure will be between 1 and 40, as a result of the way in which the tables of values have been compiled.

A form is supplied with the documentation accompanying the Index and this is shown in Fig 4.9. The Material Factor is inserted at the top of the form.

2. The next step is to consider hazards other than those strictly connected to the materials used in the process. These additional hazards are in two categories;

a) *General process hazards*

These are features which could increase the magnitude of the loss and include such items as:

- the handling and transfer of materials
- types of reactions in the process
- access
- drainage

Penalties are applied as appropriate and inserted at the relevant place on the form in Fig 4.9.

b) *Special process hazards*

These are hazards which are known to contribute to incidents which increase the probability of fire or explosion and so they include:

- temperature
- dust
- pressure
- quantity of flammable material
- heaters

Penalties are again applied and inserted on the form at the appropriate place.

Fig 4.9

FIRE AND EXPLOSION INDEX ◆Dow				
	LOCATION		DATE	
PLANT	UNIT		CHARGE	
MATERIALS AND PROCESS				
MATERIALS				
CATALYSTS		SOLVENTS		

	PENALTY	PENALTY USED	
MATERIAL FACTOR (SEE TABLE I APPENDIX A) ──────────▶			
1. GENERAL PROCESS HAZARDS (SEE TABLE II)			
BASE FACTOR ────────────────▶	1.00	1.00	
A EXOTHERMIC REACTIONS (FACTOR .30 TO 1.25)			
B ENDOTHERMIC REACTIONS (FACTOR .20 TO .40)			
C MATERIAL HANDLING & TRANSFER (FACTOR .25 TO .85)			
D ENCLOSED PROCESS UNITS (FACTOR .30 TO .90)			
E ACCESS	.35		
F DRAINAGE (FACTOR .25 TO .50)			
GENERAL PROCESS HAZARD FACTOR ────────────▶			
2. SPECIAL PROCESS HAZARDS			
BASE FACTOR ────────────────▶	1.00	1.00	
A PROCESS TEMPERATURE (USE ONLY ONE)			
1 ABOVE FLASH POINT	.30		
2 ABOVE BOILING POINT	.60		
3 ABOVE AUTOIGNITION	.75		
B LOW PRESSURE (SUB ATMOSPHERIC)	50		
C OPERATION IN OR NEAR FLAMMABLE RANGE			
1 TANK FARM STORAGE FLAMMABLE LIQUIDS	.50		
2 PROCESS UPSET OR PURGE FAILURE	.30		
3 ALWAYS IN FLAMMABLE RANGE	.80		
D DUST EXPLOSION (FACTOR 25 TO 2.00) (SEE TABLE III)			
E PRESSURE (SEE FIGURE 2)			
F LOW TEMPERATURE (FACTOR .20 TO .50)			
G QUANTITY OF FLAMMABLE MATERIAL			
1 LIQUIDS OR GASES IN PROCESS (SEE FIG 3)			
2 LIQUIDS OR GASES IN STORAGE (SEE FIG 4)			
3 COMBUSTIBLE SOLIDS IN STORAGE (SEE FIG 5)			
H CORROSION AND EROSION (FACTOR .10 TO .75)			
J LEAKAGE – JOINTS AND PACKING (FACTOR .10 TO 1.50)			
K USE OF FIRED HEATERS (SEE FIG 6)			
L HOT OIL HEAT EXCHANGE SYSTEM (FACTOR .15 TO 1.15) (SEE TABLE IV)			
M ROTATING EQUIPMENT PUMPS COMPRESSORS	.50		
SPECIAL PROCESS HAZARD FACTOR (F_2) ──────────▶			
UNIT HAZARD FACTOR (F_1 x F_2 ÷ F_3) ──────────▶			
FIRE AND EXPLOSION INDEX (F_3 x MF) (F & E I) ──────────▶			

The Dow Fire and Explosion Index Form

3. Once all the general and special factors have been calculated they are multiplied together to produce the Unit Hazard Factor. The individual penalty factors of a general nature are added and this gives F(1). The special hazard factors are added and this gives F(2). The Unit Hazard Factor, F(3), is F(1) x F(2).

4. This Unit Factor is then applied to the Material Factor to produce the Fire and Explosion Index. Let us say that we have a Material Factor of 30 in a particular Process Unit. The general hazards come to a penalty of 2, and the special hazards aggregate to 1.5. This would mean that the Unit Hazard Factor, i.e. the hazard rate associated with the particular unit under consideration, would be 2 x 1.5 = 3. We then multiply this factor, which is a measure of the riskiness of the unit, by the Material Factor, which is a measure of the riskiness of the materials we are using. This gives a figure of 3 x 30 = 90. The Fire and Explosion Index is therefore 90.

5. It is possible that we could have two Process Units which had the same Unit Hazard Factor, i.e. two units which had the same general and special hazards associated with their processes. We could therefore have ended up with another unit having the same Unit Factor of 3. This however would not in itself tell us that the two plants presented the same hazard as they may both process entirely different materials. It is necessary then to relate the Unit Hazard Factor to the materials. The table in Fig 4.10 does this.

The vertical axis is a measure of the overall effect of a fire or a blast and is a scale from 0 to 1. The graph simply converts the Unit Hazard factor into an estimate of effect by relating it to the materials used. In our example we had a Unit Hazard Factor of 3 and a Material Factor of 30. From the graph we can see that the Damage Factor is approximately 0.74. What this means is that a fire could have no effect at all, at one extreme, or could result in total destruction, at the other extreme. We have estimated that the combination of process hazards and materials at this unit could result in a fire representing 74% destruction. This figure of 0.74 or 74% is known as the Damage Factor.

Fig 4.10

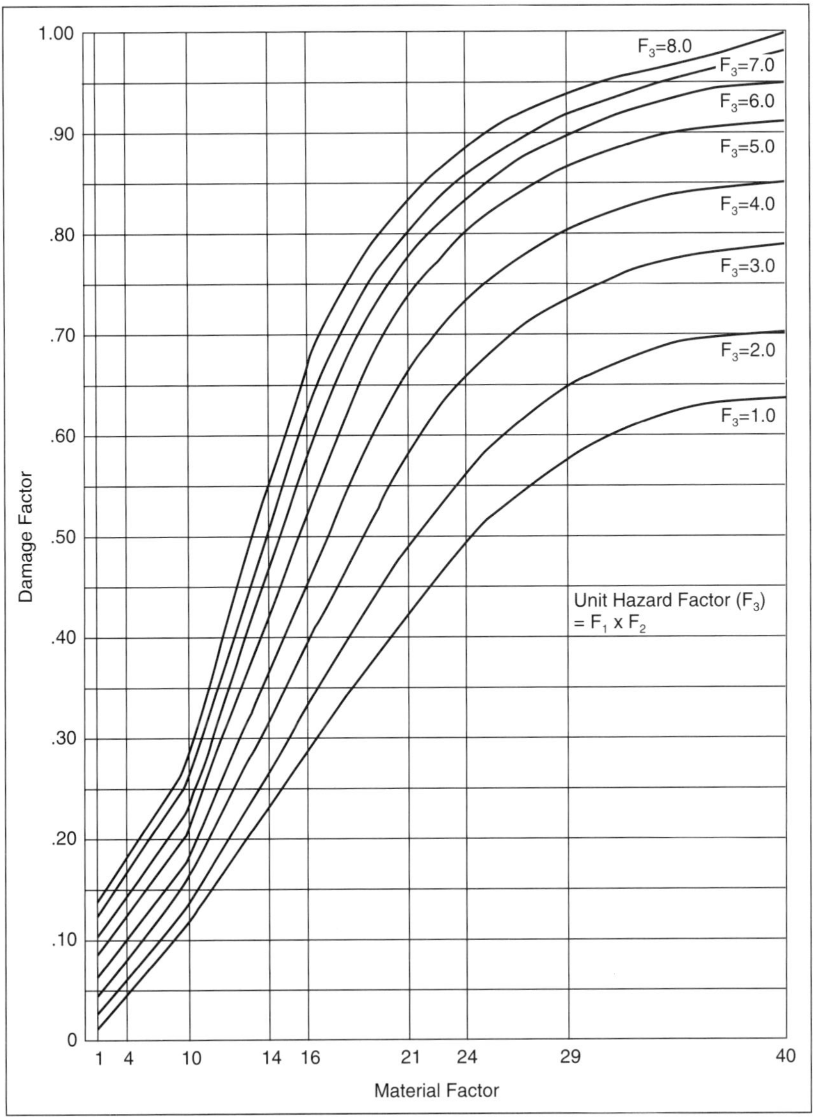

Relating the Unit Hazard Factor to the Materials

It is clearly the combination of the general and special process hazards and the materials used in the process which increases the potential for damage. The Damage Factor combines these aspects of risk and provides some measure of hazard. As we said earlier it would not be accurate simply to take either the process hazards or the material on their own. This would not result in a true reflection of hazard. We can illustrate this by looking at two Process Units which happen to have the same Unit Hazard Factor, i.e. the hazards associated with the process are the same but the materials are different:

	Process Unit One	Process Unit Two
Unit Hazard Factor	3	3
Material Factor	30	14
Damage Factor	0.74	0.32
Fire & Explosion Index	90	42

The probable extent of damage at Process Unit Two is very much smaller than at Unit One and this is due solely to the different Material Factor brought about by the different materials which must be used in the process.

6. You will see from the example above that the Fire and Explosion Index for the two units is also different. This index figure is now used to find the area of exposure which is likely to be affected by the fire or explosion. The graph in Fig 4.11 is used to convert the Fire and Explosion figure into an Area of Exposure.

The Index is plotted along the horizontal axis and the Area is read off. For our Unit One the Index is 90 and hence the radius of exposure is found to be approximately 76 feet. The Area of Exposure is therefore 18,152 square feet (the area of any circle is π times the radius squared or 3.1427 x 5776). We can now consult our plans and see what plant is within this area as there is 74% damage probability from the Process Unit we are considering. In the same way we can see that the other Process Unit represents a 32% damage probability to an area of about 3,633 square feet surrounding it.

The documentation provides a rough qualitative equivalent of the severity of the Fire and Explosion Index similar to the one shown in Table 4.6:

Fig 4.11

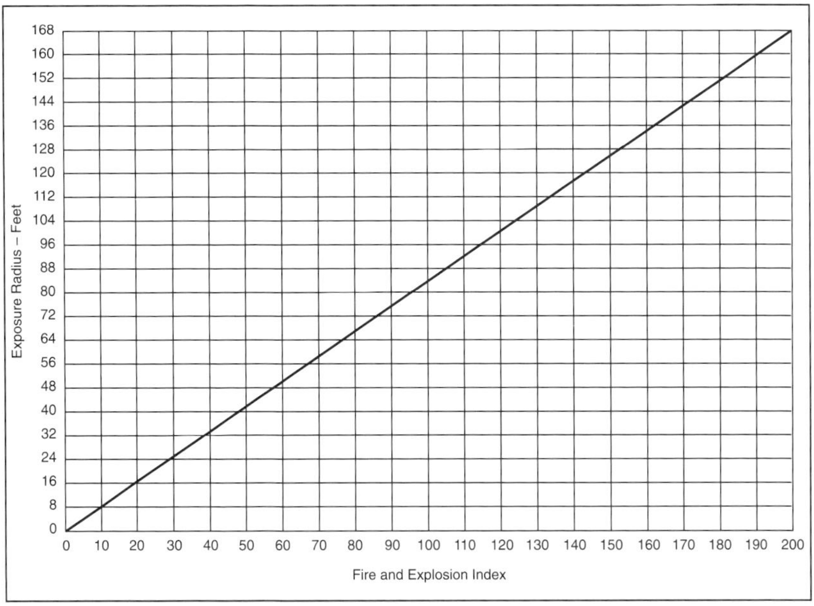

Converting the Fire and Explosion Index into an Area of Exposure

Table 4.6

Fire and Explosion Index Range	Degree of Hazard
1 – 60	Light
61 – 96	Moderate
97 – 127	Intermediate
128 – 158	Heavy
159 +	Severe

7. The Damage Factor represents the probable extent of any fire or explosion and so if we calculate the value of property within the Area of Exposure we could have some idea of what such an incident may cost. This is done by taking the replacement value of all such plant and multiplying it by the Damage Factor. Let us say that we had £280,000 in the Area then the Maximum Probable Property Damage, MPPD, would be £280,000 x 0.74 for the first Process Unit. This gives an expected damage figure, an MPPD, of £207,200.

8. The MPPD is very much a base figure as no account has been taken of any good features of the plant. So far we have concentrated on all those features which could increase the chance of loss. Now we can turn to the credit features and allow certain reductions in the MPPD as a result. A long list of credit points are given which include:

- sprinklers
- emergency shutdown systems
- drainage
- certain good operating procedures

These various features produce a credit allowance of a figure between 0 and 1. All allowances to which the unit is entitled are multiplied together and the result is a Credit Factor. The MPPD is multiplied by the Credit Factor in order to reflect the good points in the plant or process and this provides us with the actual MPPD. In our example let us say we have a Credit Factor of 0.45. This would then produce an actual MPPD of £207,200 x 0.45 = £93,240. This is much lower than the base MPPD and reflects the good points for which credit has now been allowed.

9. We could pull all the work we have done on Process Unit One together in one summary table as follows:

Fire and Explosion Index	=	90
Radius of exposure	=	76ft
Value inside Area of Exposure	=	£280,000
Damage Factor	=	0.74
Base MPPD	=	£207,200
Credit Factor	=	0.45
Actual MPPD	=	£93,240

The steps are as we have outlined them above but clearly some experience in constructing the index is desirable, and again the team approach may well be the best way to go about the whole job. The index does not identify individual risks but it does try to put some measure on the level of exposure arising out of the activities at the plant. With the index the risk manager can make comparisons across all the plant his company may operate and can monitor changes from year to year.

5

IDENTIFYING RISK 3

5.1   INTRODUCTION

So far a range of tried and tested risk identification and analysis techniques have been examined. These have ranged from the relatively straightforward, such as site visits and inspections, to the more complex such as Hazard and Operability Studies (HAZOPS) and Hazard Indices. One of the common characteristics linking all of these methods is that they are all well established risk identification and analysis methods.

We will now, however, go on to look at the more recent and emergent techniques of risk identification which are finding favour in risk management. The techniques we will be looking at will have some familiar and common elements as many are inspired by and developed from existing tried and tested techniques in risk management and wider business disciplines. For example Risk Scorecards have their roots in the familiar Balanced Scorecard methods used to measure general business performance for the last decade or so, while the methodology of Process Mapping has its origins in the field of Quality Management and relies heavily on the familiar Flow Diagram techniques which we have already examined earlier. It is equally fair to say that each of these methods have found their origins in particular disciplines, such as quality management, however, each has grown beyond these beginnings to find genuine applicability and usefulness in the field of business risk management.

As discussed in the introduction to Chapter 3, this is not the place for a debate on the distinction between risk identification and analysis, as each of the techniques discussed have characteristics of both stages of the risk management process. Rather, the techniques discussed all generally have elements both of recognition and measurement of risk with a view to leading to the effective control and ultimately management of the risk.

Four separate emerging methodologies will be considered: Process Mapping, Risk Scorecards, Risk Ranking and finally Risk Profiling. It should be noted that this does not promise to be an exhaustive consideration of these topics and that other relevant techniques exist and are emerging and developing all the time. These four methods do however best reflect the evolution of the discipline of risk management in the context of the wider business community.

For each of the four methods which will be studied the origins of the technique will be considered and the common applications of the technique will be discussed. A synopsis of the application of the technique itself will then be given and a practical example will be presented. The strengths and weaknesses of each of the methods will then be considered.

5.2   PROCESS MAPPING

All businesses are made up of a whole variety of processes. By representing these processes diagrammatically – or mapping them – we can see the way to improve things. If we apply this to the management of risks we can see clearly the potential for losses or the opportunities to maximise potential in the way that risks are dealt with.

This technique has its beginnings in the realms of quality management and the vogue for process re-engineering, which swept through companies in mainly the USA and Europe during the 1980s and 90s. The by-line of this movement was "If it ain't broke – fix it!" i.e. even if a business is operating effectively and efficiently it could still benefit from an in-depth analysis of its processes with a view to improvement. Some analysts now argue that such an approach led to a situation where businesses over-engineered to their detriment; however, it must be acknowledged that the technique itself has real benefits when applied correctly.

Business processes are a set of activities that convert inputs coming into the business into outputs which meet agreed customer needs. Inputs are the things needed to be able to carry out the activity, for example physical and human resources, knowledge, technology, etc. Outputs are the results of the process, for example products, services, information and by-products. This idea can be summarised in a diagram such as the one reproduced overleaf.

Fig 5.1

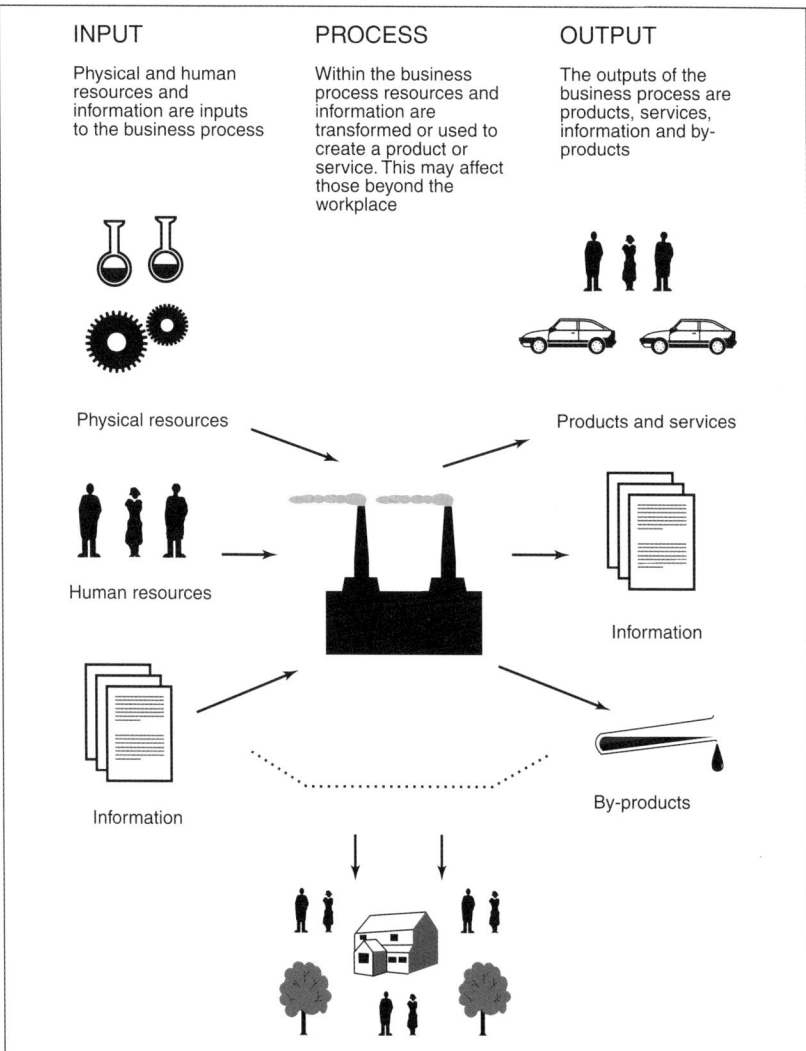

INPUT

Physical and human resources and information are inputs to the business process

PROCESS

Within the business process resources and information are transformed or used to create a product or service. This may affect those beyond the workplace

OUTPUT

The outputs of the business process are products, services, information and by-products

Physical resources

Human resources

Information

Products and services

Information

By-products

(c) Crown Copyright. Reproduced by permission of the Health and Safety Executive.

For example, if we consider a notional business such as the Imperial Rubber Company, they might have inputs of raw rubber and a variety of chemicals, their workforce provides the human resource, and information comes from their research and development department. The process will take place in their factory for example at their Manchester site. Their outputs will be their rubber products, information such as instructions for their products, and by-products such as waste from their various industrial processes.

So, what are process maps? Process maps are diagrams that show, to varying levels of detail, what the organisation does and how it goes about doing it. The process map is often likened to a road map. It shows the major elements of the operation, the most important activities of each process, the order of the elements, the inputs and resources required to carry out each activity along with the associated outputs. The main aim of the process map is to visualise the work process so that weaknesses and risks can be identified clearly, and to prompt new thinking about how work is done so that it can be done more efficiently, safer or more cost effectively.

As stated in the introduction the actual operation of process mapping also has its origins in the flow chart which we have already examined. This technique takes the basic idea that all operations can be split into discreet elements and further develops it so that specific risk issues can be identified and quantified. In process mapping the concepts behind flowcharts have probably most notably been exemplified in relation to the management of health and safety risks. In 1991 in their landmark publication *Successful Health and Safety Management* the UK Health and Safety Executive (HSE) represented the 'process' of managing workplace safety risks using a three-tier flowchart/process map as depicted overleaf.

This diagram shows that workplace safety risks can only be managed effectively by a systematic layered approach to management, with a high-level overview of management processes which are required to ensure that the correct mid-level activities or 'Risk Control Systems' are in place, to ensure that the appropriate task processes or 'Workplace Precautions' are implemented to protect everyone who may be affected by the work of the organisation. Again this process or systems approach to the management of risks would be wholly appropriate for an organisation such as IRC.

Fig 5.2

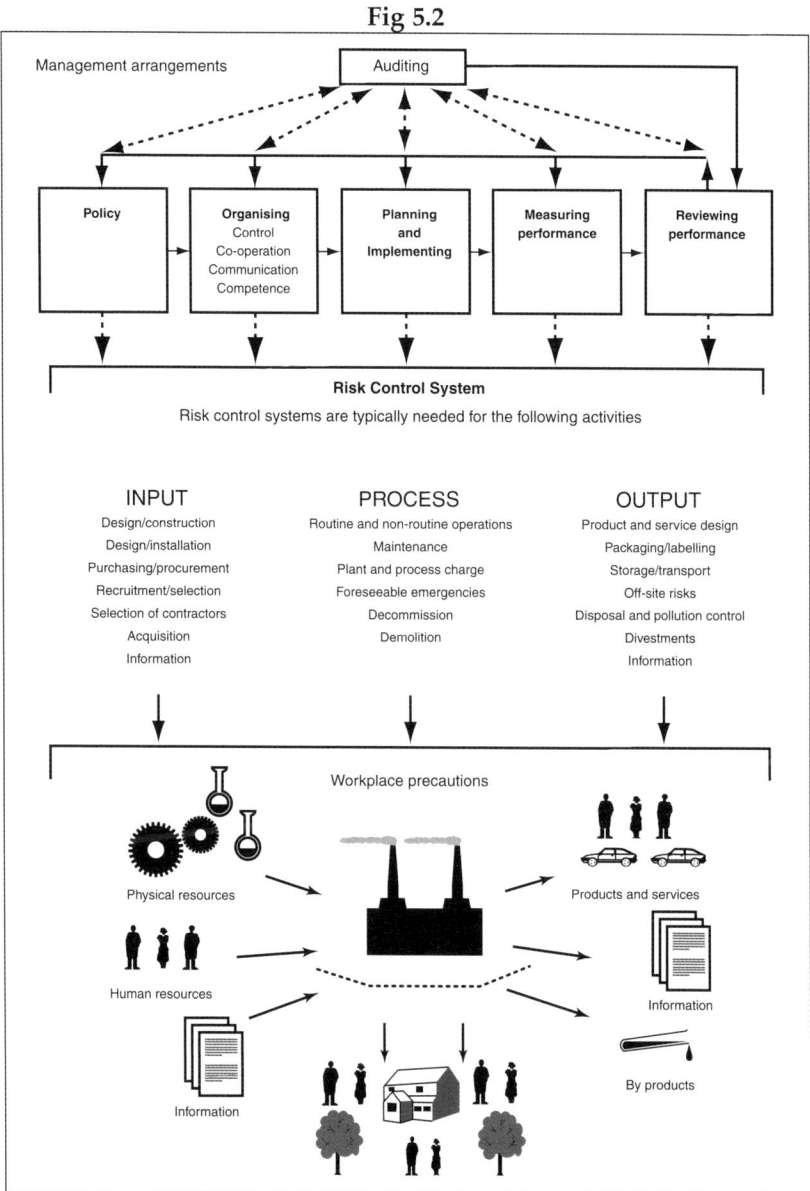

In some organisations flowcharts may be all that is needed to manage risks effectively. Obviously this would not develop the idea of process maps much beyond the now familiar concept of flow charts.

The major difference that process mapping introduces is the use of what are known as 'Process Definition Charts' (PDC). PDCs focus into processes in a much more detailed way and identify four key components for the delivery of any process or activity in the following way:

Fig 5.3

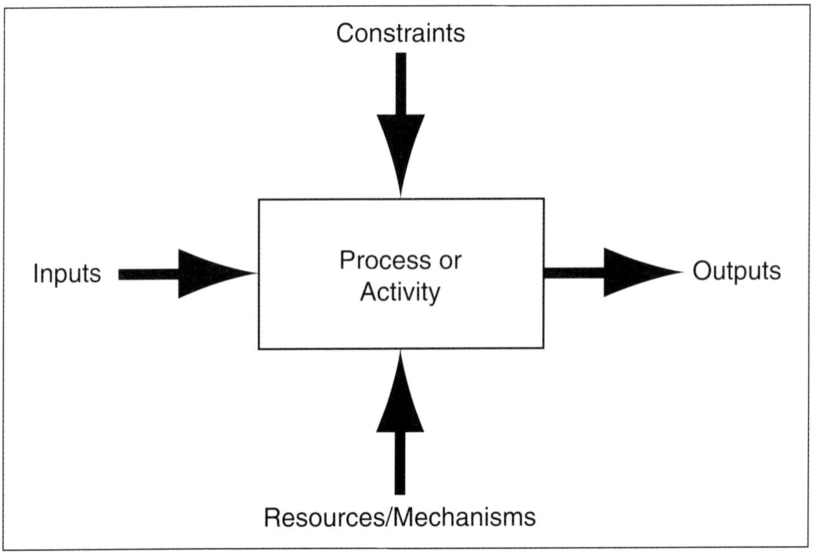

Source: Audit Scotland "The Map to Success" (2000)

Activities are the tasks or particular functions which make up the process.

Inputs are the things needed to undertake the activities and generate the outputs. In most cases inputs are changed or used up by the process. Examples might include raw materials, employees' time, money, etc.

Outputs are produced by the process. They would normally be products or services.

Constraints or controls moderate the process. These might be organisational, such as procedures, standards or a set budget, or external, such as applicable laws, imposed standards or a set amount of resources.

Resources or mechanisms are needed to produce the outputs. They differ from inputs as they are not altered or used up by the process. Examples might include equipment, buildings or people.

Staying with the example of health and safety risks, a PDC for carrying out health and safety risk assessments, one of a range of safety activities carried out by an organisation such as IRC, would perhaps look like this:

Fig 5.4

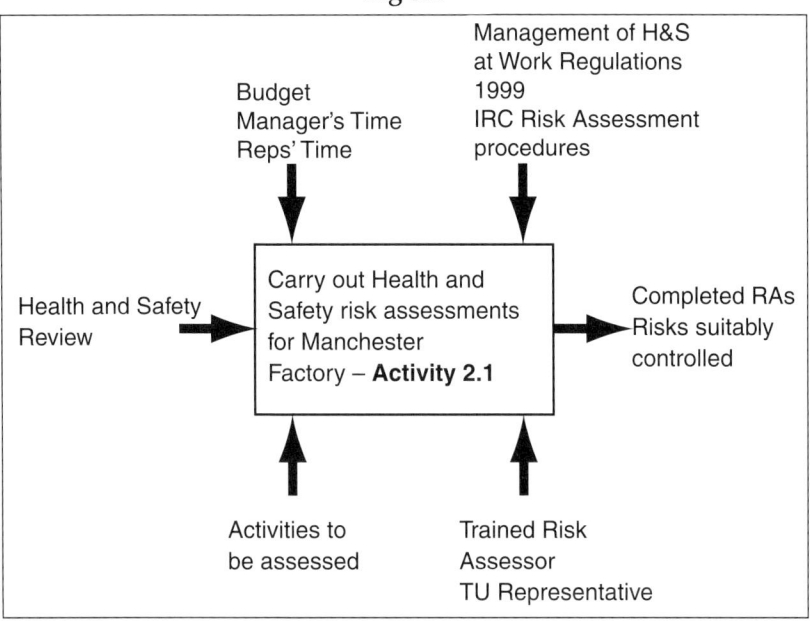

Potentially PDCs such as these flowcharts can be combined, as shown in Fig 5.5 to give a complete map of a particular process such as the management of health and safety within IRC. In this way key inputs and resources can be highlighted and significant constraints can be detailed so that the process can be undertaken correctly.

In practice such complete process maps are generally produced utilising a standard methodology known as Integration Definition for Function Modelling (IDEF) and commercially available software systems. Very soon these maps can become extremely complex; however, an essential purpose is served by making the organisation consider the following points:

- will the inputs be available, if so, where do they come from? This allows the consideration of which earlier process or activity creates outputs which will feed into the process under consideration.

Fig 5.5

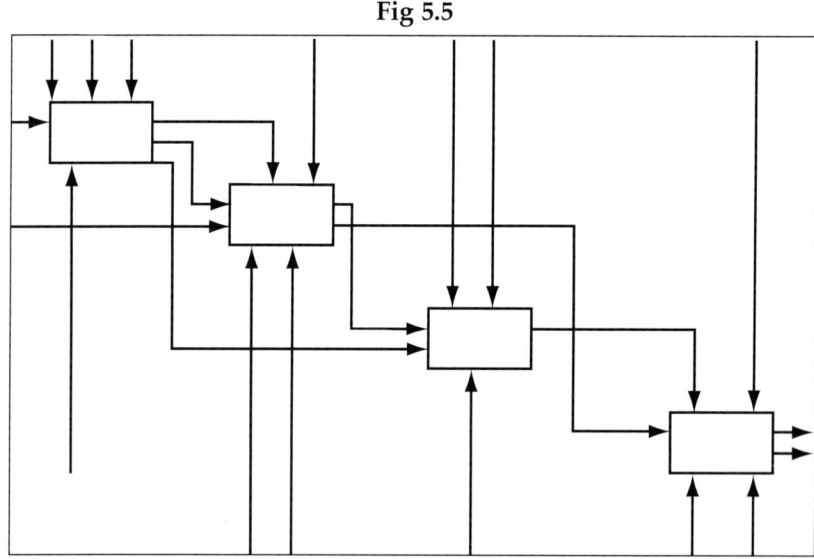

Source: Audit Scotland "The Map to Success" (2000)

- are the resources available to allow us to complete the process?

- do the process owners and their staff understand the critical constraints for this process? In this case a full understanding of legislative and organisational risk assessment requirements.

- have the expected outputs of the process been clearly understood? Do these meet 'customer' requirements (understanding that the next process, for example in this case training of operatives, will require these outputs as inputs)?

Now that the basics of the technique have been covered, the way that businesses should go about undertaking process mapping will be considered. Essentially this should be undertaken by following a simple step by step approach.

Firstly organisations should decide why they would want to process map. This allows crucial decisions on resourcing to be made at the outset. At its most basic, process mapping can be a framework for carrying out informal work reviews. At its most complex, involving

IDEF as outlined above, process mapping is a very complicated and formal system requiring much effort, investment and time. For example if IRC were to commit to this technique for their entire organisation then this would be significant business decision.

The next stage is to decide which processes to map. Many organisations, considering the commitment and complexity involved, may only focus on key operations or aspects of their business. So considering IRC, they may have decided that the health and safety of their employees and customers was so important that safety management deserved to be process mapped, to ensure that is was as effective as possible. This will basically be decided by a process of prioritisation, focusing on core or critical processes. Areas of the business which might be performing poorly may also be likely candidates. It should, however, be recognised that sometimes the most obvious processes may not be the ones upon which we should focus. For example the safety management process may be being undermined by weaknesses in related but independent processes in areas such as training or recruitment processes.

The personnel involved should then be considered. As process mapping is essentially about improving the way things are done, it is vital to involve the people involved in carrying out the activity. This will obviously vary according to the business and the activity under consideration. Using our example, IRC may want to include their Safety Manager (the process owner), the Risk and Insurance Manager, Managers who will be undertaking risk assessments (process members), the person who instigates the process, in this case a Safety consultant or the enforcement authorities (the process supplier), and finally a representative of the employees who will be being protected by the risk assessments (the process customer).

The flowcharts and maps will then have to be produced. Again, depending upon the organisation and what is being mapped, the process will vary. It has been recognised that the following is an indication of established 'success factors':

- management commitment
- effective communication
- development of a systematic approach
- training those involved in the methodology
- providing adequate resources in time and money

- looking for quick wins which will show immediate benefits to those involved.

There are further more complex process mapping techniques which allow for the introduction of a quantitative element; for example budgetary estimates could be assigned to the various factors to allow an estimation of the costs involved in the process to be considered. The value at risk could also be assigned to the risk element of the process map. This would allow for a more in-depth analysis of the process. These more advanced uses are, however, beyond the scope of this publication.

Notable risk management uses of process maps include the fields of safety management as explained here, environmental management, quality management, supply chain risk management and project management. Specific examples include the engineering industry, the public sector including local authorities, health care and law enforcement, the financial sector, in particular auditing, and interestingly enough insurance management.

As may already have become apparent, process mapping has numerous advantages. These include the ability to make sense of inter-related and complex processes, allowing focus on critical areas and ensuring delivery of quality processes, products or services. When related to risks critical to most organisations, such as safety of staff and the public and environmental concerns, the benefits could be crucial. Other less obvious advantages include the actual process of constructing the process maps themselves. If this is carried out in the manner suggested, it encourages understanding of all the activities required to deliver the product or service amongst the members of the organisation involved. Specific roles and responsibilities can be identified clearly, ensuring that everyone within the business knows the part they play in activities, thus avoiding situations where the wrong people may be involved or the worst case scenario when no one takes responsibility.

Most business operations require the integration of multiple elements of the organisation to deliver their product or service; process mapping facilitates these operations by ensuring more effective integration of the various parts of the business. As process mapping is output driven, focusing upon the desired outcome of the process, whether a new rubber product or a safer system of work, the technique helps ensure that the customer requirements, whether internal or external, are properly understood. It has been said that process mapping encourages what is known as a 'challenge culture' within organisations; this can only have positive benefits for risk management within an organisation as it will encourage staff to question why things have gone wrong, why losses have occurred and also encourage them to think how losses could be avoided in the first place or in future. With its origins in quality management and the search for performance improvement within organisations, there is an obvious synergy with risk management, which fundamentally seeks to avoid waste and loss to the organisation. Process mapping should deliver a business advantage to any organisation undertaking the method.

Obviously it would be unfair to talk solely about the advantages of the technique. More perceptive readers will no doubt have formed the view that the technique could appear overly complex, producing numerous complex diagrams that could easily confuse the uninitiated. It must also by accepted that there is the possibility that without the proper support and knowledge, a poorly conceived attempt at process mapping could potentially do more damage than good. Without the appropriate thought, planning, resourcing and buy-in from management, the exercise could at best be undermined and at worst be an extremely damaging waste of time, effort and resources. It is therefore essential that a decision to utilise process mapping is thoroughly considered before a commitment is made.

In conclusion it must be recognised that when thoughtfully and properly applied, process mapping could bring real benefits to the management of risk, particularly in the areas highlighted earlier in the section. The fact that the methodology is also currently very much in vogue across a broad range of business should not be underestimated.

5.3 RISK RANKING

The prioritisation of risk is fundamental to our analysis of risks. There are a number of ways in which this can be done and these will vary depending upon the risks under consideration and the particular methodology being employed. An in-depth study of these various methods is outwith the scope of this publication; however it will be worthwhile to examine one relatively new methodology in detail. Risk assessment methodologies have long been established as a predominant risk management tool with a broad range of uses ranging from emergency planning through to societal risk issues. Probably the area that has benefited most from risk assessment is the field of occupational health and safety. For example in the United Kingdom (UK) there have been wide ranging risk assessment legal requirements relating to almost all businesses for well over a decade now.

Many readers will be familiar with the simple 5-step approach to risk assessment advocated by the UK Health and Safety Executive (HSE), shown below:

1. Look for the hazards
2. Decide who might be harmed and how
3. Evaluate the risks and decide whether the existing precautions are adequate or whether more should be done
4. Record your findings
5. Review your assessment and revise it if necessary

(Those unfamiliar with the method should refer to guidance freely available from the HSE and on their website.)

While this methodology has numerous advantages it has been criticised in some circles for being over simplistic, in particular not providing the complexity needed to prioritise the wide ranging workplace risks present in many organisations. It is also criticised for relying too heavily upon the subjective judgement of the assessor at step three to make a judgement on the adequacy of existing controls. As the setting of control priorities is one of the fundamental reasons why we analyse risk, this could be viewed as a major drawback. We will therefore now examine a more advanced method which has been researched by the HSE to address risk assessment in such situations – risk ranking, or more specifically Risk Priority Assessment (RPA).

RPA focuses upon the ranking of various risks dependent upon their significance, based upon the likelihood of incidents causing particular consequences of varying seriousness, the typical example being an accident causing an injury. It does not claim to be able to assess more complex and long lasting risks such as work related ill health. The methodology was developed by reviewing a range of risk assessment and ranking methods suggested in a range of official and unofficial guidance from a variety of sources. It has taken these ideas and further developed them by focussing upon a range of different types of accidents and has weighted their relative significance using historical UK accident statistics. It is aimed at the assessment of acute risk in small and medium sized enterprises. It could be suggested that Imperial Rubber Company (or at least parts of it) fall within this definition, therefore we will again use the company as a case study to demonstrate the methodology in practice.

The technique suggests that risks be assessed and ranked following a six-step process:

Step 1: What Could Happen?
Step 2: How Likely is it to Happen?
Step 3: Decide How Someone Might be Harmed
Step 4: Decide How Many are Likely to be Affected
Step 5: Evaluate the Risks
Step 6: Rank, Plan and Review

The method relies upon a scoring system based upon the seriousness of past accidents in UK workplaces. In many ways it could be said to be similar in its methodology to other methods discussed in this book, i.e. it relies upon past incident data to project future losses, probably most notably Hazard Indices. The key difference being that these projections are based upon national statistics perhaps for the first time. Fundamentally the method dictates that the bigger the risk score the greater the problem, this then allows structured decisions to be made on the reduction of risk. The strategy does however advocate that the aim of managing health and safety hazards in the workplace is to reduce the overall risk score in the workplaces, discouraging organisations focussing only on the big risks to the detriment of the more mundane issues which can also be of significance.

We shall now examine the six-step process in more detail by applying it to IRC.

Step 1: 'What Could Happen?'

In this step IRC would have to consider a variety of accidents from the table shown overleaf which might apply in their workplace.

Type of Accident	'Historical Importance Value'
Drowning or asphyxiation	19
Fall from height over 2m	18
Trapped by something collapsing or overturning	16
Contact with electricity or electrical discharge	12
Exposure to an explosion	11
Struck by moving vehicle	7
Fall from height up to 2m	7
Contact with moving machinery	6
Exposure to fire	6
Slip, trip or fall on the same level	5
Struck by moving including flying/falling object	5
Exposure to or contact with a harmful substance	4
Strike against something fixed or stationary	4
Injured by animal	3
Acts of violence	3
Injured while handling, lifting or carrying	3

(c) Crown Copyright. Reproduced by permission of the
Health and Safety Executive.

The importance value is based upon the historical importance of each accident in terms of the number of deaths and major injuries that have resulted from past accidents.

For each of the relevant accidents, anything within IRC which could cause these types of accidents should be considered. These are the hazards, and these should be recorded on the form shown at the end of this section (Fig 5.6). The importance value from the table should also be entered in column **A** on the form. The methodology suggests that this exercise will probably be best achieved utilising a team approach and consulting widely, involving employees and their representatives. For example within IRC this might involve the Risk Manager, Safety Manager, Production Manager and Trade Union Safety Representative. Once all the possibilities have been considered then the team should move on to the next type of accident until all potential hazards have been identified. An example is given below:

Type of Accident	Score A	Hazards
Fall from height over 2m	18	Maintenance of factory roof
Ditto	18	Retrieval of items from warehouse racking
Ditto	18	Maintenance of rubber vats

(c) Crown Copyright. Reproduced by permission of the
Health and Safety Executive.

Step 2: 'How Likely is it to Happen?'

Once step 1 is complete we then have to consider the likelihood of each of the hazards. RPA uses a list of phrases, as described in the table below, to describe the likelihood of an incident occurring and assigns scores to each of these descriptions.

How Likely is it to Happen	Score
Effectively impossible	1
Unlikely	2
Plausible	3
Possible	4
Probable	5
Very Likely	6
Almost Certain	7

(c) Crown Copyright. Reproduced by permission of the
Health and Safety Executive.

For each of the hazards that have been identified a score should be selected which best describes its likelihood. The relevant phrases should be written in the column marked Step 2 in the RPA form and the scores should be placed in the box marked score C as shown at the end of this section. It should be noted that the ordering of the values inserted in the table runs Step 1, Step 3, Step 2...; this is to reflect the risk score formula explained later in the section.

Step 3: 'Decide How Someone Might be Harmed'

Following on from this the result of the accident will have to be considered. Again a range of accident injury/illness outcomes have been ranked and scored to reflect past experience in order of importance, see table below. The scores are based upon the number of fatalities and major injuries that have occurred in the past.

Death	491
Ill health – permanently incapacitating	99
Amputation	26
Other injuries caused by contact with electricity	20
Concussion/internal injuries	19
Damage to eyesight	18
Bone fractures	18
Dislocation	16
Natural causes (heart attack)	15
Poisonings and gassings	14
Burns	4
Lacerations and open wounds	2
Contusions/severe bruising; superficial injuries; sprains and strains; ill health (non incapacitating e.g. dermatitis)	1

In relation to each of the hazards previously identified the most likely injury/illness outcome should be considered and the score should be selected and placed in the box labelled Score **B**.

Step 4: 'Decide How Many are Likely to be Affected'

The number of people who might be affected by each of the hazards should then be entered in the column labelled step 4. It is likely in many cases that this might only be a single person but obviously the greater the number of people exposed to the hazard the greater the risk.

Step 5: 'Evaluate the Risks'

Once steps 1-4 are complete for each of the hazards an attempt can then be made to evaluate the risk rating for each. To rate the risk the following simple formula is used:

$$\textbf{RISK RATING} = \textbf{(A + B)} \times \textbf{C} \times \textbf{D}$$

So for one of our examples, the hazard of the fall from a height of over 2m while carrying out maintenance of the rubber vats, the following scores could possibly be given:

Step 1 Fall from height of over 2m   Score A = 18
    Step 2   Possible   Score C = 4
    Step 3   Bone fractures   Score B = 18
    Step 4   One person affected   Score D = 1

Risk Rating = $(18 + 18) \times 4 \times 1 = 144$

The appropriate risk rating scores for each of the hazards can then be inserted in the appropriate column on the form.

Step 6: 'Rank, Plan and Review'

This step completes the process. The preceding five steps will have allowed a score rating to be assigned to each of the hazards which IRC might face – the higher the score the greater the risk. This allows the organisation to consider their most significant risks and then make reasoned decisions on how each will be controlled. Obviously it would be recommended that focus should be placed on the highest ranked risks first. The actual decisions on risk control are obviously outwith the scope of this publication therefore we shall leave the risk ranking process at this point.

One final point before we move on to consider the benefits and drawbacks of the methodology is that users might want to include an analysis of the cost effectiveness of the actions taken so that the cost/benefit of risk reduction measures can be considered.

Obvious advantages of the system are that it is based upon national experiential data, therefore it has real relevance in a wide range of workplaces. It is also based upon existing and familiar methodologies so it could be said to be tried and tested to a certain extent. The method is also relatively simple, following a step by step process, and only very basic calculations are required. Therefore it is probable that the ranking could be undertaken without the need for extensive knowledge or competency in risk management theories and applications. It also reflects the wide range of accident risks which might be present within many working environments and allows them to be ranked and compared in a fair, unbiased and systematic fashion.

The major disadvantage of this system from a risk management perspective is that it only considers health and safety risks and pays no attention to the various other risks business organisations might face.

The methodology also has other drawbacks even within its own limited scope. The first and most important of these is that it pays little regard to more chronic workplace health and safety issues such as ill health. As these issues have such an unfortunate cost particularly to individuals, but also to businesses and society in general, then this has to be a major flaw. This would be a particular problem to IRC as they face many such hazards associated with the industrial processes carried out in the rubber industry. The system also does not highlight potential risk to people other than employees, for example customers, members of the public, although perhaps its 'bolt-on' nature in relation to the HSE's 5-steps approach takes this into consideration. Other disadvantages are that certain judgement calls required by the system will involve an amount of subjectivity on the part of the person making the assessment, probably most notably when deciding the most likely injury outcome. Although we have cited its simplicity as a virtue of the system, given its target audience of small and medium sized businesses, the methodology may appear too complex to some.

Taking all these factors into consideration it must be acknowledged that the technique does have definite merits; however, the fact that it has not yet been adopted by the HSE for widespread dissemination is perhaps particularly noteworthy. The principles of assigning scores to past loss events based upon experiential information and then using these to calculate risk ranking is not new, however, this type of simplified approach could also be adopted in relation to other business risks such as environmental or financial risks. Indeed, an organisation or a group of organisations such as a trade association could devise something similar. Where an association has pooled statistics on types of losses for its members it may be able to use them in the way we have shown above, for any form of risk.

5.4   RISK SCORECARDS

The two techniques considered so far in this chapter have been quite focussed in their application: process mapping to particular operations in an organisation and risk ranking to a particular risk – health and safety. Now we will move on to consider more strategic and wide ranging methods to identify and analyse risk. The first technique which will be considered is the use of Risk Scorecards.

Fig 5.6

Risk Assessment for: Imperial Rubber Company		Date: 23/3/03		Assessed by:				Page: 1	
	STEP 1		**STEP 3**		**STEP 2**		**STEP 4**		**STEP 5**
Type of Accident	Score A	Hazards	Nature of Injury	Score B	Likelihood	Score C	Number Affected D		Risk Score (A+B) x C x D

© Crown Copyright. Reproduced by permission of the Health and Safety Executive.

The scorecard approach to improving business performance is well established and is based on the idea that performance improvement can only be achieved by measuring Key Performance Indicators (KPIs). This idea is summed up in the following well used phrase – "If you can't measure, you can't manage – and if you can't manage, you can't perform". Probably the most notable example of this approach is Kaplan and Norton's Balanced Scorecard, which was introduced in 1993 and is used today by a wide range of successful businesses and public sector bodies. This technique uses a range of performance measures to benchmark organisational effectiveness with a view to helping to meet business objectives. The most commonly used performance indicators are with issues such as Customer Management, Internal Operations Management, Employee Management, Financial Management and Organisational Learning/Innovation. Obviously all of these KPIs have applicability to Risk Management, however, we are not limited to this list and the approach can be further developed to consider risk KPIs. The most notable example of this approach is the FIRM Risk Scorecard which has recently been suggested by Paul Hopkin in his new text book *Holistic Risk Management in Practice* (also available from Witherbys). As the name of the book suggests the technique is part of a much more wide ranging approach to risk management than can be considered in this text, however, it will be useful to consider the scorecard in more detail as an example of another way to analyse business risks.

The FIRM Risk Scorecard suggested by Hopkin is essentially a strategic risk assessment tool. It provides a framework for the systematic identification of risks to an organisation. In particular the method focuses upon the timescale of the effect of risk, the character of the risk's impact on the organisation and relates this to the risk exposure and overall risk capacity of the business. By doing this the scorecard highlights the complex and interdependent nature of risk within businesses and the effect that it can have over the whole organisation. The methodology does this by considering risk in the following classifications: **F**inancial, **I**nfrastructure, **R**eputation and **M**arketplace (FIRM). The method considers risk as external (reputation and marketplace) and internal (financial and infrastructure). This allows a cross disciplinary mix or quantitative and qualitative factors to be considered when assessing the risk the organisation faces. The characteristics of each of the headings of the FIRM Risk Scorecard are summarised on the table shown overleaf.

Following the now familiar process we will now take a closer look at the technique by demonstrating its use in Imperial Rubber Company.

We will now consider the characteristics of each of the FIRM headings as they might relate to IRC.

Financial Risks

These are risks which can have an impact upon the organisation's financial resources and balance sheet, specifically how available funds and/or earnings are placed and controlled, financial procedural failures relating to loss mitigation, and budgeting and matters relating to sound internal financial control. We can usually quantify these risks relatively easily with reference to measuring the value of any losses and/or estimations of the value of lost opportunities relating to poor financial management. An example may be IRC being unable to invest in new equipment to competitively tender for a new contract because of unavailability of funds due to internal accounting delays.

The level of financial risk will obviously vary between companies and Hopkin suggests a way to benchmark this is to correlate it to internal financial triggers, such as the capital expenditure above which Chief Executive Officer authorisation is required. For a medium to large organisation such as IRC this may be within the range £100,000 to £1 million.

Obviously the key people to involve when considering risks in this category are the Finance Director, the Insurance and Risk Manager, and accountants and internal auditors, as they will hopefully fully understand the organisation's internal financial control systems. Examples of these risk control systems are Capital Expenditure (CapEx) authorisation and internal financial control procedures. Weaknesses, infringements and deviations from these procedures will highlight weaknesses and loss potential in the system.

Fig 5.7

	Financial	Infrastructure	Reputational	Marketplace
Description	Risks that will impact the way in which money is managed and profitability is achieved.	Risks that will impact the level of efficiency and dysfunction within the core processes.	Risks that will impact desire of stakeholders to deal or trade and level of customer retention.	Risks that will impact the level of stakeholder trade or expenditure and customer retention.
Desired State	An effective and adequate system of internal financial management and control.	An infrastructure which has no unplanned dysfunctional events and efficiently satisfies customer requirements.	A reputation that ensures a positive image for the organisation with stakeholders.	Adequate funding of activities and adequate ongoing income from the marketplace.
Internal or External Risk	Internal	Internal	External	External
Quantifiable	Usually	Sometimes	Not always	Yes
Measurement of Risk Productivity Indicator	Gains and losses from internal financial control.	Level of efficiency in processes and operations.	Nature of publicity and effectiveness of marketing profile.	Income from commercial and market activities.
Performance Gap	PROCEDURES Failure of procedures to control internal financial risks.	PROCESS Failure of processes to operate without dysfunction.	PERCEPTION Failure to achieve the desired perception of the organisation.	PRESENCE Failure to achieve the required presence in the marketplace.
Control Mechanisms	• CapEx standards • Internal Control • Delegation of Authority	• Process Control • Loss Control • Insurance and risk financing	• Marketing • Advertising • Reputation and brand protection	• Strategic plans • Business plans • Opportunity assessment

Summary of attributes under each heading of the FIRM Risk Scorecard

Source: Paul Hopkin *Holistic Risk Management* p82 Witherby (2002)

Infrastructure Risks

The type of risk which falls within this category are what could perhaps be labelled as established risks, the kind of loss exposures which would normally be covered by insurance risk transfer and financing control strategies similar to insurance. Typical examples include physical assets such as buildings, machinery and equipment, manufacturing equipment and IT hardware, and employees and members of the public who may be affected by the organisation's activities.

Risks in this area of the scorecard will affect the normal operation and efficiency of the company and are usually connected to non-routine events impacting the infrastructure in place to support the organisation's business activities. An example of this type of risk to IRC may be fire damage to an area of their plant or a workplace injury to an employee. Normally we can estimate the financial impact of these risks relatively easily as they are usually internal in nature; however, complications can occur when external factors come into play. A typical example of this would be the failure of a key supplier to provide essential raw materials due to a major incident at their premises causing delays to IRC's production.

Hopkin suggests that the benchmark for significance of these risks will also vary between companies; however it is generally related to the time of effect of the infrastructure risk event or a more detailed consideration of the financial impact on future profitability or earning capacity. This can be closely linked to the organisation's performance upon financial markets and a benchmark key performance indicator in this case would be a 10% movement in share price. IRC would obviously be able to monitor this type of event.

Key personnel for assessing risks in this area within IRC would perhaps be the Operations or Production Manager or Director, Risk and Insurance Manager and the Safety Manager, as they will most fully understand the company's infrastructure which is at risk. They will also have the greatest say in the control mechanisms for these risks such as policies, procedures, maintenance and insurance mechanisms, therefore will be able to identify any potential problems in these areas.

Reputational Risks

These risks are obviously closely related to the company's image in relation to customers, suppliers, shareholders and society in general – in other words, stakeholders. Reputation risks are linked to IRC's brand image, however, risks which can damage this are very wide ranging and difficult to understand and quantify. Examples of these types of risks could be corporate governance and ethical issues, ensuring business continuity, and legal compliance issues. Typical examples for IRC may be Enron-style financial and accounting irregularities, letting down customers due to a production interruption because of a major incident at one of their plants, or the culpable workplace death of an employee. Any of these examples could attract unwanted and negative publicity which could adversely affect the company's image and reputation. This obviously focuses on the negative aspects of these types of risk, however, the positive aspects of publicity and marketing should also not be underestimated.

Risks to this area of the company can be characterised as risks which affect the relationship with the company's customers and suppliers, the perceptions of the organisation's stakeholders, and the company's positive image and brand strength. The complex nature of these risks makes measurement problematic; however, an obvious key performance indicator in this area is the effect of reputational risk issues on the company's financial market performance.

In many companies, and IRC would probably be no exception, it might be difficult to identify the key personnel to assess risks in this area, as the issue has such complex and cross-disciplinary impact. IRC may wish to assign this area to a particular director to champion marketing and brand issues and would rely upon guidance from the company Marketing Manager or marketing agency. As this area is an emergent one within the field of Risk Management, control regimes are in their infancy. There are possible insurance mechanisms along with robust business continuity and crisis management procedures. The Risk and Insurance Manager would play an integral role in these areas.

Marketplace Risks

These types of risks could be described as being competitive in nature as they relate to the company's positioning within the marketplace and the commercial risks that all businesses face.

Quantification of these risks is possible via indicators such as revenue levels, turnover, commercial costs, and profits.

Marketplace risks can be characterised as those which effect client and customer spending and the ability to hold on to trading partners, commercial risks relating to the company's poor market profile and performance, and risks to objectives relating to revenue and business growth. A typical example for a company such as IRC would be decisions to invest in new rubber product development, to enter new export markets, or to raise capital via a new shares option.

Within IRC it would most likely be the Commercial Director or Manager with responsibility for sales and marketing who would take ownership of this area, and they would call upon key staff to identify and help quantify risks in this area. Typical controls for these types of risks are robust business planning and strategy, and risk and opportunity assessments of new projects and business opportunities.

The FIRM Risk Scorecard, when quantified, can be used to graphically represent risk management within the company, as shown in Fig 5.8.

This represents what Hopkin refers to as the risk capacity of the company, in this case IRC. It represents the level of risk, or opportunity appetite added to hazard tolerance and control acceptance, that IRC would be willing to accept and breaks it down into the four areas of the FIRM Risk Scorecard. If the theory is taken to its full and logical conclusion, IRC would be able to quantify its risk capacity and make decisions based on how much it is prepared to risk, meaning that they will not receive any unexpected or unpredicted surprises and that the company's capacity for risk is used to maximum benefit. This will help IRC make the most of the opportunities and threats which the wide variety of risks they face present.

Hopkin identifies a range of advantages to the methodology under each of the FIRM headings. Obviously a whole range of benefits could be gained by adopting such a strategic and wide ranging approach, from better marketplace presence to brand improvements, improved stakeholder relations to enhanced corporate governance. In general it would appear to offer increased efficiency, security, stability and effectiveness for the organisation through improving its handling, dealing with and management of risk.

Fig 5.8

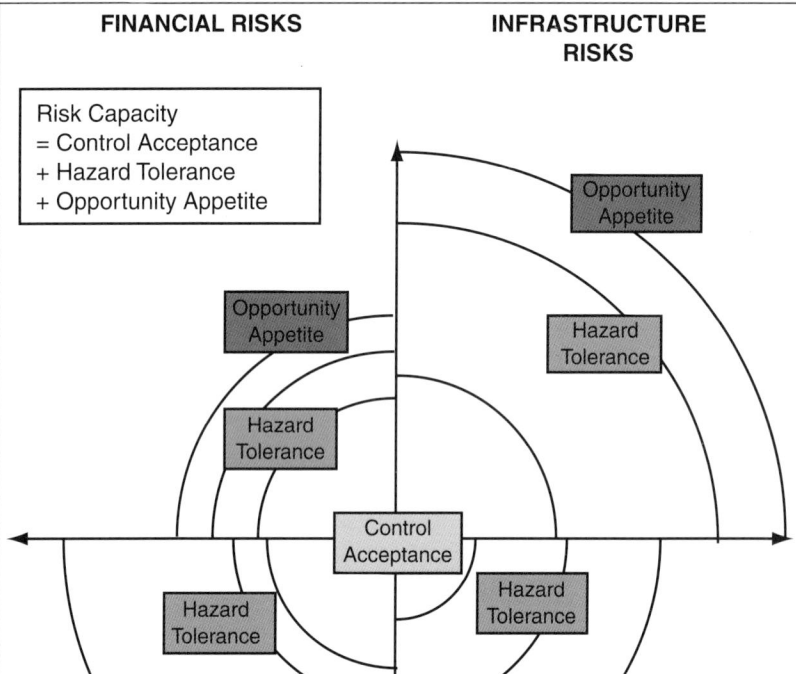

Source: Adapted from Hopkin *Holistic Risk Management in Practice*
p90 Witherby (2002)

In terms of disadvantages, we could say that it will only really be of applicability and benefit to large businesses. It may also be fair to question if the FIRM framework truly represents the wide ranging and complex risks that many companies face in today's business environment. The technique's value as a stand alone risk identification and/or analysis method must also be called into question, as it may only be of true value when used within an holistic approach to risk management as proposed by Hopkin and others.

Most readers will, however, recognise that this type of approach could reap real benefits when used as a strategic risk assessment tool around which to hang consideration of risk management issues. Its similarity to and influences from such widely used business improvement techniques as Balanced Scorecard, alone would make it of real benefit within organisations that are utilising such strategies.

5.5   RISK PROFILING

Due to the wide ranging perspectives on risk in the business world today, ask five different professionals "What is meant by the term risk profiling?" and you will usually get five different answers. This is because the term will have different definitions depending upon the background of the person being asked. To a scientist it may mean the environmental toxicity of a particular chemical, to a doctor the particular characteristics of a particular health risk, and to someone working in the world of finance it may be related to the way financial institutions assess the credit worthiness of investment decisions. In the field of Risk Management, however, its most relevant definition is probably as a strategic risk identification and assessment methodology.

Risk profiling has possibly emerged due to the influence of the Turnbull Report and the London Stock Exchange's combined code, which has introduced strict business risk management controls to all listed companies, along with requirements for annual public reporting on risk management controls. These have placed a much greater, and perhaps for some even a completely new, emphasis on sound risk management. One way to tackle these issues is through the use of risk profiling. Risk profiling provides a framework for meeting these requirements by allowing for the strategic, systematic, structured assessment and monitoring of business risks.

Obviously the technique has attractions other than purely Turnbull compliance. Even without these requirements the method will bring the same business benefits of improved efficiency, competitive advantage and profitability that all risk management activities bring. The technique also provides additional security against disastrous losses, effective control of business risks during periods of change and growth, and smooth management of risk during merger or takeovers. In addition it can also be used to allow transparency to the process linking directors' business rewards to key performance indicators, particularly re-assuring during times of controversy relating to 'fat-cat' director salaries. The technique can also be used to address requirements to demonstrate compliance to enforcement agencies or governing bodies, such as those relating to charitable organisations.

One particular organisation that leads the field in the application of this particular technique are AEA Technology, a world renowned UK based innovation business which provides risk management solutions to worldwide clients. They suggest a five-step approach to corporate risk profiling as shown in Fig 5.9.

Fig 5.9

```
        ┌─────────────────────────────┐
        │      Define risk units      │
        └─────────────────────────────┘
                     ▼
  ┌───────────────────────────────────────────┐
  │ Establish a risk ranking and prioritisation scheme │
  └───────────────────────────────────────────┘
                     ▼
      ┌─────────────────────────────┐
      │   Identify threats and assess   │
      └─────────────────────────────┘
                     ▼
    ┌─────────────────────────────────┐
    │ Categorise risks and identify controls │
    └─────────────────────────────────┘
                     ▼
  ┌─────────────────────────────────────┐
  │ Action plans for risk control and monitoring │
  └─────────────────────────────────────┘
```

Source: AEA Technology, http://www.aeat.com/consulting/corprk.htm. (2003)

Let us now imagine that Imperial Rubber Company have been elevated to being listed on the London Stock Exchange and once more use the company as an example to illustrate this process in operation.

Step 1 – Define Risk Units

At this stage the aim is to split the business into more manageable risk categories with a view to undertaking the Risk Profiling exercise. This can be achieved in a variety of ways. In relation to IRC the risk units could simply be in line with the various business units as follows:

IRC Manufacturing (Manchester) incorporating industrial coatings

IRC Retail – National Bounce Company

Subsidiaries – Imperial Rubber (Civil Engineering)
Imperial Pipes and Hoses plc

Alternatively the identification of risk units could be common to all operations and related to business disciplines such as Finance, Human Resources, Operations, etc, however for the purposes of this exercise we will utilise the various business units. One method suggested by AEAT is to broadly split the business into four broad categories: Values, Processes, People, and Assets. Each of these areas can be further subdivided as shown on the diagram in Fig 5.10. Another approach is to carry out techniques such as brainstorming in an attempt to identify all the risks the business might face.

Fig 5.10

Mission, vision, values and strategy	Responding to market
Corporate Management	Business Continuity
Legal and Regulatory	Crisis Management
Mergers, acquisitions and	Operational Risks
divestments	Financial Control
Subsidiaries	Reputation
Expansion	Suppliers
Expansion	Customers
IP	HR
IT	Key Personnel
Security	Key Personnel
Facilities	Outsourcing
Plant, offices, premises	Environment
Confidential Information	Health and Safety
Company Relationship/Image	Ethical Behaviour
Branding	Neighbours/3rd Parties

Values   Processes

Assets   People

Source:
AEA Technology, http://www.aeat.com/consulting/flyers/crppresentation.pdf (2001)

Step 2 – Establish a Risk Ranking and Prioritisation Scheme

There are obviously a variety of techniques which can be considered; for example the risk ranking methodology outlined earlier in this chapter could be adapted to rank a broader range of risks than health and safety alone. Suitable guidance, such as that issued by the Institute of Chartered Accountants in England and Wales (ICA), or by consultants such as AEA Technology suggests that a far simpler approach should be taken. They suggest that risk be rated straightforwardly and qualitatively in terms of impact (severity) and likelihood (frequency) and that the rating should be kept as simple as possible. AEAT suggest classification such as that shown on the table in Fig 5.11 and we will use this for IRC's Risk Profiling exercise. Whatever ranking method is chosen it is suggested that the approach be considered and tailored to the particular organisational requirements and characteristics.

Fig 5.11

IMPACT		LIKELIHOOD	
None	Negligible and impact recoverable	**Incredible**	Is not judged to be credible
Minor	0.1% reduction in turnover or 1% reduction in contribution	**Improbable**	Is not likely to occur over the next ten years
Moderate	1% reduction in turnover or 10% reduction in contribution	**Remote**	Is likely to occur about once every ten years
Significant	10% reduction in turnover contribution wiped out	**Occasional**	Is likely to occur about once a year
Substantial	Business unit posts significant losses		

Source: Adapted from AEA Technology,
http://www.aeat.com/consulting/flyers/crppresentation.pdf (2001)

The results of this rating can then be placed on a suitable risk matrix such as the one shown below, relating to the ranking system above. Use of the matrix allows prioritisation of actions. The two attributes of severity and likelihood have become rows and columns of the matrix and so we can read off, for example an occasional likelihood and substantial impact, as 'high' risk.

	None	Minor	Moderate	Significant	Substantial
Occasional	**Medium**	**Medium**	**High**	**High**	**High**
Remote	**Low**	**Medium**	**Medium**	**High**	**High**
Improbable	**Low**	**Low**	**Medium**	**Medium**	**High**
Incredible	**Low**	**Low**	**Low**	**Low**	**Medium**

The prioritisation can be depicted on a matrix in a variety of ways in addition to the High, Medium and Low categorisation shown above. For example AEA Technology use a traffic light system of Red, Amber and Green, mirroring approaches used in a variety of sectors including, probably most notably, health care. Alternatively the priorities could be assigned numbers, 1 relating to high and so on.

An overall approach should now also be considered to address each category of risk, detailing the emphasis and priority each will receive.

Step 3 – Identify Threats and Assess Risks

Now that the business has been organised into units and the ranking system has been chosen we must now systematically identify and assess all the potential opportunities and threats faced by each of IRC's three units. In this case it will be useful to break the overall risk faced by each of the units into a variety of categories such as those outlined on the diagram shown earlier in this section. For each of the units the risks can be rated by likelihood and impact, based on knowledge within the company and perhaps assistance from Risk Management Consultancies such as AEA Technology. A table such as the one overleaf can be drawn up to illustrate the key areas of risk and potential for improvement.

The results can also be represented graphically to better demonstrate areas requiring most attention.

Step 4 – Categorise Risks and Identify Controls

At this stage we prioritise our actions in line with the ratings we have carried out. Risks with the greatest effect on the business must be addressed effectively. In the case of IRC most attention must be focussed on the Manufacturing Division and on the Processes, Assets and People therein. Obviously the other areas of the business and their inherent risks must not be ignored, however, they would perhaps receive less priority on a sliding scale, to the level where no action other than to closely monitor the risk to ensure that it does not deteriorate may be all that is required. For all areas the most effective and cost effective controls should be selected. This process will be greatly assisted by the risk profiling process undertaken so far, as the company will have a fundamentally improved appreciation of the risks they face.

Business Unit	Risk Unit	Impact	Likelihood	Risk Ranking
IRC Manufacturing	**Values**	Significant	Improbable	Medium
	Processes	Substantial	Improbable	High
	Assets	Significant	Occasional	High
	People	Moderate	Occasional	High
IRC Retail	**Values**	Minor	Incredible	Low
	Processes	Moderate	Occasional	High
	Assets	Minor	Improbable	Low
	People	Moderate	Occasional	High
IRC Subsidiaries	**Values**	Minor	Remote	Medium
	Processes	Minor	Remote	Medium
	Assets	Significant	Improbable	Medium
	People	Moderate	Occasional	High

Fig 5.12

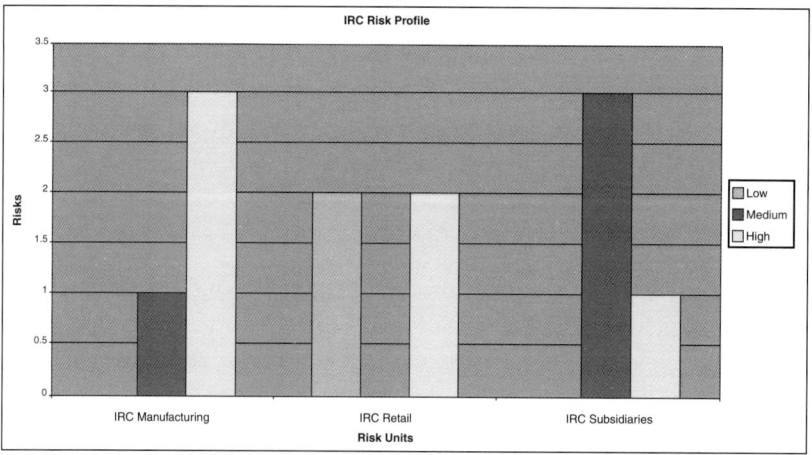

Obviously the selection and implementation of suitable controls is outwith the remit of this publication.

Step 5 – Action Plans for Risk Control and Monitoring

This stage is primarily concerned with putting into effect the result of the technique undertaken so far and is therefore probably beyond the scope of this work. It should, however, be noted though that there is a requirement to feed back progress so that the company can maintain an ongoing awareness of the risks that they are facing and influence future risk decisions. It could be argued that this monitoring stage is fundamental to the identification of new and developing risks for the company.

Obviously this has been a much simplified consideration of the methodology and to undertake a full Corporate Risk Profiling exercise would be a great challenge for any company. That is why the use of consultants such as AEAT would appear so attractive; there is also the additional benefit that advice from consultants is often held in higher esteem within an organisation than internal advice.

The most obvious benefit of risk profiling is its truly comprehensive, cross-discipline and strategic approach. Risk profiling provides for the transparent, comparable and consistent assessment of risk across all parts of the business. A company-wide picture of risk is built up and this addresses the differing and competing risk priorities that many large businesses can face. The process is tailored to individual businesses as every company is different and therefore each will face a different risk profile for a whole variety of reasons. The prioritisation process allows for the focus of what are often scarce resources on the key risks which might affect the aims and objectives of a particular business. Another advantage is that the on-going and flexible nature of the process also allows for the identification and integration of new or evolving risk issues into the system. Finally, the methodology provides peace of mind as it provides auditable proof demonstrating that stringent requirements such as those set out by the Turnbull Report have been met.

As ever it would be unfair to paint such a one-sided view of the process, therefore we must also now consider potential drawbacks to the technique. Readers may form their own opinions, however, it could be suggested that the technique is not really a new methodology at all, merely an amalgamation of a range of tried and trusted methods applied in a slightly different cross-enterprise, strategic fashion. There may also be a suspicion that the technique is too broad in its approach, leading to large complex organisations perhaps missing or misinterpreting certain risks. There is also perhaps a danger of ignoring or down-playing the lower priority risks, as we know if these risks are neglected they can often be the ones which sneak up to take us by surprise. Many of these weaknesses are, however, perhaps more attributable to a flawed and questionable application of the process rather than real drawbacks to the process itself.

The technique is possibly also too ambitious and complex for smaller businesses or organisations and they could be better served by taking a much more piecemeal approach to risk issues.

6

STATISTICAL ANALYSIS OF RISK 1

6.1 INTRODUCTION

In the previous chapters we have concentrated on the analysis of risk. This has involved both identification and then the formal analysis of the identified risk. We noted, as we did this, that some techniques were more concerned with identification than analysis, that others adopted a broad view of risk and that some concentrated on the qualitative rather than the quantitative analysis of risk.

In the end we agreed that the most important thing was that risk was brought to light and that a number of different techniques could be used to satisfy individual problems. Once risks have been identified we are often left with a large volume of information and can use this information in statistical analysis.

This chapter and the next are concerned with statistical risk analysis. The approach which has been adopted is, it is hoped, a practical one. Certain basic concepts in statistics will be introduced with the aid of a practical problem and the relevance of statistics should emerge.

Before introducing the example and beginning the chapter, let us make one or two points of a very general nature:

- what we will do in this chapter will be of an introductory nature. It is not possible, nor would it be worthwhile, in this study guide to provide a comprehensive text on statistics. This chapter and the one which follows will only be an introduction to a much wider topic.

- in addition to being introductory in nature these chapters are also selective. They will concentrate on techniques which seem to have some relevance for risk management. This means of necessity that certain topics will be left out.

- the chapters are written on the assumption that the reader has very little knowledge of statistics already. In fact a person with no previous knowledge should be able to read them without too much difficulty.

- finally these chapters recognise the fact that statistics and quantitative risk analyses may not be the most popular topics among risk and insurance managers. However we live in an increasingly quantitative world and the risk manager must endeavour to keep abreast of developments.

6.2 GATHERING DATA

The first stage in statistical risk analysis is the gathering of data. Risk and insurance departments do generate large volumes of information on claims, policies, premiums, etc. Consider for a moment all the data that is collected by and kept in your own department.

Very often this data is collected more as a matter of routine than by definite conscious decision to gather it. The risk manager has data and must look over it and see to what uses it can be put. In the unique case of a risk manager starting from scratch he can decide himself what he wants to collect, but this will be unusual. However the data is gathered, one point still remains. The end result will only be as good as the data with which you start. For example you will not be able to analyse employee injuries by shift if you do not record the shift during which the accident occurred. By the same token there is as much danger in gathering unnecessary information. Why ask for the employee number when recording accident details if you do not intend to use this in some later analysis?

In deciding on what information to collect it is essential to have a clear picture of what the end result is likely to be. This is often best achieved by imagining what kind of statements you would like your analysis to produce at the end of the day. For example if you want to make statements such as:

"Forty-three percent of all back injuries, many of which involved lifting sheet metal, occurred in the moulding plant during the early shift."

If this is the kind of statement, among many others, which you could imagine including in some report at a certain stage in the future then the correct data must be gathered. This simple statement implies that you must collect data on employee injuries which includes the type of injury, agent of injury, place of injury and time. It is therefore a useful discipline to consider all that you might want to say by way of a report at the end of your statistical analysis and then make sure you gather the appropriate data to begin with.

There are a number of techniques which can be employed in the gathering of data and most text books on statistics will include a comprehensive list of them. In the risk management situation it is likely that the data set already exists. In only a few cases will the risk manager have to set about devising a system for collecting data.

What may be necessary is some adjustment in the format in which the data is gathered. If we take claims information as an example, it may well be that a report of, let us say, industrial injuries, is submitted to the insurance department. The risk manager will want to ensure that this report contains all the information he will need for his own analysis in addition to whatever is required by the insurers for their purposes.

The design of forms for gathering information then becomes quite important and this is an aspect of gathering data with which he may be concerned. The design of any form will depend on the nature of the data being collected, what the risk manager hopes to do with the data, and any style which the company as a whole may normally adopt for reporting. There are however a number of general points we could make about documents which are intended to be used for gathering risk data.

The following points should be considered when designing any form for gathering information. This could be any form of information which the risk manager may want to collect, e.g. information on accidents, fires, thefts, revisions to sums insured, staff lists, payroll and turnover figures, etc, etc.

- the form should contain full instructions. The one thing which will ensure the non-return of a form is some problem which makes completion difficult. For example, if the questions are listed but the person completing the form is not clear as to whether he is to tick a correct statement or provide a full answer. Similarly if the person to whom the form is to be returned is not shown on the form then this could cause unnecessary delays.

Included in the instructions should be some indication of why the form is required, what its objectives are and how it will be used.

- ambiguities must be avoided. Each question must be clear, and this means clear from the point of view of the person asked to answer it. A question asking for details of any industrial accidents would have to clearly indicate what was meant by 'details' and what constituted an 'industrial accident'. Where ambiguities creep in and different respondents answer according to their own interpretation then the data is of little value.

It may also be in certain circumstances that pieces of machinery or processes have names which are in the form of a 'slang' term or are shop floor names. In these cases it is best to use such terms and avoid ambiguities.

- leading questions should be avoided. Street market researchers should not frame a question such as, "All reasonable people watch the ten o'clock news. Do you watch the ten o'clock news?" In the same way we cannot put on our form for gathering data a question such as, "All the plant managers within the company who are really anxious to minimise industrial accidents make a great deal of use of the recent safety posters sent. What use have you made of them?" Leading a person, by whatever means, is not acceptable.

- the form should be no more complicated than necessary. One possible disadvantage of the ease with which computers can handle large volumes of data is that people designing forms ask far more than they need. When forms were analysed manually there was a definite incentive to keep the form brief and we must try to stick to this idea. Long and complicated forms do tend to 'put people off', there is no doubt about that. Our endeavour is to have the form completed quickly and accurately. Short crisp questions are more likely to achieve this end than lengthy, wordy forms.

- when designing the form, remember how the information is to be analysed. In many cases the data will be recorded on a computer and this will greatly speed up the eventual analysis. However, the designer of the form must remember this and gather data in a suitable way.

Generally speaking computers use numbers when analysing data gathering forms. The computer does not, for example, read in sentences and interpret them. It can read in a number which corresponds to a pre-defined sentence however. Take a simple question asking for the shift during which an accident took place. We could think of three ways, among others, in which such a question could be put:

"During which shift did the accident occur?"

This will involve the respondent in answering: back shift, early shift, night shift or whatever shifts the company operates. The computer cannot however accept the words 'back shift'. It works with numbers and analyses them. What you can do is to provide alternatives for the person, from which he picks the correct one:

"Please indicate during which shift the accident occurred by ticking the appropriate box."

Early shift ☐ 1

Day shift ☐ 2

Back shift ☐ 3

Night shift ☐ 4

You can see a number against each box. When the computer is being fed the answer for this question it will be given the answer for each respondent in terms of the box number. The computer can then count the number of times the number '2' was given as the answer. If this turns out to be 55 times out of 100 forms completed then 55% of all incidents occurred during the day shift. In addition to this the computer has the capability to extract other information from those forms where the number '2' was answered in this question. For example it could calculate the location of the incidents. Another question may ask for location and provide five or six alternative locations. The computer can look at all the forms, where '2' was given as the answer in the shift question, and work out where they had their incidents.

A third alternative would be to ask for the exact time, a question which would be asked in any case, and then have the computer programmed to interpret the time in terms of shifts. The starting and stopping times of shifts would be entered into the computer programme and the machine would then convert each answer into a shift. This would be much more difficult where shifts, for example, overlap.

All that we have said here relates to those circumstances when forms are being designed. It may well be that in the majority of cases the data is already being sent to you by others. In these cases all you can do is take what is being sent and make sure that how it was gathered, by others, is satisfactory.

It may seem that we have spent a lot of time on the gathering of data. However, if the data is suspect before you begin the analysis then the whole exercise will be of little value.

Let us now create an example which we can follow through this chapter and the next. It is an example based on the claims register of a hotel company. Two pages from the register are shown in Fig 6.1.

The hotel company has two hotels, one in Glasgow, the other in London, and the register is only concerned with claims made by hotel guests. These claims are either claims for personal injury or loss or damage to personal effects. All claims paid to guests for injury or lost or damaged effects are met by the hotel itself without reference to any insurance.

This is a simple example and there are many other pieces of information which you may consider it to have been valuable to gather. However, the pages we have provided will be sufficient for our purposes at the moment.

6.3   REPRESENTATION OF DATA

Now we have data! What will we do with it? In our example we have a settlement cost and four variables: location, type, age, and sex. Our first task is to represent this in the most appropriate way for our own purposes. There are a number of different ways we can represent the data and we will look at each in turn. The main point is that the method chosen must match the need at the time. If your need

Fig 6.1 CLAIMS REGISTER

Name	Sex	Age	Nature	Location	Cost
Evant, J	F	18	Ankle Sprain	Glasgow	25
Smith, F	M	38	Baggage	Glasgow	650
Gardner, P	F	50	Car	London	1900
Swan, I	F	30	Clothes	Glasgow	1600
Bolton, T	F	60	Broken leg	London	2850
Chalmers, S	F	21	Back injury	London	1400
Anderson, B	M	60	Cut hand	London	250
Black, Y	M	60	Personal Effects	Glasgow	850
Thomson, F	M	40	Baggage	Glasgow	350
Dickson, S	M	30	Clothing	Glasgow	425
McCrum, T	F	35	Foot injury	London	2050
Boyd, L	F	36	Car	London	2100
Davidson, T	M	25	Camera lost	Glasgow	550
Elder, B	M	38	Lost effects	Glasgow	610
Smith, V	F	19	Cut hand	Glasgow	70
Brown, G	F	23	Ankle strain	London	1500
Gray, T	F	23	Stolen baggage	London	1600
Cox, T	M	18	Hand injury	Glasgow	600
Young, O	F	40	Car stolen	London	2425
Robertson, S	M	18	Back injury	London	2000
Cowan, V	F	50	Facial injury	London	2525
Cruickshank, L	F	60	Car stolen	London	2750
Simms, L	M	40	Foot injury	Glasgow	700
Roy, B	M	19	Damaged clothing	Glasgow	900
Lamont, J	F	65	Broken wrist	London	2850
Dion, T	M	60	Cut finger	Glasgow	100
Cobb, B	F	40	Jewellery	London	1700
White, L	F	39	Cut leg	London	2350
Williams, T	F	57	Leg injury	London	2600
Muir, L	M	18	Bruise	Glasgow	100
Morrison, S	M	60	Jewellery	London	750
Merchant, L	M	20	Sprained ankle	London	1000
Watson, R	F	62	Neck injury	Glasgow	2900
Reid, T	F	37	Car damage	Glasgow	2100
Todd, L	F	40	Clothes	London	2400
Russell, V	M	55	Leg cut	Glasgow	1100
Sharples, L	M	30	Cases lost	Glasgow	1200

Name	Sex	Age	Nature	Location	Cost
Logan, A	F	65	Broken leg	London	2875
Calder, B	M	42	Hand injury	Glasgow	1300
Stewart, R	M	25	Cameras	Glasgow	1150
Rutherford, L	F	31	Facial injury	Glasgow	1650
McKinnon, D	F	55	Car damage	London	2550
McKenzie, L	F	38	Jewellery	London	2200
Edwards, S	M	50	Personal effects	Glasgow	540
King, R	M	42	Sprain	Glasgow	400
Larson, R	F	25	Cash stolen	London	1850
Noble, E	M	40	Hand injury	Glasgow	1500
Windsor, D	F	32	Clothing lost	Glasgow	1675
Thatcher, F	F	32	Cases stolen	Glasgow	1700
Bennett, T	F	34	Leg injury	Glasgow	2000
Ford, M	M	50	Car damage	London	1300
Steele, D	M	20	Cut finger	Glasgow	100
Owen, J	M	19	Hand cut	Glasgow	530
Johnston, R	M	55	Cut leg	Glasgow	500
Wallace, S	F	59	Broken ankle	London	2700
White, W	F	41	Clothing	Glasgow	1900
Kinloch, N	M	50	Car damage	Glasgow	1175
Shore, P	M	21	Leg cut	Glasgow	870
Paterson, E	M	50	Money	Glasgow	260
West, N	M	60	Cases lost	Glasgow	300

is to provide an overall picture of fire losses in your company for some annual report then a different method would be selected from one which you may use when providing a technical report for your insurers.

The most elementary step is to prepare an un-ordered array concentrating on cost of settlement, then we could provide a straight listing of settlement costs as shown in Fig 6.2.

At least this gives some basic idea of how the costs are distributed. It still requires careful reading to be able to interpret how the costs are distributed and has severe limitation if large numbers are involved. We have sixty costs but you may be dealing with 500 claims and an unordered array would be of little or no value. Fig 6.3 shows the ordered array.

To overcome these problems we can construct a frequency distribution. This simply condenses the array and is much easier to interpret. A frequency distribution of claims costs is shown in Fig 6.4.

Fig 6.2
Un-ordered Array of Data

25	1500	750	1850
650	1600	1000	1500
1900	600	2900	1675
1600	2425	2100	1700
2850	2000	2400	2000
1400	2525	1100	1300
250	2750	1200	100
850	700	2875	530
350	900	1300	500
425	2850	1150	2700
2050	100	1650	1900
2100	1700	2550	1175
550	2350	2200	870
610	2600	540	260
70	100	400	300

Fig 6.3
Ordered Array of Data

25	600	1400	2100
70	610	1500	2100
100	650	1500	2200
100	700	1600	2350
100	750	1600	2400
250	850	1650	2425
260	870	1675	2525
300	900	1700	2550
350	1000	1700	2600
400	1100	1850	2700
425	1150	1900	2750
500	1175	1900	2850
530	1200	2000	2850
540	1300	2000	2875
550	1300	2050	2900

Fig 6.4

Claims cost £	No
0 < 600	15
600 < 1200	12
1200 < 1800	12
1800 < 2400	10
2400 < 3000	11
	60

We can look at this distribution and see that claims costs are fairly evenly spread. The name 'frequency distribution' simply describes what we have done. We have counted the number of times, or frequency, with which each claim has occurred and how these claims are distributed. Compiling these frequency distributions is a fairly simple matter.

1. Find the highest and lowest value
2. Divide by the number of groups or classes you want
3. Create the classes
4. Assign each value to a class or group.

In our example, if we do this we find:

1. The highest value of claim is £2,900 and the lowest is £25. £2,900 – £25 = £2,875.

2. The reason for constructing the distribution is so that it can represent the data easily. There is therefore no point in having 25 classes or, at the other end, 2 classes. There must be a reasonable spread and in most cases about five to six classes is adequate. We will settle on five classes £2,875 ÷ 5 = £575.

3. In creating the classes we have to think what the final distribution will look like. It would be very cumbersome if we started at the lowest value, £25 and rose in units of £575. By rounding the £575 up to £600 and starting at £0 then we created the classes shown in Fig 6.4.

When creating the classes we use the symbol '<' which means "less than". And so the first class goes from £0 to less than £600. Theoretically this means £599.99. In practice it means that a claim of £600 exactly will go in the second class and anything less than that will be put in the first class.

4. The sixty claims were then assigned to the classes, by methodically going down the register pages. It is wise to use a method like 'five bar gates' or some other, to keep a note of how many values are being assigned to each class. Once we have done this we can count all the frequencies and they should add to 60.

The frequency distribution does give a clearer picture of what the data is telling us. It is also useful when comparing our data with someone else's or indeed when comparing sub-sets within the data. We could, for example, construct two distributions, one for Glasgow and one for London claims.

We can tell right away that there are more Glasgow claims than London ones and that the distribution of these claims is quite different. The bulk of the Glasgow claims are small but the bulk of the London claims are at the higher end of the range of values.

Fig 6.5

Claims cost £	All	Glasgow	London
0 < 600	15 (25)	14 (40)	1 (4)
600 < 1200	12 (20)	10 (28)	2 (8)
1200 < 1800	12 (20)	7 (20)	5 (20)
1800 < 2400	10 (17)	3 (9)	7 (28)
2400 < 3000	11 (18)	1 (3)	10 (40)
	60	35	25

These frequency distributions are much clearer than the un-ordered array but there is still more that we can do to make the data easier to interpret. Often it is necessary to express values as percentages. We can say that a certain percentage of all claims cost between £600 and £1,200 and another percentage cost between £1,200 and £1,800 and so on.

We can achieve this by constructing a relative frequency distribution. In the distribution in Fig 6.5 we have shown the relative frequencies in brackets. From this we can say immediately that 18% of all claims cost more than £2,400. We can also see that the Glasgow hotel had 7 claims between £1,200 and £1,800 and the London hotel had two fewer. The relative frequencies however show that for both hotels, 20% of their claims were in the bracket £1,200 to £1,800.

We can also see, quite markedly, that while 40% of Glasgow claims cost less than £600 only 4% of London claims were in this range.

One other interpretation which is often made of data is to state the number of incidents up to a certain figure, or greater than some value, etc. We could for example say that a certain percentage of all incidents cost more than £2,400, or a certain percentage cost at least £1,800.

These conclusions can be made if we construct a cumulative frequency distribution. Such a distribution is shown in Fig 6.6.

Fig 6.6

Claims cost £	f	Cum. freq.
0 < 600	15	15 60
600 < 1200	12	27 45
1200 < 1800	12	39 33
1800 < 2400	10	49 21
2400 < 3000	11	60 11
	60	

A Cumulative Frequency Distribution

You can see that we have two columns of cumulative frequencies. The first is in ascending order. There are 15 claims costing less than £600 and 12 incidents costing between £600 and less than £1,200. There are therefore 27 incidents costing less than £1,200. This procedure is carried out all through the distribution and so we have 39 claims costing less than £1,800, 49 costing less than £2,400 and 60 costing less than £3,000.

The second column shows the descending cumulative frequencies. We have 60, or all claims, costing more than £0. There are 45 claims costing more than £600 and so on.

We can also express these cumulative frequencies as relative cumulative frequencies if we want. We could say that 100% of all claims cost less than £3,000; 75% of claims [45/60] cost more than £600; 25% of claims [15/60] cost less than £600.

The techniques we have used so far are all based on the frequency distribution and we simply re-arranged the data in an effort to make it clearer to the reader. Another method of representing data would be to draw it. There is a range of methods we could use for drawing our data, some based on the frequency distribution and others not.

Fig 6.7

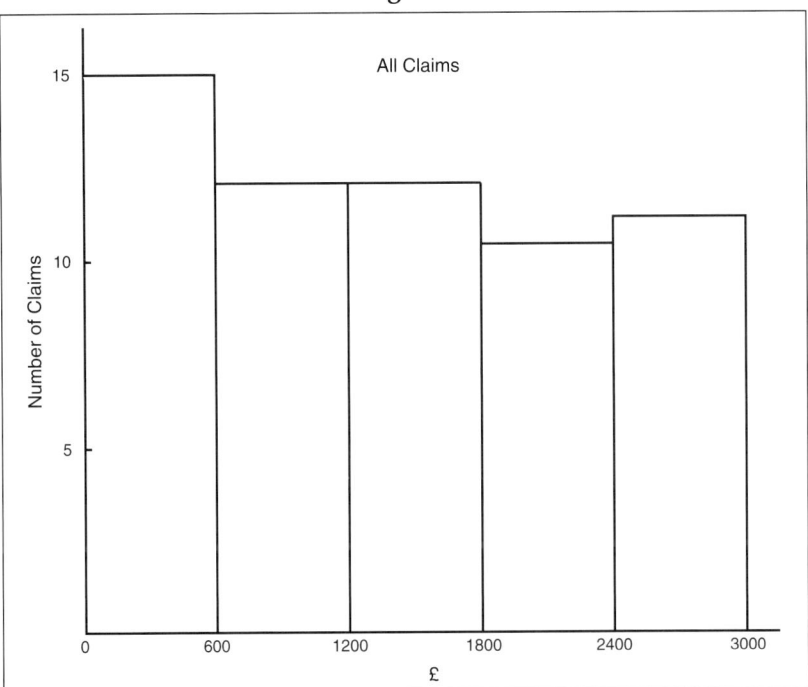

Frequency Distribution of all Claims

Fig 6.7 shows one drawing based on the frequency distribution of all claims. This method of representation is known as a histogram. The variable we are measuring is shown along the horizontal axis and the frequency with which the variable occurred is noted on the vertical axis. You can see that the horizontal axis shows the limits of the classes we used earlier in the frequency distribution shown in Fig 6.5.

From this histogram we can see immediately that the frequency with which claims arise is fairly evenly spread over the range of values from £0 to £3,000. You may want to include this histogram in a report you are compiling on claims within the group or some note you are sending to hotel managers. You may, however, be more interested in comparing the two hotels in the group.

Fig 6.8

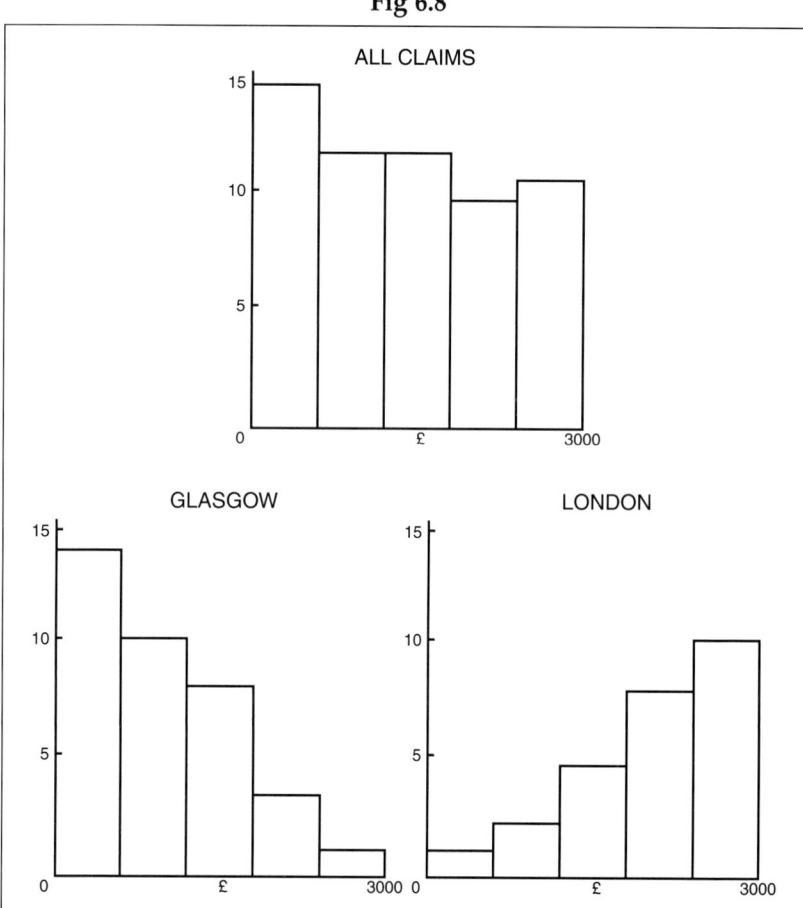

Histograms Showing Different Patterns of Claims

The three drawings in Fig 6.8 show the differences quite clearly. Neither hotel conforms with the pattern for all claims. When we contrast the two histograms for Glasgow and London we see that the bulk of Glasgow claims are small in value whereas the majority of London incidents are much more expensive. Histograms like this are a compelling way to make your point and will probably have much more impact than either of the frequency distributions shown in Fig 6.6 or the pages from the register shown in Fig 6.1.

The cumulative frequency distribution can also be drawn; when this is done the drawing is referred to as an ogive.

Fig 6.9

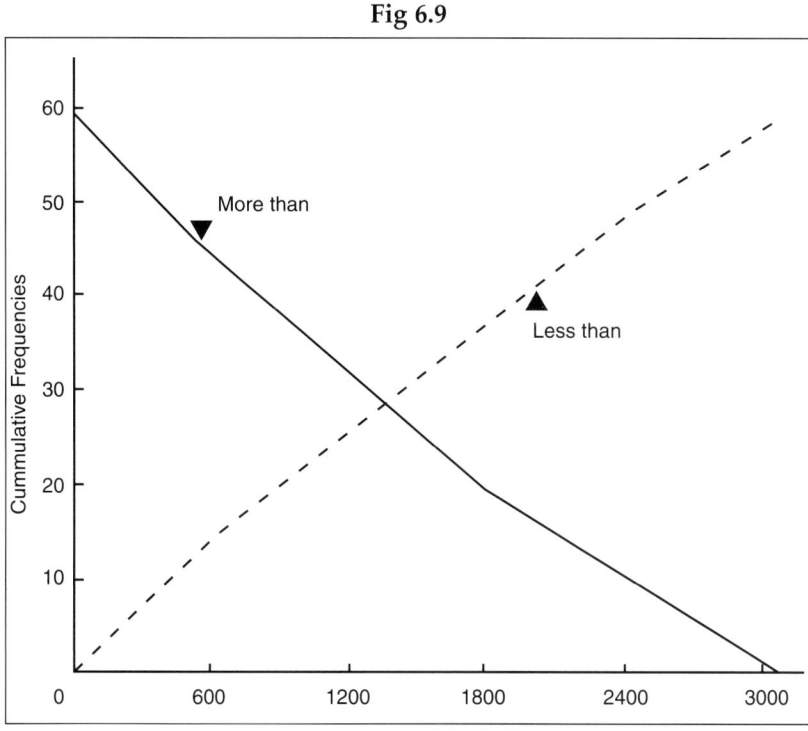

An Ogive of all Claims Costs

An ogive of all claims costs is shown in Fig 6.9. The horizontal axis is labelled with the cost of claims, in the same way as the histogram. The vertical axis now shows the cumulative frequencies. The lines, "more than" and "less than" are drawn using the limits of the various classes of the frequency distribution. For the "less than" line we have plotted the figures from the first column of the cumulative frequency distribution shown in Fig 6.6. When plotting the figures we use the top end of the classes, i.e. the cumulative frequency of 15 is plotted against £600, 27 against £1,200 and so on. The "more than" curve uses the lower end of each class, i.e. the 60 is plotted against £0, 45 against £600 and so on.

This means that when we use the lines to make interpretations for use we can say, using the "less than" line, that about 22 claims cost less than £1,000, or using the "more than" curve, that approximately 14 claims cost more than £2,000.

Notice that the lines cross at a point which has a monetary equivalent of £1,300 to £1,400. This value, let us say for the moment that it is £1,350, must therefore be the value above and below which lie half of the claims. On the "more than" curve £1,350 corresponds to a cumulative frequency of 30 and on the "less than" curve it also corresponds to 30. Later we will see that this point, the point which splits the data itself, has a special significance for us.

All of the techniques used above are based on the frequency distribution. There are also a range of more pictorial methods which we can use and which may be appropriate.

The choice of a particular method of representing data does depend on the use to which you want to put it and the following methods are often seen in company reports, newspapers, magazines, and internal company reports. They are less 'scientific' in nature but nevertheless provide a means of representing the data and giving some other person an insight into what the data reveals.

The first of these more pictorial methods is the pie chart and an example is shown in Fig 6.10.

This chart shows the division into male and female claimants. The entire circle represents all claimants and the segments are drawn to represent the proportions of the particular variables you want to show.

A second method is the bar chart. This is often seen in company publications. The one great advantage of the bar chart is that it is capable of illustrating more than one feature of the variable. The histogram, you will recall, illustrated the frequency with which a variable occurred. The bar chart can however show more than this. Fig 6.11 shows a bar chart.

This chart shows the values of injury and property claims, sub-divided into the two hotels. On the one drawing we have value, type and location of claims. You can see how this could be valuable for displaying, for example, loss figures for various forms of risk and various plants.

Finally, we could draw a graph representing the pattern of claims for the two hotels over a certain period. Fig 6.12 shows such a graph. The years are on the horizontal axis and the cost on the vertical axis. The trend over these years is clearly shown for the two hotels.

Fig 6.10

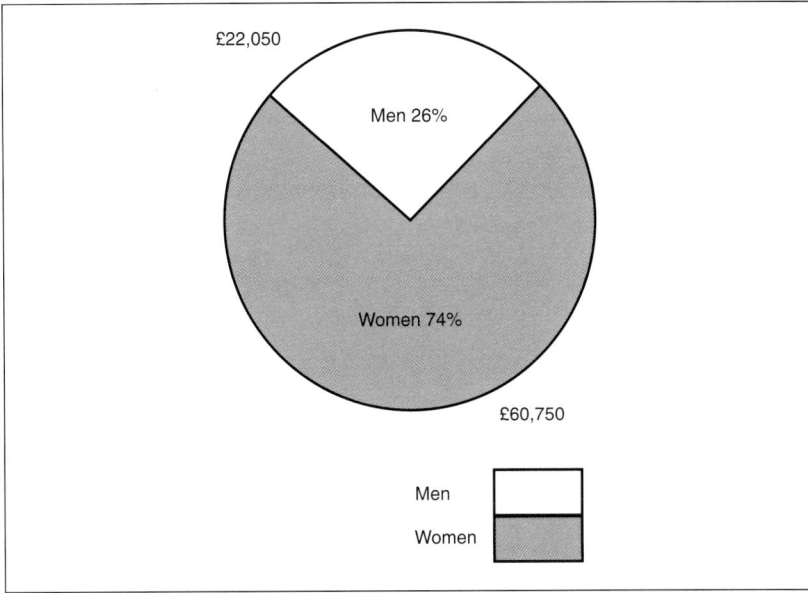

All Claims Total Costs

Fig 6.11

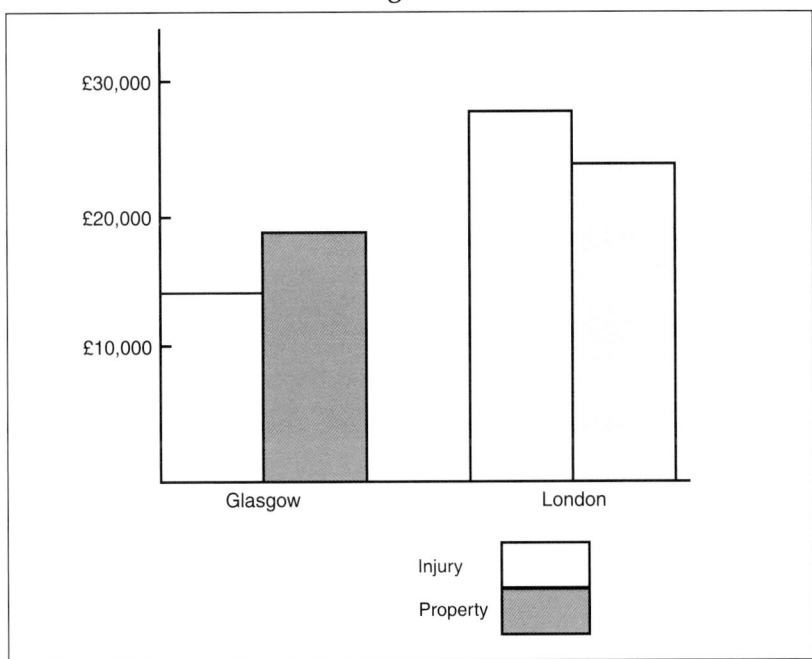

Breakdown of Cost of Claims

Fig 6.12

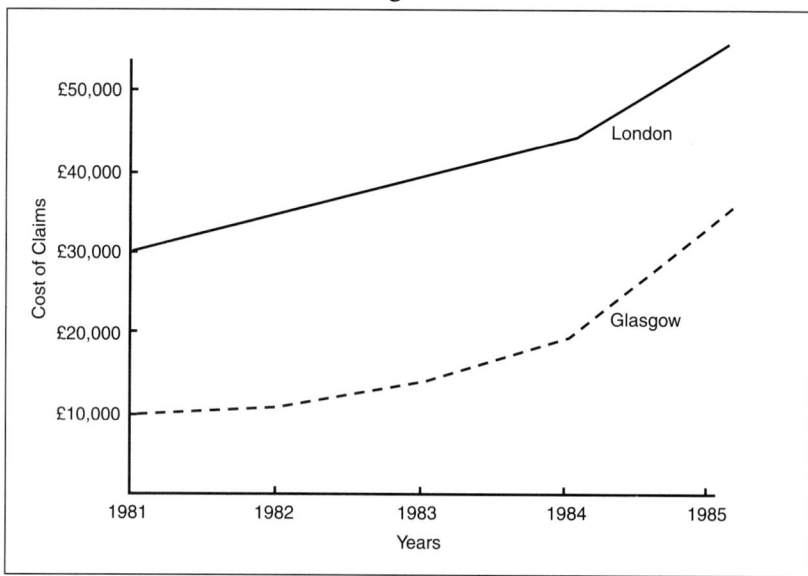

The Pattern of Claims Over Time

Fig 6.13

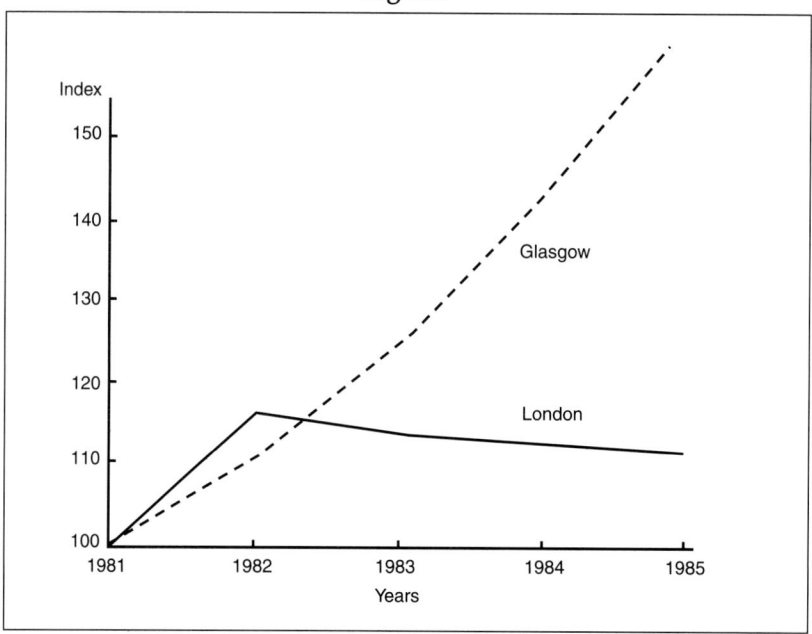

Claims Year-on-Year

What we must be careful to avoid is any misleading impressions which our graph may give. On looking at the graph we could easily come to the conclusion that the London hotel is really in a much worse position than the Glasgow hotel.

The claims are larger in size and increasing. The Glasgow claims are also increasing but they are much smaller. This is a fairly classic case of how simple it is to mislead the reader. The actual figures upon which the graph was drawn are:

	£ Glasgow	£ London
1981	10,000	30,000
1982	11,000	35,000
1983	14,000	40,000
1984	20,000	45,000
1985	32,000	50,000

These figures actually tell a different story from that implied by the graph. It would seem from the figures that the Glasgow claims are increasing at a much faster rate than London claims. If this is what you want to show then a slightly different graph would be more appropriate.

The graph in Fig 6.13 shows the same data as Fig 6.12 but this time the figures have been linked to a common base and expressed as increases year on year. For example, the 1981 figure for Glasgow was £10,000. By 1982 the figure was £11,000. If we let the 1981 figure equal 100 then the 1982 figure would be:

$\frac{11,000}{10,000} \times 100$ or 110. The 1983 figure of £14,000 would then become:

$\frac{14,000}{11,000} \times 100$ or 127 and so on.

When we change all of the figures for London and Glasgow we end up with:

	Glasgow	London
1981	100	100
1982	110	117
1983	127	114
1984	143	112
1985	160	111

When we plot these figures a quite different picture emerges as shown in Fig 6.13. This time the Glasgow claims are seen to overtake the London claims. The graph is now reflective of the rate at which claims are increasing. It all depends on what you want to show and what objectives you wish to satisfy, as to how the data should be displayed.

7

STATISTICAL ANALYSIS OF RISK 2

7.1   INTRODUCTION

In the previous chapter we looked at the basic steps involved in gathering information and in representing that information in the best manner possible. We identified a number of techniques which can be used, each one having particular validity depending upon the objectives you had set for the exercise. When we represented data however, we were not carrying out any measurement of what we had found. All we were doing was drawing or representing the data in a suitable manner. In this chapter we turn to the business of taking measurements of the data in order that we can begin to make conclusions about what our data is telling us.

Taking measurements of the data is a little like taking a snapshot of the data. We will make some calculations which will be like a picture to us of what the data is like. We will for example want to know where in the whole spectrum of values our data lies. In other words where is our data located? If we are talking about claims then we will want to locate our claims in the spectrum of money values which claims could possibly assume. Is our data around the £200 mark or is it up around the £2,000 level? This is a basic statement which we would want to be able to make. In addition to locating the data we may also want to say something about how the data is spread out. It may be that we decide the data is located around the £500 mark and that it is tightly grouped around this figure. Alternatively we could find that our data is very widely dispersed around the general location of £500, with some claims down about £20 and others much higher at about £950. We will then need a way of measuring this dispersion, as saying where the data is located will not tell us the whole story. Even with location and dispersion described, there is still one other aspect of the data which we may want to measure and that is the nature of the dispersion, that is, whether the data is grouped at one end of the scale of values or the other. Most insurance-type statistics on claims produce data which is grouped around lower monetary values. Most claims are reasonably small with only a very few extremely large ones in any year. What we will need then is some way of measuring this phenomenon. We will want to be able to say whether the data is grouped at the lower end or the higher end of the scale of values we are using. From what we have said it is clear that we require at least three measures of our data in order to have a picture of what the data is telling us. We will need a measure of location, of dispersion, and of skew. This chapter takes each of these in turn, gives a brief introduction to them and illustrates their use by means of the hotel data from Chapter six.

7.2 MEASURES OF LOCATION

What we want is some way to describe where the data is located. If someone asks what our claims at the hotel are like we want to be able to answer by giving a figure which locates our claims in the whole spectrum of money. The only one hundred percent accurate way of answering the question would be to list the entire number of claims and say to the questioner that this is what the claims costs are like. What we need is the snapshot idea which will capture the general thrust of the data and give the person a good idea of where the claims are located.

The normal method of measuring location is to express the data in the form of an average. There are however at least three forms of average and so we must be careful in our use of the term. We will look at each of these three averages in turn: the mean, median, and mode.

7.2.1 The Mean

This is the form of average with which most people will be familiar. It is found by adding all the values of the variable under consideration and then dividing by the total number of variables. In the hotel data we have 60 claims which sum to £82,800. This gives an arithmetic mean of £1,380. And so we have now located the data in the sense that we can say the claims are around the £1,380 mark. This is the kind of snapshot we were looking for earlier; at least now the data can be described to anyone in a simple manner. What we have done can be described by a simple formula:

$$\bar{x} = \frac{\Sigma x}{n}$$

Where $\bar{x}$ is the arithmetic mean

Σx is the sum of all the values of the variable x

n is the number of values of x.

The simplicity of the arithmetic mean does bring some problems and we will look at them later.

Calculating the arithmetic mean is rarely as straightforward as adding all values and dividing by the total number. One of the main problems we will experience right at the start is that in many cases we do not have all the values of every variable. What we will most likely have is a grouped frequency distribution, as we have described in Chapter six. The frequency distribution which we created for all claims was:

£	f
0 < 600	15
600 < 1200	12
1200 < 1800	12
1800 < 2400	10
2400 < 3000	11
	60

The difficulty which the frequency distribution causes is that we now do not have a value of each variable. In the frequency distribution we have a class or an interval of values in place of an individual value.

What we require is a single number to insert in the formula for the arithmetic mean. The number would have to be representative of all the values in the class. A reasonable number to select is the mid-point and this is in fact the value most often chosen to represent the class. In our example the mid-point of the first class would be £300, of the second would be £900 and so on. What we have to remember is that the mid-point only represents the values in the class. In other words, the value £300 represents the values in the first class. There are actually 15 numbers in the first class and they are 'each' being represented by the value £300. There are therefore 15 £300s in the first class, 12 £900s in the second and so on. When we use these mid-points in the formula for the arithmetic mean we will have to reflect this fact somehow.

The formula for the arithmetic mean of a grouped frequency distribution is:

$$\bar{x} = \frac{\Sigma fx}{\Sigma f}$$

Where Σfx is the sum of all values of x multiplied by the frequency with which those values arose. In our example we will have to multiply all the mid-points by the frequencies with which they occur and then sum these products. The calculations are shown below.

£	X	f	fx
0 < 600	300	15	4500
600 < 1200	900	12	10800
1200 < 1800	1500	12	18000
1800 < 2400	2100	10	21000
2400 < 3000	2700	11	29700
			84000

$$\bar{x} = \frac{\Sigma fx}{\Sigma f} = \frac{84000}{60} = 1400$$

And so the arithmetic mean of the grouped frequency distribution is £1400. You will see that this is slightly different from the arithmetic mean which we calculated from the raw data. This is clearly due to the fact that we have lost some of the accuracy of the data by placing the claims in groups. The value of x which we used was the mid-point, which is only a representative value and not the actual value. The true mean and the mean from the grouped distribution are not all that far apart and the figure of £1400 will be good enough for most purposes.

There are a number of problems which flow from using the arithmetic mean and we could spend a great deal of time looking into them. However we are mainly concerned with the use of statistics, not the theory, and so we mention two problems only of which users should be aware.

The first is that the arithmetic mean is not so suitable for certain types of figures. Take for example the following set of figures.

Year	Claims	% Increase
1984	20	–
1985	30	150
1986	60	200

The final column shows the percentage increase in claims, and so in 1985 there was a 50% increase over the previous year. We could say that the average percentage increase has been 175%, i.e. $\frac{(150+200)}{2}$

We can check this figure by applying it to the actual figures. When we do this we find:

Year	Claims
1984	20
1985	20 x 175% = 35
1986	35 x 175% = 61.25

These calculations, however, produce an incorrect answer. The actual figure for 1986 is 60 not 61.25. The problem is that the arithmetic mean is not suitable for averaging out figures which are related to each other in the way that ours are, i.e. one figure being a percentage of the one before. What we need for these situations is the 'Geometric Mean' rather than the arithmetic mean. The geometric mean is found by the following formula:

$$\sqrt[n]{X_1 \times X_2 \times X_3 \times \dots X_n}$$

In our small example we would have:

$\sqrt[2]{150 \times 200}$
$= 173.21\%$

If we test this on our figures we find:

Year	Claims
1984	20
1985	20 x 173.21% = 34.642
1986	34.642 x 173.21% = 60

This now corresponds exactly with what actually happened. The average annual percentage increase is therefore 73.21% and not 75%.

The second problem with the arithmetic mean is that it is easily distorted by extremely large or small values. The calculations for the arithmetic mean involve all values in the distribution and if there happens to be a very large value, for example, then this distorts the answer. In our hotel data we have 60 claims which total £82,800 giving an arithmetic mean of £1,380. If we had had 61 claims and the additional claim was £20,000 then the mean would have been £1,685. The mean has been pulled up by the one claim which was much higher than any other. If there are a few values in a distribution which are either much smaller or larger than the others then some mention should be made of this in any synopsis of findings.

7.2.2 The Median

The second form of average is the median. The median is the value which is exactly half way through the data, 50% of all values lie above it and 50% lie below. The median in the following list of figures is 10.

$$5, 7, 9, 10, 13, 15, 17$$

The median splits the data in half and so you are just as likely to have a value above it as below it. In our hotel data we had 60 claims and so there is no natural middle value. What we can do is to take the two values which straddle the middle, i.e. the 30th and 31st values of £1,300 and £1,400. The mid-point between these is a good enough measure of the middle point of our entire distribution. The £1,300 and £1,400 were found from the ordered array in Fig 6.3. The data must be ordered before finding the median. You cannot just pick the middle value of an unordered array, as this would not give the value which is exceeded by half the values and which itself exceeds half.

The median for our data is therefore £1,350, which is fairly close to the arithmetic mean of £1,380. Notice, however, that if we had had the 61 claims mentioned earlier, with the additional claim being £20,000, the median would have been £1,400. This is a valuable quality of the median. It is not affected by extreme values in the distribution. It is always the value of the middle item, regardless of any extremes which there are.

We saw that the calculation of the arithmetic mean was slightly different when the data was grouped. Exactly the same is the case for the median. When we have a grouped distribution we cannot place the data in an ordered array. You might say, well why not unravel the data and just create the ordered array? We could certainly do this for our 60 claims but we would be much more reluctant to do it for 2,000 claims. What we need is a method of finding the median from the grouped frequency distribution. The grouped frequency distribution is:

£	f	Cumulative f
0 < 600	15	15
600 < 1200	12	27
1200 < 1800	12	39
1800 < 2400	10	49
2400 < 3000	11	60

We know that the median is the value associated with the middle claim. We have sixty claims; let us take 30 as the middle one for our purposes at the moment. The median is therefore the value associated with the 30th claim. Using the cumulative frequency distribution we know that the 30th claim will be in the class £1,200 < £1,800. There are 27 claims up to £1,200 and 39 up to £1,800, therefore the 30th must be in the class £1,200 < £1,800.

In fact the 30th claim is 3 claims into that class. There are 27 claims up to £1,200 and we want to move on another 3 claims to find the 30th. The class £1,200 < £1,800 has 12 claims in it and so we want to move 3/12ths of the way along the class. The width or interval of the class is £600 and so we want to go 3/12 x £600, i.e. £150 into the class. The class itself starts at £1,200 and £150 into it would bring us to £1,350.

This is exactly what we found earlier when we used the ordered array of data. The median found in this way will not always coincide with the true median but it will not be far out.

We can generalise what we have done in the following formula:

$$L_m + C_m \left[\frac{\frac{N}{2} - F_{m-1}}{f_m} \right]$$

Where:

L_m = lower limit of the class having the median in it, i.e. the median class

C_m = the width of the median class

N = the number of values

F_{m-1} = the cumulative frequency of the class immediately before the median class

f_m = the frequency of the median class.

We can use the formula in our example to find:

$$1200 + 600 \left[\frac{\dfrac{60}{2} - 27}{12} \right]$$

$$1200 + 600 \left[\frac{3}{12} \right]$$

$$= 1200 + 150$$

$$= 1350$$

If you look back to Fig 6.9 and what we said about it on page 155 you will see that the ogive also gave us a median of approximately £1,350.

An extension of the thinking which went into the median can be used to find other interesting statistics. It may be useful for you to know the value which is exceeded by only 25% of claims rather than 50%. You could be considering some alternative risk financing mechanisms, new insurance covers, deductible levels, etc. By altering our formula slightly we could find this value. What we are now looking for is the upper quartile, the value which splits your data so that 75% of all claims lie below it and 25% are above. The lower quartile would split your data the other way; it would give you the value above which lie 75% of all claims and below which lie 25%.

The upper quartile will be 3N/4 way through the data, i.e. it will be the value associated with the 45th claim. In our previous formula we need only substitute "Qu" for "m":

$$L_{Qu} + C_{Qu} \left[\frac{\dfrac{3N}{2} - F_{Qu-1}}{f_{Qu}} \right]$$

$$= 1800 + 600 \left[\frac{45-39}{10} \right]$$

$$= 1800 + 600 \left[\frac{6}{10} \right]$$

= 2160

25% of all claims lie above £2,160.

We can do similar calculations to find deciles and percentiles, i.e. to find the value which split the data into tenths or percentages. We might want to know the value below which lie only 10% of all claims. This would be the 1st decile. We can have the 2nd, 3rd, 4th, 5th, 6th, 7th, 8th and 9th decile. In the same way we can have individual percentiles which split the data in more precise ways. We could find the 33rd percentile. This would be the point below which lie one third of your claims.

We mentioned earlier that the median had the advantage of not being affected by extreme values. There is one other useful feature which we should mention. The median and its off-shoots such as quartiles, deciles and percentiles can be used even where the data is incomplete.

Let us say that our grouped frequency distribution had a final class of:

£	f
greater than 2400	11

This is an open-ended class and such classes are often seen in real life. We know that there are eleven claims greater than £2,400 but we do not know what they are individually. Notice that in such circumstances the median will still be £1,350. All we have to know is the total number of claims and enough information to pinpoint the middle claim. You could not have calculated the arithmetic mean in such circumstances.

Depending on the circumstances therefore, it may be more appropriate to locate our data by describing the middle value rather than the arithmetic mean. But even the median is not appropriate in all circumstances.

Take the following numbers:

12, 12, 12, 12, 12, 12, 12, 12, 15, 17, 18, 19, 20, 20, 21, 23, 25.

The arithmetic mean is 16.12 and the median is 15. However, both of these statistics conceal one vital aspect of the data: there are eight values of 12. Almost half the data is made up of the one number.

7.2.3 The Mode

The solution to the above problem would be to use the mode. The mode is the most common number. It is quite common to use the mode in ordinary everyday language. When we talk of average holiday entitlement, average family size, we are really expressing the modal holiday entitlement or the modal family size.

Many statistics text books give practical examples of when the mode should have been used in preference to the arithmetic mean. We could imagine an example in a simple planning decision. Let us say you are making provision for the supply of accident record forms at twenty different factories. You could work out the average number of forms used by twenty factories and send each one that number. This would be of no value if in fact most factories either have a very small number of accidents or a very large number. In such a case the distribution would be said to be bi-modal, it would have two modes. It would have been better to identify this first and despatch forms accordingly.

7.3 MEASURES OF DISPERSION

What we have done so far is to locate where our data is. In our case we were locating our claims in the whole spectrum of money. We saw that there were three main measures of location.

Location, however, is only one part of the story. We must add to it the question of dispersion. Take the following two sets of numbers:

A	B
10	1
11	11
12	21
$\bar{x} = 11$	$\bar{x} = 11$
median = 11	median = 11

Both have identical arithmetic means and medians but they are really quite different in the extent to which they are spread out around the measure of location. Series A is tightly grouped and is no more than 1 away from the mean. On the other hand series B is widely dispersed with a space of 10 between the mean and the other numbers.

We can think of this in terms of risk. If you had two factories and one produced claims according to series A and the other according to series B, then which is the riskier? It all depends on what you mean by 'risk' but if you had to fund losses or charge them out, in advance, to the two factories then series A is much less risky. Claims will only be 1 away from the average.

Much the same problem faces the insurance underwriter. If he knew that claims would be tightly grouped around the mean then he could charge a premium and know that it would probably be sufficient.

However, if claims are widely dispersed around the mean then it becomes much more difficult to know what to charge. Claims could be low but they could be high and the underwriter does not know ahead of time whether you are one of those who will have low or high value claims, or whether this year the claims will produce a similar mean.

What we need is some measure of dispersion. The simplest measure is to calculate the range of values. The range is the space between the highest and lowest value. In our hotel data this is £2,900 – £25 = £2,875.

A much more valuable figure is the standard deviation. This measures the extent to which the values are dispersed around the arithmetic mean. It is possibly one of the best known of all statistical tools but probably not well understood.

We will illustrate how to calculate the standard deviation with a simple example and then return to our hotel data to show its application.

7.3.1   The Standard Deviation

Let us take the following figures:

x
4
7
11
12
15
23

The arithmetic mean is 12. Standard deviation measures dispersion around the mean and so we can see that 4 is 8 from the mean, 15 is 3 from it and so on. If we compile a separate column of deviation from the mean we get:

x	$\bar{x}$	$(x - \bar{x})$
4	12	−8
7	12	−5
11	12	−1
12	12	0
15	12	3
23	12	11

We cannot simply add these dispersions as this would sum to zero. What we could do to avoid the zero sum is to square the values:

$$(x - \bar{x})^2$$

64
25
1
0
9
$\overline{121}$

If we now add these squared deviations from the mean and divide by the number of values we have, we get an 'average' squared dispersion:

$$\frac{\Sigma (x - \bar{x})^2}{n}$$

$$= \frac{220}{6}$$

$$= 36.667$$

However, squared values are not much use to anyone, i.e. squared accidents, squared fires, etc. We must take the square root to return to normal values.

$$\sqrt{36.667}$$

$$= 6.05$$

The formula for all of this is:

$$s = \sqrt{\frac{\Sigma (x - \bar{x})^2}{n}}$$

If the data is in the form of a grouped frequency we then have:

$$s = \sqrt{\frac{\Sigma f (x - \bar{x})^2}{\Sigma f}}$$

In this case we multiply each deviation by the frequency with which it occurred. An alternative formula for the standard deviation, and one which takes a little less time to calculate is:

$$s = \sqrt{\frac{\Sigma f x^2}{\Sigma f} - \left[\frac{\Sigma f x}{\Sigma f}\right]^2}$$

It gives exactly the same answer as the other formula.

Today it is becoming less and less important to remember formulae or even to know them. The use of computers, even business micros which are so common, mean that we can concentrate on the application of all the computational work, rather than the computations themselves. What we must understand are the conditions under which a particular statistic can be used and the interpretation of what we find.

Let us return now to the hotel data and see if we can illustrate the value of the standard deviation. The claims register shown in Fig 6.1 shows the nature of the claims. There are two types recorded, either injury or property. What we could do is to examine each of these two types of claim to see what the data can tell us.

Taking the two types of claims, we have the following frequency distribution:

£	Injury	Property
0 < 600	9	6
600 < 1200	5	7
1200 < 1800	5	7
1800 < 2400	4	6
2400 < 3000	7	4

The standard deviation is found by one of the two formulae we showed above. Let us take the injury claims and use the formula:

$$s = \sqrt{\frac{\Sigma f x^2}{\Sigma f} - \left[\frac{\Sigma f x}{\Sigma f}\right]^2}$$

We need to find Σfx, x^2 and fx^2.

x Mid-point	f	fx	x²	fx²
300	9	2,700	90,000	810,000
900	5	4,500	810,000	4,050,000
1,500	5	7,500	2,250,000	11,250,000
2,100	4	8,400	4,410,000	17,640,000
2,700	7	18,900	7,290,000	51,030,000
	30	42,000		84,780,000

We can put these figures into the formula:

$$s = \sqrt{\frac{84,780,000}{30} - \left[\frac{42,000}{30}\right]^2}$$

$$= \sqrt{2,826,000 - 1,400^2}$$

$$= \sqrt{866,000}$$

$$= 930$$

You can do exactly the same for the property claims and you should find a standard deviation of 791.

What do these two standard deviations actually tell us?

On its own the standard deviation is really very difficult to interpret. However it can be useful when comparing two different distributions and it is certainly useful in a whole range of statistical work far beyond what we might cover in this book.

In our example the means of both distributions, injury and property, are identical. The mean of the injury claims is seen in the standard deviation formula:

$$\frac{\Sigma fx}{\Sigma f} = 1400$$

If we calculate the mean property claim we find:

x Mid-point	f	fx
300	6	1,800
900	7	6,300
1,500	7	10,500
2,100	6	12,600
2,700	4	10,800
		42,000

$$\frac{\Sigma fx}{\Sigma f} = \frac{42,000}{30} = 1400$$

Both types of claims are therefore located at the same place, but their dispersion is different. The injury claims are more widely dispersed than property claims. The difference is not very marked but it does exist. This takes us back to the point we made earlier. If we have two distributions with the same mean but one has a wider dispersion then it is the riskier of the two. The extent of the dispersion will determine just how risky the distribution is.

This direct comparison of the standard deviations was possible because the means were the same. Remember that the standard deviation measures dispersion around the mean and so if the mean for one distribution was substantially higher than another, the standard deviation would also be measured in larger figures. This may be due solely to the size of the numbers and not to a larger dispersion.

For example take the following two distributions:

A	B
4	40
7	70
9	90
10	100
$\bar{x} = 7.5$	$\bar{x} = 75$
$s = 22.9$	$s = 22.9$

Distribution B has a standard deviation of 22.9, which is much larger than the standard deviation for distribution A, but this is due solely to the fact that the size of the numbers in distribution B is 10 times that of A. The dispersion is in fact exactly the same. One way to compare this dispersion when the means are different is to express the standard deviation as a percentage of the mean. If we do this for the two distributions we get:

A	B
$\frac{s}{\bar{x}} \times 100$	$\frac{s}{\bar{x}} \times 100$
$\frac{2.29}{7.5} \times 100$	$\frac{22.9}{7.5} \times 100$
30.53%	30.53%

This figure is called the "coefficient of variation" and it allows us to compare different standard deviations even where the arithmetic means are quite different.

In our hotel data we would separate out the Glasgow injury claims from the London injury claims; when we do this we find:

Glasgow $\bar{x} = 850$
London $\bar{x} = 2069$

The Glasgow injury claims have a much lower mean than the London injury claims but what about their dispersion? The respective standard deviations are:

Glasgow $s = 804$
London $s = 816$

The standard deviations are not all that dissimilar but remember that the means are quite different. The coefficients of variation are:

Glasgow $\dfrac{804}{850} \times 100 = 94.59\%$

London $\dfrac{816}{2069} \times 100 = 39.44\%$

This shows quite clearly that the Glasgow injury claims, while having a lower mean cost than London, have a substantially higher dispersion. This implies that the range of claims in Glasgow is much wider than for London. The size of injury claims will cover a wide range, unlike London injury claims which are more tightly grouped around the mean, albeit a higher mean.

The coefficient of variation allowed us to make this comparison and can be useful whenever there are distributions of varying sizes. One such situation is comparison of costs for different currencies. When comparing sterling costs and dollar costs we have to take account of the differing values of the currencies themselves and avoid misleading conclusions. The coefficient of variation allows this to be done. Say that we have the following figures:

Britain $\bar{x} = £500$
            $s = £350$

USA $\bar{x} = \$720$
            $s = \$500$

It is difficult to compare these figures in a direct fashion. We could transfer all the values into either pounds or dollars but we could calculate the coefficient of variation and avoid that extra work:

Britain $\dfrac{£350}{£500} \times 100 = 70\%$

USA $\dfrac{\$500}{\$720} \times 100 = 69.4\%$

The dispersion within the two distributions is almost identical.

7.3.2   Skew

There is one final measure we must add, in order to describe our data fully. We have located our data and measured its dispersion around the mean. Look at these key statistics for all Glasgow and London claims.

Fig 7.1(a)

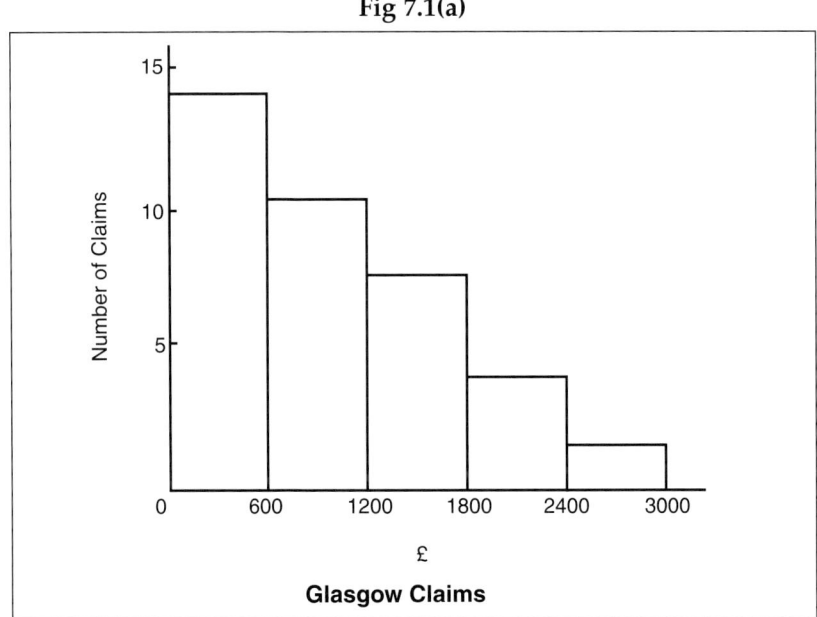

Glasgow Claims

Fig 7.1(b)

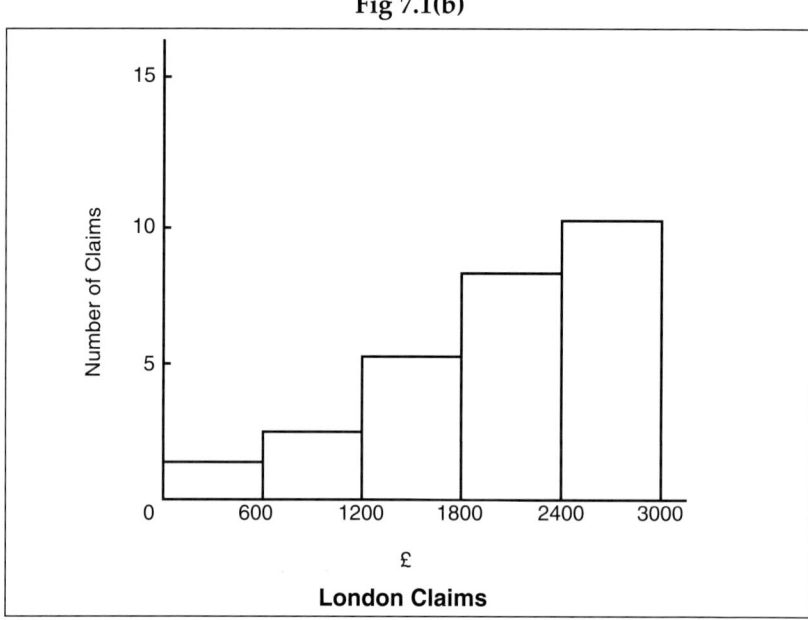

London Claims

Glasgow $\bar{x}$ = £925   s = £696   Coefficient of variation = 75%
London $\bar{x}$ = £2019 s = £699   Coefficient of variation = 35%

Glasgow and London claims have roughly the same standard deviation but we know this is meaningless until we relate it to the arithmetic mean. When we do this we see that Glasgow claims are much more widely dispersed around a lower arithmetic mean. Going on our earlier comments we might say that Glasgow claims cost less but there is a high variation, while London claims cost more on average but are more predictable, as they are more tightly grouped around the mean.

We have drawn both distributions in Fig 7.1(a) and 7.1(b). From these two histograms you can see that the two distributions are really quite different. There is one feature we have not yet discussed, which can be observed from the two drawings. We have not yet measured the extent to which the data may be bunched or grouped at the lower or higher end of the distribution. We have not yet measured skew.

You can see from the drawings that the Glasgow claims are bunched at the lower end of the distribution. The frequency is highest over the lower values. This is the opposite of the London claims, where the highest frequencies are measured over the high value claims. This bunching is what we refer to as skew and we must look now for some way of measuring it in a distribution.

In Fig 7.2 we have drawn a distribution which has no skew, it is in fact symmetrical. The frequency distribution for this drawing is:

x	f
10	2
20	6
30	10
40	6
50	2
	$\Sigma f = 26$

The arithmetic mean is 30. The median is the value associated with 13th number, and this is also 30. We can see here that when the distribution is symmetrical, as we have shown in Fig 7.2, the mean and the median will coincide.

When a distribution is skewed, either to the left or to the right, then the mean and median will not be the same values. The key to measuring skew lies with this fact. When the mean and the median are the same we have no skew; we could say we have zero skew. When the mean is greater than the median then the distribution will be bunched at the lower end of the values. Think about this – the mean is being pulled up by a few high values when in fact the majority of values are much lower.

The following distribution shows this:

x	f
10	10
20	7
30	5
40	3
50	1
	$\Sigma f = 26$

The mean is $\dfrac{\Sigma fx}{\Sigma f} = \dfrac{560}{26} = 21.54$. The median is the value of the 13th number and this is 20. The mean is therefore greater than the median and the distribution is skewed to the right-hand side of the distribution as we can see in Fig 7.3. One formula for measuring skew is:

$$\frac{3(mean - median)}{St.\ Dev.}$$

Fig 7.2

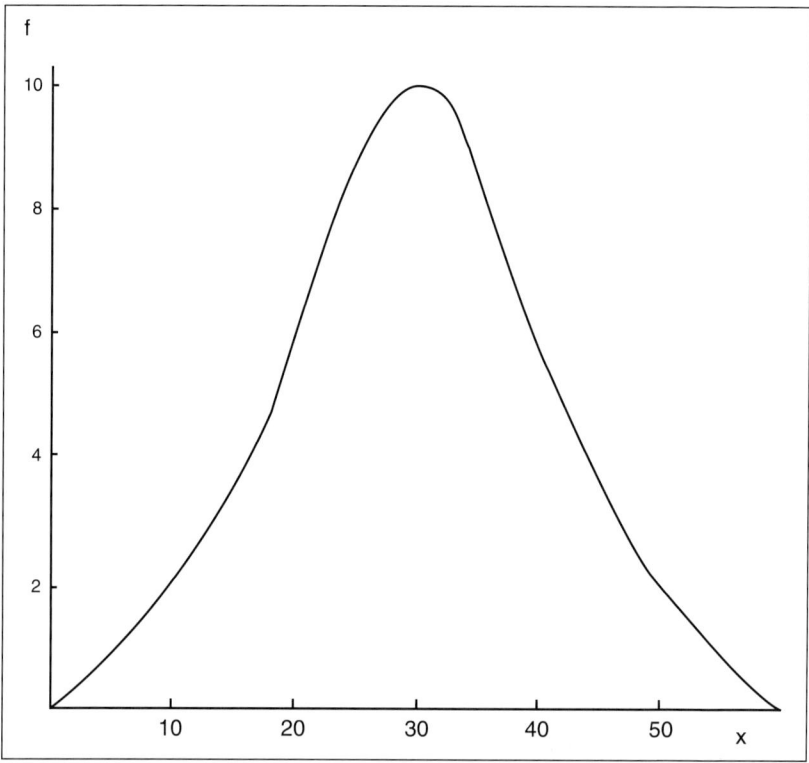

A Symmetrical Distribution Without Skew

We are expressing the difference between the mean and the median in terms of the standard deviation. When the mean and median are the same then the formula produces "0" which we term zero skew.

In the distribution which is skewed to the right we find that an answer will always be positive. This is because the mean will be larger than the median in view of the high values, even though the bulk of values are bunched at the lower end. For the distribution in Fig 7.3 we can calculate the standard deviation to be 11.67. Skew, known as Pearson's coefficient of skew, is therefore:

Fig 7.3

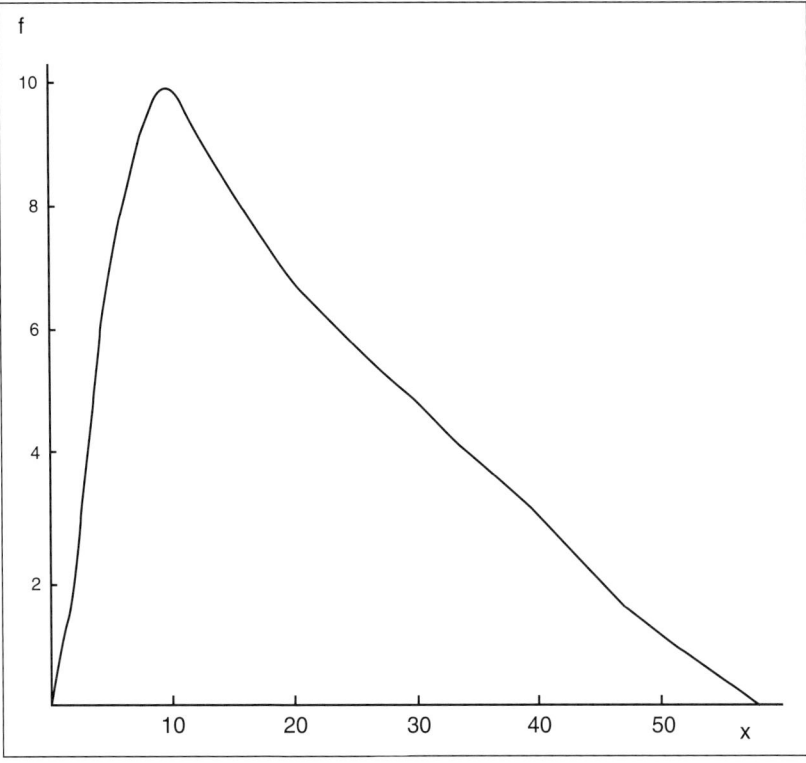

A Distribution With Skew

$$\frac{3\,(21.54 - 20)}{11.67} = 0.4$$

This positive figure of 0.4 is the measure of skew. The most important thing is that the coefficient is positive, thus indicating that the distribution is bunched at the left and slopes down to the right.

The alternative to this 'positive skew' would be negative skew. The following distribution shows this:

x	f
10	1
20	3
30	5
40	7
50	10
	$\Sigma f = 26$

Fig 7.4

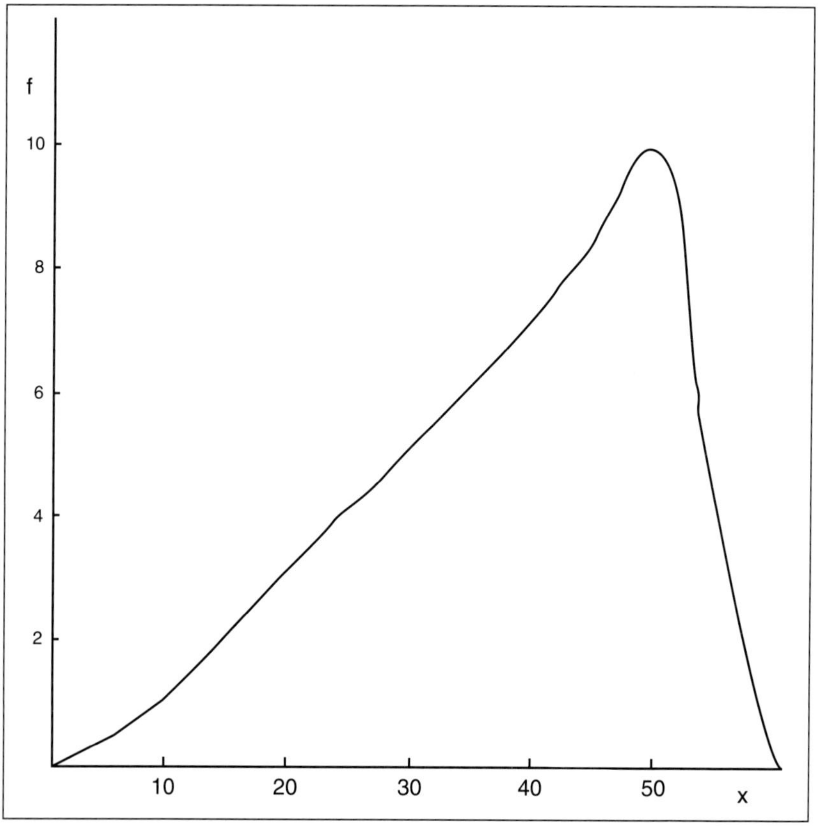

An Illustration of Negative Skew

The drawing in Fig 7.4 illustrates this distribution and we can see that it is skewed the other way. The highest frequencies are associated with high values and this time the mean will be pulled down by the few low values.

The arithmetic mean is $\dfrac{\Sigma fx}{\Sigma f} = \dfrac{1000}{26} = 38.46$. The median is again the value of the 13th number which is 40. The standard deviation can be calculated to be 11.67. (We could have guessed that the standard deviation would have been the same because the actual dispersion is exactly the same for this distribution as it was for the distribution in Fig 7.3. The only difference is the skew.)

The coefficient of skew is therefore:

$$\frac{3\,(38.46-40)}{11.67} = -0.4$$

This is also the same, except that now it is negative, which implies that the distribution is bunched at the higher end of the scale of values.

If we now return to our hotel data and try to apply what we have discovered, the figures necessary to calculate skew for the Glasgow and London claims distributions, shown in Figs 7.1(a) and 7.1(b) are:

Glasgow: mean 925   median 700   standard deviation 696
London: mean 2019   median 2100   standard deviation 699

Using Pearson's formula we have:

Glasgow $$\frac{3(925-700)}{696} = +0.97$$

London $$\frac{3(2019-2100)}{699} = -0.35$$

The Glasgow figures are positively skewed and the London claims negatively skewed.

We now have the three measures we need of our data, and in fact any data. We have measured location, dispersion and skew and it is only when all three have been found, as we saw, that we have a comprehensive picture of the data. In this chapter we have taken the time to draw distributions and indeed follow through formulae. However, in the real world this is not what is done. In most cases there will be too many figures to start drawing distributions, and there will be no need to carry out calculations by hand when computers can do all of the computational work for you. In fact many simple pocket calculators will compute standard deviations, for example, at the press of a single button.

What is important are two things. Firstly, that we can understand what our data is like without having to take the extra time required in drawing it and, secondly, that we can interpret the statistics we compute.

8

PROBABILITY

8.1   INTRODUCTION

There is one aspect of the statistical analysis of risk that we have not yet discussed in detail and that is probability. Measurement of the likelihood of loss is clearly an important aspect of the analysis of risk and is one with which risk managers should be familiar.

Discussion of likelihood inevitably leads on to measuring likelihood and measuring likelihood is what probability theory is all about. This chapter will introduce the whole idea of probability theory, the ways in which probabilities are derived, their uses, and conclude with a discussion on probability distributions.

8.2   THE MEANING OF PROBABILITIES

Probability theory is a topic which often causes confusion in the mind of those who are trying to get to grips with it for the first time. It is often the case that those people who are very good with statistical calculations find probabilities a real problem, and vice versa.

Probability theory sets out to attach a numerical value to our measurement of the likelihood of an event occurring. This probability figure must be between 0 and 1. A probability of 0 implies that the event is impossible, while a figure of 1 shows that it is certain to occur. Clearly there are few, if any, events which are either impossible or certain and most events therefore have a probability which lies between these two extremes.

A probability cannot exceed 1 or be a negative figure and if any calculations produce such a figure then the calculations are wrong. Where the probability lies on the range from 0 to 1 is an indication of how likely the event is. An event with a probability of 0.001 is quite unlikely: there is a one in a thousand chance of it occurring. An event with a probability of 0.95, on the other hand, is 95% certain to occur.

We can now use these statements to express the likelihood of different events occurring and will be able to rank different events according to how likely they are. We could say that the probability of fire at a particular plant is 0.2; of one of our vehicles being in a motor accident is 0.1; of theft from our shops is 0.01, and so on. Each statement expresses the likelihood of the event. In the above examples, fire seems the most likely event with theft being least likely.

If that was all there was to probability theory then people would not have the fear of it that they do. What we have to look at are the ways in which these probabilities are derived and then used.

8.3   DERIVATION OF PROBABILITIES

8.3.1   A Priori

The first method is the simplest to understand, but unfortunately is not very realistic. It had its origin in games of chance, where for example a person wanted to know the likelihood of getting a particular playing card or a specific number on the roll of dice, etc.

The a priori method expresses likelihood by taking the number of outcomes which you want and dividing this by the total number of all possible outcomes. And so if you wanted to know the probability of getting a red card from a pack of playing cards you would take the 26 red cards and divide by all cards to get 26/52 or 0.5. The total number of outcomes which you wanted is 26 – there are 26 red cards – and the total number of all possible outcomes is 52 as there are 52 cards in the pack.

The same thinking can be used to find the probability of getting a 3 on the roll of a dice. There are six sides on a dice and each has a different number. Only one outcome corresponds to what you want and so the a priori probability is 1/6 or 0.1666.

In general terms we can say that we can calculate an a priori probability where all the events are equally likely to occur and all possible outcomes are known.

In the two examples we used above these rules certainly applied. You are just as likely to pick one card as another and just as likely to roll the dice and get a 3 as any other number. In the same way, you knew in the playing card example that there were 52 possible outcomes when you selected a card and six possible outcomes when you rolled the dice.

These two assumptions are rather unrealistic in practical business situations. In most business problems the various events or outcomes to a problem are rarely equally likely and, in addition, it is often the case that the whole range of outcomes is not, or cannot be, known. In a very general sense we can see this in the problem of estimating losses. A risk manager may be trying to evaluate the cost of losses at a particular plant. In addition to the probability of various types of losses being unequal, there is also inequality within types. For example, the probability of having a large fire loss is not the same as the probability of there being a very small incident. We know that small incidents are really quite common whereas high fire losses are, fortunately, unlikely. It would not be possible therefore to use the a priori method of determining probabilities as the events with which we are concerned are not all equally likely.

The other condition which had to be satisfied before we could use the a priori method was that all possible outcomes had to be known. It is this condition which is really the most unrealistic in normal risk management problems. You will recall that in order to calculate the a priori probability we divided the desired number of outcomes by all possible outcomes. Using this approach to find the probability of there being three fires at your plant next year, you would divide 3, the number of desired outcomes, by the total number of all possible outcomes, which would be the total number of all possible fires. This figure just cannot be found!

At the end of any time period we will be able to calculate the number of fires we have had but we will never know the number of fires we did not have, and the total number of all possible fires is the sum of all those which took place and those which could have occurred but did not. It is similar to asking someone how many goals were not scored in a football match. We know how many were scored and that is all.

8.3.2 Relative Frequency

What was required was a method of determining probabilities which was based on the information we had. The relative frequency concept expresses likelihood in terms of the relative frequency with which similar events have occurred in the past.

A risk manager with 100 vehicles in a fleet would determine the probability of one of these vehicles being in an accident next year by looking back over the previous year and noting the number of vehicles that had been in an accident. If five vehicles had been involved in an accident in the previous year then we would say that the relative frequency with which vehicles were in accidents was 5/100 or 0.05.

We could do the same for fires. Let us say we had 50 fire incidents last year distributed as follows:

Cost	Number
$0 < 100$	25
$100 < 200$	15
$200 < 300$	6
≥ 300	4
	50

The relative frequency with which fires costing £300 or more occurred was 4 in 50 or 0.08. Assuming that there are no factors which alter the likelihood of loss then the probability of fires costing £300 or more next year is 0.08.

This method of determining probabilities also has its difficulties. There may be factors which change likelihood from year to year, or exact details of accidents in the past may not have been recorded. These two problems relate to cases where there was some previous record, albeit not suitable for deriving probabilities, but what of the case where no previous knowledge exists?

This could easily occur in the case of some new production process, chemical, or building material. The process, chemical, or material has not been used before and so the number of losses in the past from injury, disease, or fire, respectively, cannot be calculated. The relative frequency concept is therefore not appropriate. In such cases we could turn to the third method of deriving probabilities.

8.3.3 Subjective

Where inaccurate or no historical information exists we can attempt to measure degrees of belief in the likelihood of an event occurring. This involves questioning yourself or others according to one of several methods which exist for the purpose of eliciting probabilities.

It is not necessary to go into the detail of the techniques here; what we might want to remember is that such techniques exist and can be useful.

8.4 COMBINING PROBABILITIES

What we have discovered so far is the basic issue of how probabilities are derived. Having obtained a measure of the likelihood of an event or events occurring in the future, we will want to use this information in some way. There are certain rules for the manipulation of probabilities and we will look at the most important here.

8.4.1 Alternative Events

So far we have limited our examples to single events: the probability of fire, an accident, an injury, etc. Often it is necessary or desirable to calculate the likelihood of either one or another event occurring. For example we may want to know the probability of there being a fire *or* a theft at a shop; of the London *or* Birmingham plant having a computer breakdown, etc.

We call these probabilities, alternative probabilities, and a rule exists to help us calculate them. The particular rule is known as the additions rule, for reasons which will become clear shortly.

Let us say that we operate a three shift system: early, late, and night shifts. We want to know the probability of an accident occurring on either the early or late shifts. Without looking at probabilities at all we could imagine that if 20% of all accidents took place during the early shift, 25% during the late shift and 55% during the night shift, we could say that 45% of all accidents occurred during either the early or late shifts. This should be obvious from the information we have available: 20% of all accidents were during the early shift, 25% during the late shift and 45%, the total of these two, occurred during either the early or late shift.

If we reduce these percentages to probabilities then we would say that the probability of an accident during the early shift is 0.20, the late shift is 0.25, and the night shift is 0.55. We use a form of probability shorthand to avoid having to write "early shift", "day shift", etc, all the time. Let us say that the event that an accident occurs during the early shift is "A", during the late shift is "B", and during the night shift is "C", and so the probability of an accident occurring during the early shift would be written as P(A).

All the probabilities would then be:

P(A) = 0.20
P(B) = 0.25
P(C) = 0.55

In passing we can see that these probabilities sum to 1. This is because we only operate three shifts, and accidents which occur will occur with certainty during one of these shifts.

We know already that the probability of (A) or (B) is 0.45. This was found by adding the individual probabilities:

$$P \text{ (A or B)} = P(A) + P(B)$$
$$= 0.20 + 0.25$$
$$= 0.45$$

In the same way we could have calculated the probability of an accident occurring on either the late shift or night shift. This would be:

$$P \text{ (B or C)} = P(B) + P(C)$$
$$= 0.25 + 0.55$$
$$= 0.80$$

We must now notice one important feature of this example. The events we have discussed are *mutually exclusive*. By this we mean that the events cannot occur at the same time, in other words it is impossible for one accident to occur in both the early shift and the night shift. An accident can only be in one shift but not both.

This idea of mutual exclusivity could also apply for example to calculating the probability of an injured employee being male or female, of damages being above or below a certain figure, of employees being injured or killed, etc. However, there are many cases where events will not be mutually exclusive.

Let us stay with the accidents to employees example. Out of 300 employees, you have, during the past year, recorded 25 accidents sustained by experienced employees, i.e. those with more than 5 years' relevant work experience, and 15 accidents sustained by those who had previously had an accident or accidents. Of the 25 experienced people, 5 had also sustained an accident in the past. We can represent this accident record in a diagram known as a Venn diagram. The square represents all employees, and the circles the two types of employees involved in accidents. This diagram is shown in Fig 8.1.

We can see in this diagram that out of the total number of employees there are the following categories:

- those who had no accidents
- those having an accident, who had work experience
- those having an accident, who had had previous accidents
- those having an accident, who had both work experience and had had previous accidents.

These four groups can be identified in the diagram. One circle represents those having an accident who had work experience, another those having an accident who had had a previous accident, and the overlap those with experience and a previous accident. The remainder of the square represents all those who had no accident.

Fig 8.1

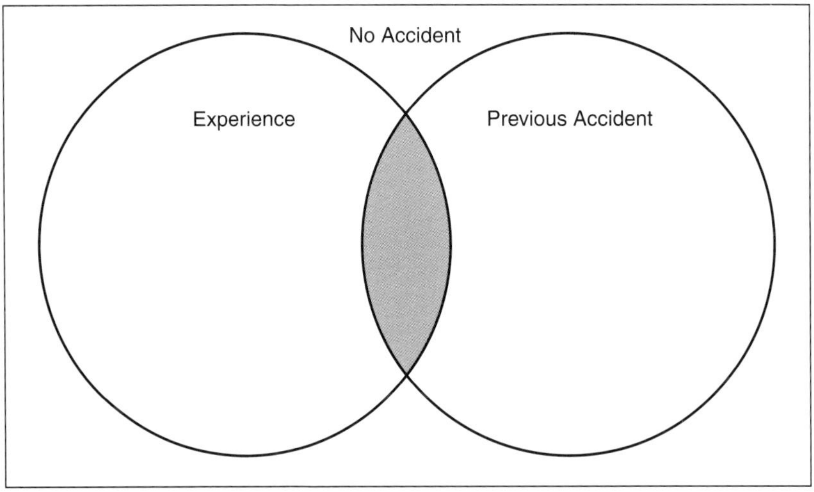

A Venn Diagram

When we insert the numbers we now end up with the diagram in Fig 8.2.

Fig 8.2

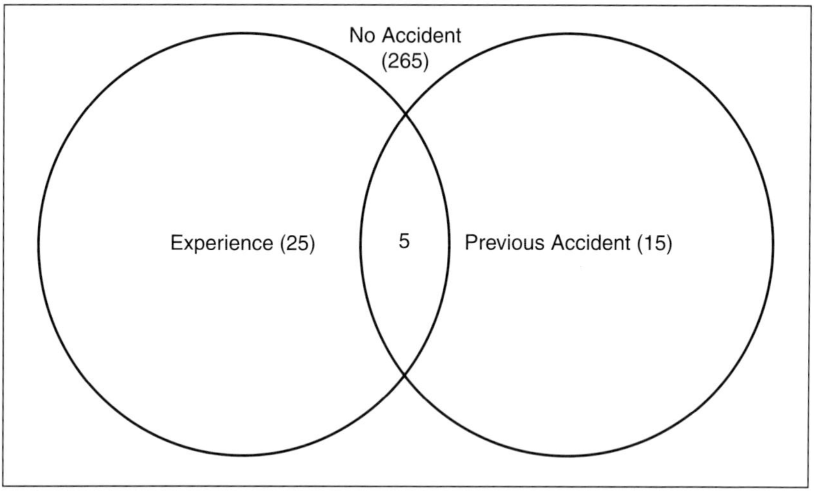

Inserting the Numbers

Five people who had an accident had both experience and a previous accident. This leaves 20 who had experience but no previous accidents and 10 who had previous accidents but no work experience.

What then is the probability of a person involved in an accident being experienced or previously having had an accident?

Using our notation of before we could let experience be (A) and previous accident be (B), and so we are looking for P(A or B). If we follow the rule we used earlier then we would say that P(A or B) = P(A) + P(B). Now P(A) is the event that a person in an accident had previous experience. We had 25 people and so the probability is 25/300; the probability of a person having an accident, who had previously had an accident, is 15/300. Therefore:

$$P(A \text{ or } B) = P(A) + P(B)$$
$$= \frac{25}{300} + \frac{15}{300}$$
$$= \frac{40}{300}$$

If this were correct it would mean that the probability of a person not having an accident would be 1 – 40/300 or 260/300, i.e. it is certain that a person either has an accident or not. If the probability of having an accident is 40/300, then when this is deducted from 1, which is the certainty we just mentioned, we are left with 260/300 as the probability of not having an accident. We can see however from Fig 8.2 that this figure of 260/300 is wrong. The correct number of people not involved in an accident is 265 not 260. The formula P(A or B) = P(A) + P(B) does not seem to have worked in this case. The reason why the formula failed is the fact that the events are not mutually exclusive. When we added the 25/300 to the 15/300 we added the overlap of 5 twice. Of the 25 with experience there were 5 who had had a previous accident. In the same way the 15 with a previous accident included 5 with experience. It is the same 5 but we included it both in the 25 and the 15.

What we need to do is to deduct it once from the total. A formula for this would be:

$$P(A \text{ or } B) = P(A) + P(B) - P(A \& B)$$

The expression P(A & B) is the probability of a person in an accident having experience *and* a previous accident. When we expand this formula we have:

$$P(A \text{ or } B) = P(A) + P(B) - P(A \& B)$$
$$= \frac{25}{300} + \frac{15}{300} - \frac{5}{300}$$
$$= \frac{35}{300}$$

and so the probability of an accident victim having work experience or a previous accident is 35/300 or 0.12. This means that the probability of a person not having an accident is 265/300 or 0.88, which is correct according to the Venn diagram.

Fig 8.3 shows the Venn diagram with all the relevant probabilities inserted.

Fig 8.3

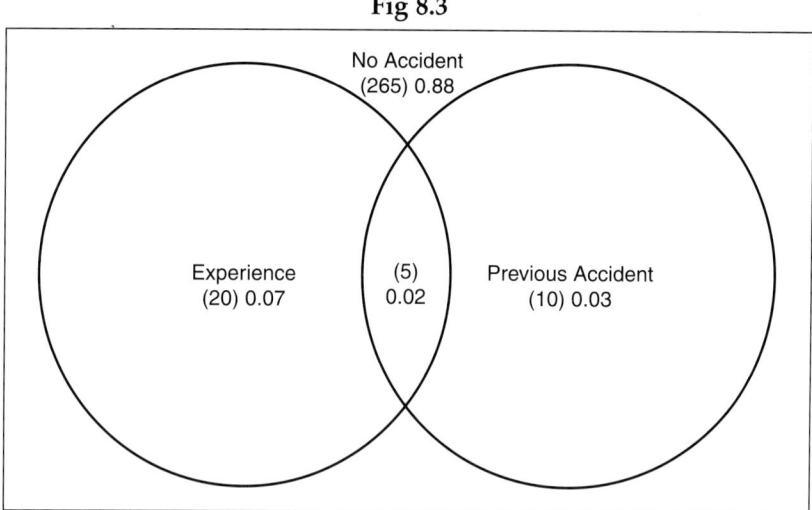

No Accident
(265) 0.88

Experience
(20) 0.07

(5)
0.02

Previous Accident
(10) 0.03

The Venn Diagram Inclusive of all Relevant Probabilities

We can now see from this that the probability of an accident victim having work experience but no previous accident is 0.07. The probability of a victim having a previous accident but not work experience is 0.03, and so on.

Apart altogether from the computation of probabilities it is often useful to illustrate complex problems in a simple diagram such as the Venn diagram, in order to clarify some of the complex relationships which may exist in certain problems.

8.4.2   Joint Events

Another common way in which individual probabilities are combined is in the computation of probabilities for joint events. We might want to calculate the likelihood of there being a fire at our London factory and Birmingham plant during the next year. Based on past records and an element of subjective thinking, we believe that the probability of a fire in Birmingham, P(B), is estimated at 0.02, and in London, P(L), is 0.04.

What we now want is the probability of a fire in London and Birmingham, P(L and B). When we stop to think about this we could imagine that the joint probability is likely to be smaller than the individual probabilities. The likelihood of a fire in both plants is less likely than a fire in one or other. In fact we multiply the individual probabilities together in order to arrive at the joint probability:

$$P(L \text{ and } B) = P(L).P(B)$$
$$= (0.04)(0.02)$$
$$= 0.0008$$

From there being a 1 in 25 chance of a fire in London and a 1 in 50 chance of a fire in Birmingham there is now a 1 in 1250 chance of a fire at both London and Birmingham. We call this rule for computing joint events, the multiplication rule.

The simple formula of $P(A \text{ and } B) = P(A).P(B)$ holds good if events are 'independent'. This word independent means that the occurrence of one event does not alter the likelihood of the other event occurring. This was the case in the example we have used so far.

Consider, however, the case where we have two buildings within very close proximity. The first building has a probability of going on fire of 0.05 and the other a probability of 0.02. The buildings are so close that if one goes on fire then the other is almost certain to ignite; in fact if one of the buildings is on fire it has been estimated that there is an 85% chance of the other catching fire.

If we now want to calculate the probability of both going on fire we will have to take account of this new information. The simple formula $P(A \text{ and } B) = P(A).P(B)$ will not suffice as it assumes independence between the events, which is not the case.

By re-writing the formula we can reflect the fact that the events are not independent.

$$P(A \text{ and } B) = P(A).P(B/A)$$

This expression $P(B/A)$ is the probability of 'B' given that 'A' has occurred. Using the figures we have above then:

$$P(A) \quad = 0.05$$
$$P(B) \quad = 0.02$$
$$P(B/A) = 0.85$$
$$P(A/B) = 0.85$$

When we calculate $P(A \text{ and } B)$ we now find:

$$P(A \text{ and } B) = P(A).P(B/A)$$
$$= (0.05)(0.85)$$
$$= 0.0425$$

There is now approximately a 1 in 24 chance of both buildings igniting. This much more likely figure, than the 1 in 1250 calculated earlier, is due to the fact that the two events are not independent.

Notice that the probability of (A and B) is not the same as the probability of (B and A).

$$P(B \text{ and } A) = P(B).P(A/B)$$
$$= (0.02)(0.85)$$
$$= 0.017$$

The figure of 0.017 is the probability that building (B) goes on fire and then building (A). Remember that building (A) was more likely to go on fire than building (B) and so it is important to remember which building goes on fire first.

8.4.3   Probability Trees

Before leaving the area of combining probabilities let us take a brief look at the use of probability trees. These trees are a useful way of illustrating the combination of events.

We can show the use of probability trees by means of a simple example. Let us say that at a particular site it is estimated that the likelihood of theft is 0.2. The likelihood of this theft then being of fixtures and fittings, stock or plant has been put at (0.3), (0.5) and (0.2) respectively. Regardless of what kind of property is stolen, the theft could be large or small. The probability of a large theft loss of fixtures and fittings is put at 0.7. The probabilities of large stock and plant thefts has been put at 0.5 and 0.1 respectively.

We can illustrate this problem by a probability tree and draw some interesting conclusions from it. Let us start with a simple tree of whether or not there will be a loss. This is shown in Fig 8.4(a). In this tree we can see the two possibilities and the respective probabilities at the tips of the branches of the tree.

In Fig 8.4(b) we have added on further branches showing the nature of the theft. The likelihood of theft was estimated at 0.2 and so the probability of no theft is 0.8. We know the probabilities of having fixtures and fittings, stock or plant stolen and these have been inserted in brackets above the relevant branches. At the tip of the tree we have now shown the combined probability of a theft being of one of the three types.

Fig 8.4(a)

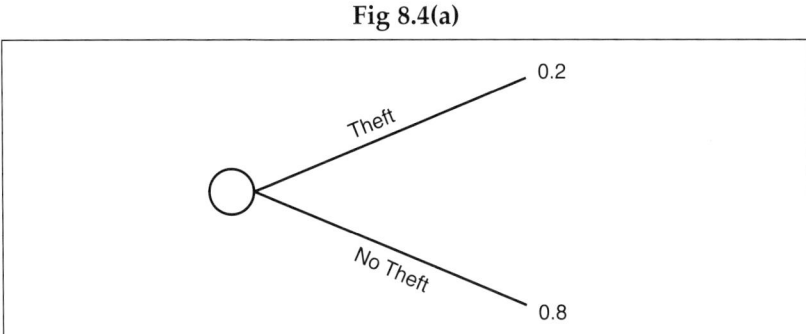

Fig 8.4(b)

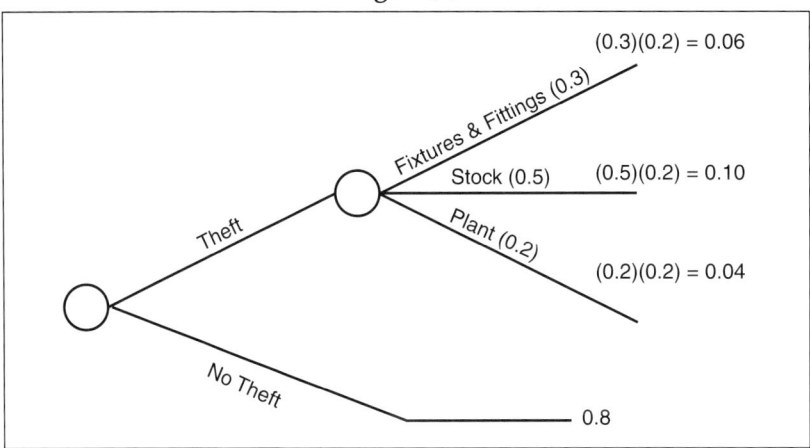

The Probabilities and Nature of Theft

What we have calculated is the probability of having a theft *and* it being of fixtures and fittings, etc. This is really just an application of the multiplication rule for joint events which we discussed earlier. We multiply the individual probabilities of the two events in order to arrive at the probability of the joint event. We can see now, for example, that the likelihood of having a theft of stock is 0.1 and of plant is 0.04.

In Fig 8.5 we have added the final aspect of the problem, whether the theft was a large theft or small theft. The probability of having a theft of fixtures is calculated as 0.06, and we see this in Fig 8.4(b). We now know that a large fixtures theft is quite likely, probably due to the nature of the fixtures and fittings, including micro computers, video machines, etc. And so, if the probability of a theft of fixtures is 0.06 and the probability of any fixtures theft being large is

0.7, then the probability of having a fixtures theft and it being large is (0.06) (0.7) or 0.042.

We can do the same for all the types of property and the probabilities are shown at the tips of the branches of the tree.

We can now use the tree to calculate various other probabilities. For example, the probability of having a large theft of anything other than stock would be 0.046. We found this by saying that any large theft other than stock must be a large theft of either fixtures or plant. The probability of a large fixtures loss is 0.042 and of a large plant loss is 0.004. The probability of either of these happening is therefore (0.042) + (0.004), an example of the addition rule for alternative events.

Fig 8.5

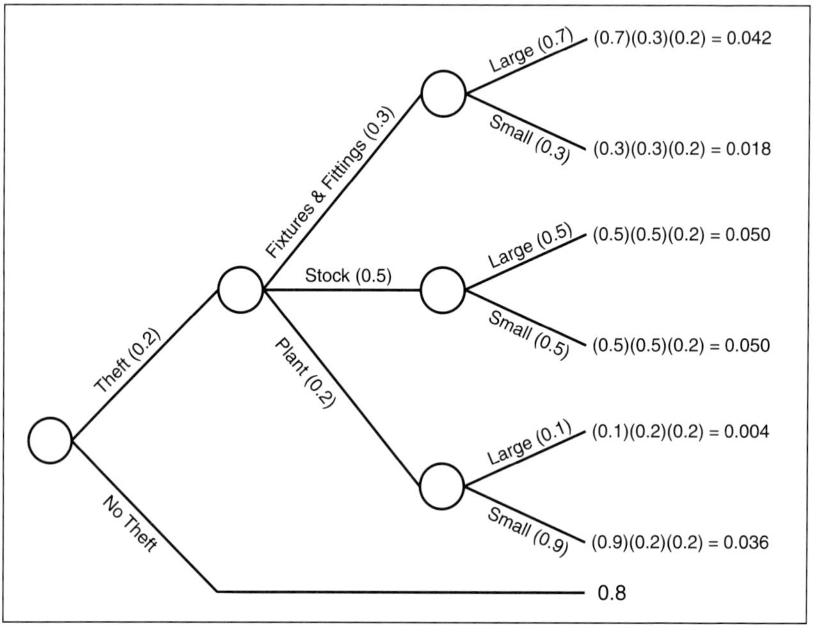

The Addition of Large or Small Thefts

Notice, just before we leave the tree, that the sum of all the probabilities at the tips of the branches is 1. We have a list of mutually exclusive events which are exhaustive of all possibilities, and so one or other must happen; one or other is certain and so the addition of them all is 1.

This may have appeared to be a rather lengthy introduction to the idea of probability theory, and it has only been an introduction, but it is an important area. Whenever we speak of risk we imply the calculation or estimation of likelihood, and we should endeavour to be familiar with the basic notion of probabilities.

8.5 PROBABILITY DISTRIBUTIONS

We move on now to a particular application of probabilities. Probability distributions will help us to carry out many of the estimates of likelihood which we will want to make.

Let us firstly create a simple example in order to illustrate some fundamental points. A company has 100 vehicles in its motor fleet and over the past year it has kept a careful record of accidents. Of the 100 vehicles, 60 were not involved in any accidents, 20 were involved in one accident, 10 in two, 7 were in three, and 3 were in four accidents during the year. This information is displayed in a frequency distribution as follows:

Number of accidents	Number of vehicles
0	60
1	20
2	10
3	7
4	3
	100

This is the kind of frequency we looked at in Chapter six. It might, however, be useful for the manager of the fleet to express the number of vehicles having accidents in relative terms rather than absolute figures. A slight alteration to the distribution can bring this about as we see below:

Number of accidents	Relative frequency
0	60%
1	20%
2	10%
3	7%
4	3%
	100%

The manager can now see that 10% of his fleet had two accidents, 20% had one accident, and so on. These relative frequencies can also be looked upon as probability statements. Imagine a pool of 100 vehicles and you were to pick one vehicle at random, what is the likelihood, the probability, that it has not been in an accident? Well 60% of all the vehicles were not involved in an accident and so the probability of selecting one is 0.6.

By re-writing the distribution we now get:

(x) Number of Accidents	P(x)
0	0.60
1	0.20
2	0.10
3	0.07
4	0.03
	1.00

This time we have defined the number of accidents as (x) and the frequency column has been altered to show the probability of x, i.e. the probability of a particular number of accidents. We could now use this historical data as the base of our probability distribution. We have to assume, of course, that there are no changes envisaged over the period for which we are calculating probabilities.

We can also draw the probability distribution and we have done this in Fig 8.6.

This is similar to the histograms we saw earlier but this time the vertical axis shows the probability with which particular values of (x) occur. The variable (x) is the number of accidents each vehicle had. The use of the word variable simply denotes the fact that (x) does not have one particular value alone. The value can vary. In fact (x) is a random variable, meaning that the exact value of (x) is not known at the outset of any time period. All we know is that there are a number of possible values which (x) could assume.

Fig 8.6

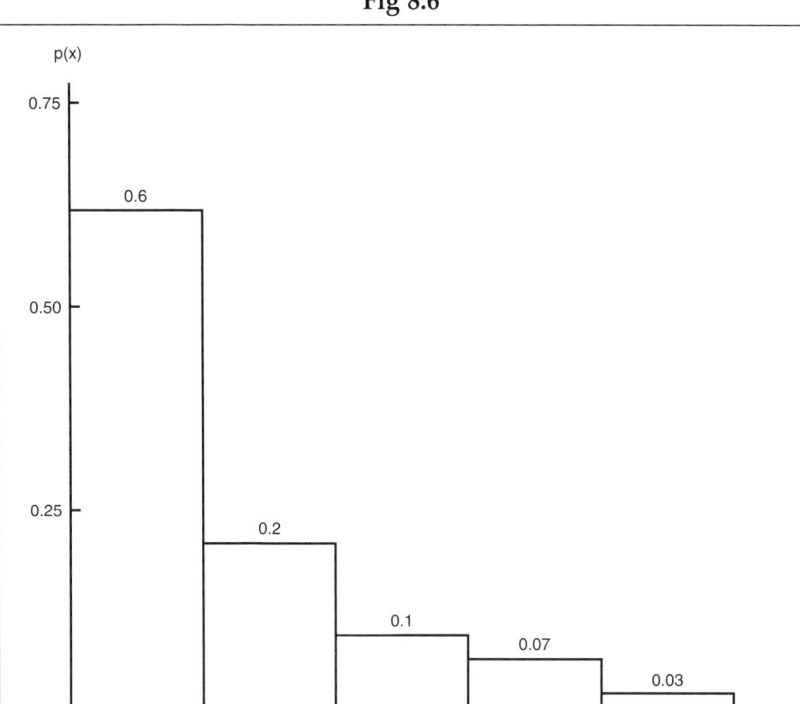

The Probability Distribution

8.5.1 Discrete and Continuous Variables

One other important feature we should mention about our variable is that it can only be a whole number. It is only possible to have 0, 1, 2, 3 or 4 accidents. It is not possible for there to be 3.84 accidents. When a variable can only be a whole number like this we call it 'discrete'. The opposite of a discrete variable is one which can be expressed in fractions. Examples of this would include salaries, claim costs, premiums, weights, volumes, temperatures, etc. Such variables are termed 'continuous'. This distinction may seem a little theoretical at this stage but its relevance should become clear as we move on.

In risk management terms we can see that, for example, the number of fires in a year is discrete but the cost of each fire is continuous.

We have looked at a probability distribution for a discrete variable, the number of accidents each vehicle in a motor fleet had. Let us look at a probability distribution for a continuous variable. The accident damage repair cost of the vehicles involved in the distribution we used earlier could be an example.

It would seem from the distribution that there were 73 individual accidents: 20 vehicles had 1 accident, 10 had 2, 7 had 3, and 3 had 4 accidents. In total this gives us:

$$20 \times 1 = 20$$
$$10 \times 2 = 20$$
$$7 \times 3 = 21$$
$$3 \times 4 = 12$$
$$\overline{73}$$

Not all of these accidents will have involved accidental damage repair costs, and those which did involve some repair would have had costs over a wide range of money. We could look at all the repair invoices and draw a frequency distribution. This we have done in the table below:

Cost of Repair	Frequency	P(x)
0 < 100	30	0.41
100 < 200	23	0.32
200 < 300	12	0.16
300 < 400	5	0.07
400 < 500	3	0.04
	$\overline{73}$	$\overline{1.00}$

The table also shows the probability of (x). In this case (x) refers to a range of money, and so the probability of accidental damage repair costs being between £200 and £300 is 0.16, while there is a 41% chance that the repairs will cost less than £100.

When this information is drawn it looks like the distribution in Fig 8.7 (ignore the shaded area for the moment).

The interpretation of this distribution in Fig 8.7 is different from the drawing in Fig 8.6. In Fig 8.6 we had a discrete variable. This meant that each value of (x), the variable, had an associated probability. We could read from the drawing and see that the probability of x being 3 was 0.07, and so on.

Fig 8.7

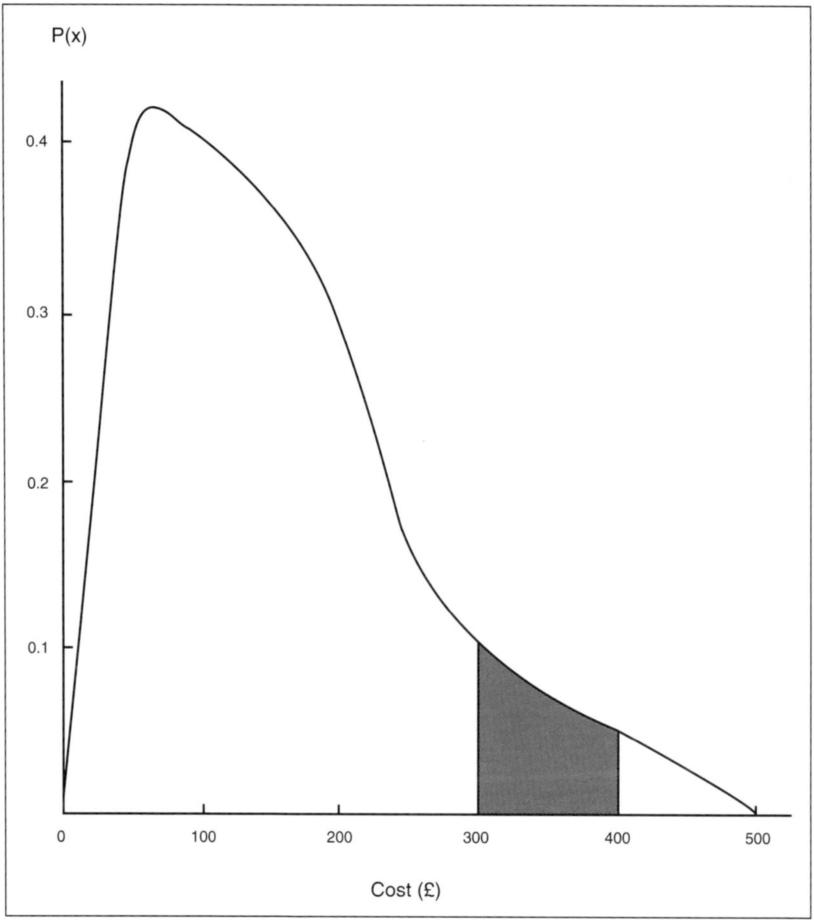

With the drawing in Fig 8.7 it is not just as simple. In Fig 8.7 we have a continuous variable. We are concerned with the cost of repairs and clearly that cost could be any fractional amount of money. It is not possible therefore to show a probability against each one of these potentially infinite number of different amounts of money. The best we can do is to assign probabilities to a range of values. In our example we grouped the different repair costs into five classes and could then express the likelihood of a claim costing between one amount and another.

Therefore, when we look at the probability distribution in Fig 8.7, we cannot look upon the y-axis as representing the probability of any specific amount of money. The scale on the y-axis indicates only the height of the curve at any point. This, again, may seem rather abstract but think for a moment about what the curve actually represents: one hundred percent of all claims costs are bounded by the curve. We know from the table we drew above that the probabilities of the various costs all summed to 1. We are sure that the cost of any one claim will be within the area bounded by the curve. We cannot however simply read off the drawing and find specific probabilities associated with certain amounts of money. For example, on our drawing in Fig 8.7 a cost of about £25 would seem to be associated with a probability of 0.2. However if we draw a horizontal line from 0.2 across the drawing we can see that it also cuts the curve at an amount equal to approximately £240. It just doesn't make sense to interpret the curve in the same way as we interpreted the drawing in Fig 8.6.

Go back then for a minute to this idea of the height of curve. If 100% of costs are bounded by the curve then the total area under the curve has a probability of 1. We can then find the probability associated with any area under the curve. A specified area under the curve will be a proportion of the total area and this will give us our probability. In Fig 8.7 we could find the probability of a claim being between £300 and £400, i.e. the area under the curve which is shaded. The actual procedure for calculating this probability can be quite complex, however, as we will see later there are ways in which we can be helped.

8.5.2   Actual and Theoretical Distributions

The distributions we have used above could all be looked upon as 'actual' or 'empirical' distributions. They are actual or empirical in the sense that we obtained actual data and then drew the distributions which matched this data. There is no doubt, therefore, that these distributions are a good representation of our data, always assuming that our records and drawings are accurate.

You can imagine that this process will take some time. Each occasion when a probability has to be drawn, someone will have to go to the sources of information and extract relevant data before drawing a probability distribution. Not only will the process take some time but we will find that many of the distributions we draw will have a general similarity.

This fact of the basic similarity of many probability distributions is not one which has escaped statisticians and, over many years now, there has developed a number of theoretical distributions which closely approximate real world situations. This idea of theoretical distributions is one which many people find extremely difficult to follow, particularly if it is some time since they last studied mathematics. Let us see if we can introduce the idea with a simple non-mathematical analogy and then try to keep the maths to a minimum.

Imagine that you are in the process of buying a new suit. (I hope this is an example with which readers from both sexes can sympathise.) One option open to you is to visit a tailor and have him take careful measurements of certain key areas such as waist, chest, arms, legs, etc. He then sets to work and produces a suit. You may even go for a try-on of the suit and final adjustments can be made. The hope, of course, is that the final suit will match your requirements exactly. Those who have one arm or leg shorter than the other will know exactly what I mean when I say how good it is to have a suit which matches these little peculiarities.

The one major drawback to this whole process is the cost. To have a suit made-to-measure will be expensive and will take some time. In the end, however, the finished product will be exactly what you need, assuming you have chosen a good tailor and you did not breathe in at the wrong time during the measurement session!

If the time and expense is too heavy you could always buy a suit off-the-peg. It may not be just as good a fit as the one made specially for you but it will be good enough. You could visit a large store and select a suit which matches, as close as possible, your own measurements. The store will have suits on racks all labelled with different sizes. Once you select the suit, you will inevitably find that it doesn't fit exactly. Well, it can't, as the same suits with the same measurements are intended to fit hundreds or even thousands of customers. It will be good enough; one arm or leg may be a little short or long but on the whole it will look quite good.

This suit story is a useful analogy with our probability distribution story. Using an actual distribution is a bit like having a suit tailor-made. It is expensive to do and time consuming but will fit your data exactly. Using a theoretical distribution is like taking a suit off-the-peg. We select a distribution according to certain key measurements and use it. It will be good enough but will not, of course, be an exact fit.

We can imagine then that there is a range of theoretical distributions which will match real world situations. What we have to know is how to select a distribution for a particular set of data we may have.

In broad terms, these theoretical distributions are in two family groups. There is a family of continuous probability distributions and a family of discrete probability distributions. We will start with what is probably the best known of all such distributions, the normal distribution.

8.6 THE NORMAL DISTRIBUTION

The normal distribution is a member of the family of continuous probability distributions and we start with it as it is well known and is perhaps the simplest to introduce.

We said earlier that theoretical distributions match very closely what happens in many real life sets of data. If we take for example the heights of males in Great Britain, we know that the vast majority are all of roughly the same height, or at least within six inches or so of each other. There are very few small people and very few large people.

In fact, if we were to draw a distribution of the heights of men it would look something like the drawing in Fig 8.8.

This shows that the bulk are of roughly the same height, with fewer people, or a lower probability of finding people, at either extreme.

If we think back now to the analogy with the suit, when we buy a suit off-the-peg we need to look for one which is roughly our size. We could say that there are some parameters which we work to. These parameters could be our height, chest size, arm length, etc. In the case of many multiple stores the parameters are often reduced to one figure such as size 10 or 12, or small, medium or large. However it is done, we will select our suit according to some key parameter or parameters.

In the same way our normal distribution is selected according to certain key parameters. It is still the same normal distribution but it will look slightly different to match different problems, just in the way that it will be the same suit which appears in size 36, 38, 42 and 44.

Fig 8.8

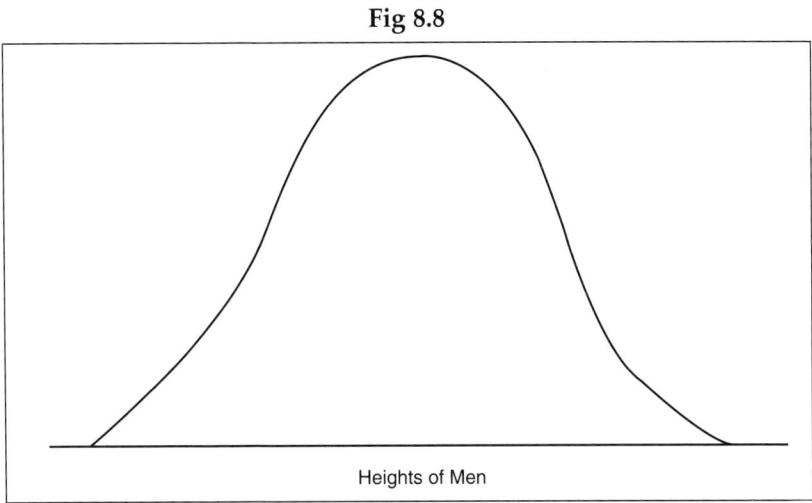

Heights of Men

The basic shape of the normal distribution, in the same way as you can talk about the basic design and colour of a suit, is the bell shape we have shown in Fig 8.8. It is symmetrical around the arithmetic mean and has a main characteristic, the bell shape. The mode and the median all coincide with the mean.

This idea of key parameters can be illustrated by thinking for a moment about temperatures. I have not calculated the annual mean temperature in London but would guess it to be about 55°F. There will be some days when it is extremely cold and some days when it is extremely hot (in those years when summer actually arrives). It is very similar to the heights data. There will be a few extremes, with the most likely temperatures being evenly spread around the mean.

In fact the London temperatures will not vary all that much from the mean; the standard deviation will be relatively low when compared to some cities. Take, for example, Moscow. The mean temperature may be very similar to London but the spread will be much wider. The distribution may still be normal in the sense that it is bell shaped with fewer at the extremes than in the middle, but it will look different from the London distribution. The two distributions are shown in Fig 8.9.

Both distributions are bell shaped and, while the means are almost the same, the spread of temperatures is quite different.

If we compared Moscow with Miami we would get quite a different picture.

Fig 8.9

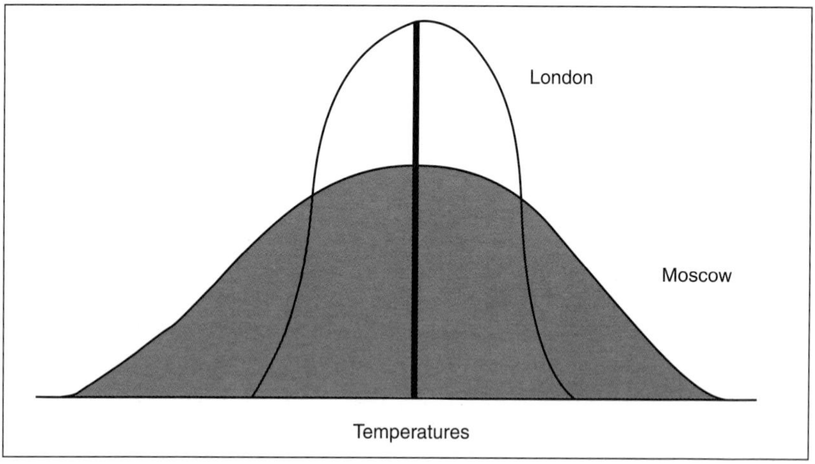

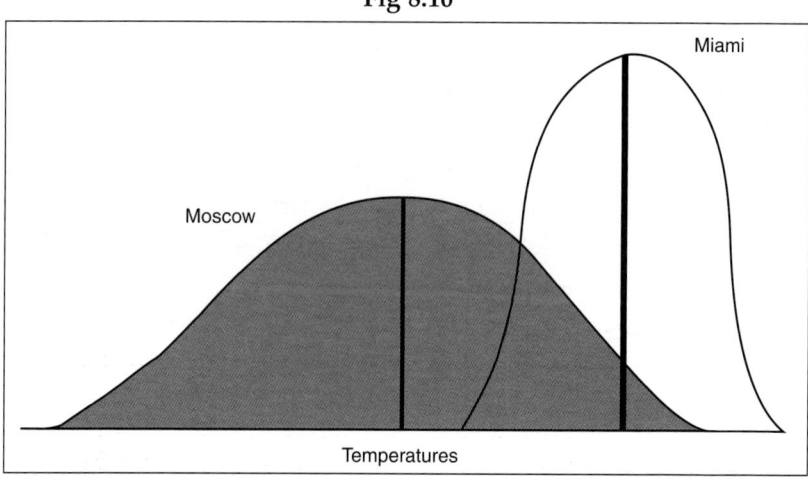

The Distribution of Temperatures Between London and Moscow

Fig 8.10

Moscow and Miami Temperature Distribution

In Fig 8.10 we have the flatter pancake distribution this time compared with the very peaked distribution for Miami. The Miami temperatures will be tightly grouped around a much higher mean than Moscow.

Looking at the drawings in Figs 8.9 and 8.10 we can begin to see the importance of the mean and standard deviation, in determining the shape of the normal distribution. All we need in order to use a normal distribution is the mean and standard deviation of our data.

What then is the value of the normal distribution? Why go through all this theory? What benefit is to be derived?

The benefit lies in the fact that the normal distribution can be explained mathematically. There is an equation, making use of the mean and standard deviation of your data, which explains the curve and allows us to calculate areas under the curve between different points. This relates back to what we said earlier about being able to express the probability of an event being within a range, that range being an area under the curve.

We do not need to bother about the mathematics of the curve but what we may be interested in is the fact that by reading standard statistical tables we can find certain areas under the curve.

8.6.1 Using the Normal Distribution

You can see from the drawings in Figs 8.8 to 8.10 that the normal distribution can be squat or peaked, depending on the parameters. In order to find areas under the curve then, we would need an infinitive number of tables to match all the possible shapes of curves.

To overcome this problem we can re-write the x-axis in a standardised way. What we do in fact is to write the x-axis in terms of standard deviations around the mean. An illustration of this is shown in Fig 8.11.

This shows a normal distribution with a mean of 30 and a standard deviation of 8. Let us say that this is a distribution of the time taken between the notification of an accidental damage claim in a motor fleet and the final settlement. On average the claim takes 30 days to clear up with a standard deviation of 8. You can see that the x-axis has two labels. The top label is the time measured in days. The lower one is the standardised measurement we mentioned earlier. This is referred to as "Z" and it measures the number of standard deviations we have moved from the mean. The value of z at the mean is obviously 0 and, as the standard deviation is 8, then the value of z at 38 is +1. Similarly the value of z at 14 is -2, as we have moved two standard deviations down from the mean.

Well how will this help? Fortunately the normal distribution is symmetrical and so movements on one side of the mean are simply the mirror image of movements on the other side. In addition, the mathematics of the curve result in us being able to calculate the area under the curve between the mean and any number of standard deviations around the mean.

Fig 8.11

6	14	22	30	38	46	54	Time in Days
−3	−2	−1	0	+1	+2	+3	Z Value

$\mu = 30$
$\sigma = 8$

X-Axis Showing Standard Deviations Around the Mean

Three well known areas are:

± 1 standard deviation embraces 68.27% of all the values
± 2 standard deviations embraces 95.45% of all the values
± 3 standard deviations embraces 99.73% of all the values

And so in our simple example we can say that 95.45% of all claims took between 14 and 46 days to settle. We found this by moving two standard deviations above and below the mean.

These areas will be so, regardless of whether the curve is peaked or squat, and so you can begin to see the great value in being able to carry out these calculations.

The standardised values come into their own when you do not want to move in neat numbers of standard deviations. Say we wanted to know the chance of a claim taking between 30 and 35 days to settle: we want the area under the curve bounded by 30 and 35. What we do is to express this range in a standardised way so that we end up with a z value which we then use to consult statistical tables.

We have covered a distance of 5, 35 − 30, and in terms of standard deviations this would be ⅝th of a standard deviation because a full standard deviation is 8. In other words what we have done is:

$$\frac{x - \mu}{\sigma}$$

where x is the value
μ is the mean
σ is the standard deviation

In our example this is:

$$\frac{35 - 30}{8} = \frac{5}{8} = 0.625$$

What this means is that the value 35 is 0.625 standard deviations away from the mean. Fortunately we have standard statistical tables which tell us the area under a normal curve for any distance around the mean. Most of these standard tables follow the same pattern.

A sample extract would be:

Areas under the normal curve

z	.00	.01	.02	.03	.04	.05	.06
0.5	.1915	.1950	.1985	.2019	.2054	.2088	.2123
0.6	.2258	.2291	.2324	.2357	.2389	.2422	.2454
1.5	.4332	.4345	.4357	.4370	.4382	.4394	.4406
1.6	.4452	.4463	.4474	.4484	.4495	.4505	.4515

We use these tables by reading down the z column to find the first number after the decimal place and then look along the columns to find the second number. In our case we had z = 0.625, which we could round to 0.63. We look down to find 0.6 and then along to .03 and find a value of 0.2357. This tells us that 23.57% of all values under the curve lie between 30 and 35 days. The probability of a claim taking between 30 and 35 days is therefore 0.2357.

Let us say that for some reason we want an estimate of the chance that claims will take longer than 42 days. It may be that our investments or access to funds changes after such a period. What is the probability of a claim taking longer than 42 days to settle?

In Fig 8.12 we have shaded the appropriate area.

We know that 50% of all claims take longer than 30 days, this is because the distribution is symmetrical around the mean. What proportion of the area is $(x - \mu)/\sigma$ greater than 42? Our formula measures distances around the mean and so we cannot find a z score for distances beyond 42. What we can do is find the area under the curve between 30 and 42 and then subtract it from the 50% which we know lies above 30. In formula terms this would be:

$$\frac{x - \mu}{\sigma} = \frac{42 - 30}{8} = 1.5$$

Fig 8.12

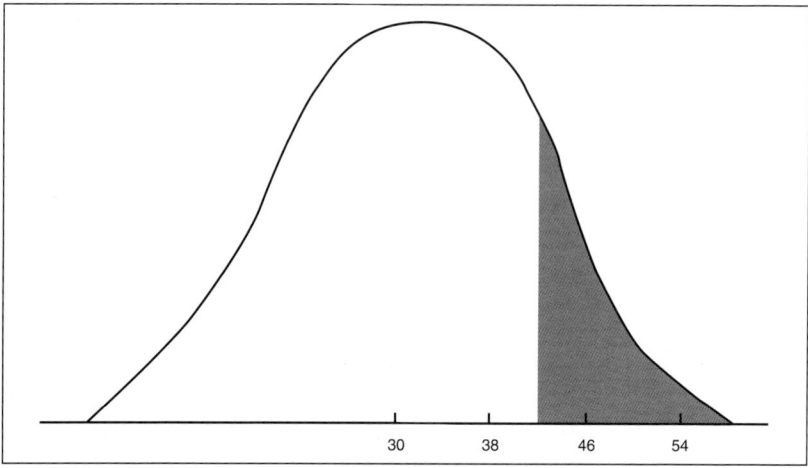

The Probability of a Claim Taking Longer Than 42 Days to Settle

We have a z value of 1.5 which, according to our brief extract, represents 43.32% of the area under the curve. And so if the area between 30 and 42 is 43.32% then the area beyond 42 must be 50% – 43.32% or 6.68%. There is only a 6.68% chance of a claim taking more than 42 days to settle. The probability is 0.0668.

The normal distribution is only one of the family of theoretical distributions which are suitable for use with continuous variables. Other distributions include the exponential.

8.7   BINOMIAL DISTRIBUTION

We must now turn to discrete variables and look at theoretical distributions suitable for these cases. Discrete distributions are very common in risk management. One particular application is in calculating the number of accidents we may expect. Accidents can only assume a whole number as we have said before, and are therefore discrete. Any distribution of discrete variables would conform more to the drawing in Fig 8.6 and would not be suitable for treatment by the normal distribution, which was confined to continuous variables.

Rather than build an actual distribution every time we want to calculate probabilities for a discrete variable, we can turn to the family of theoretical probability distributions for discrete variables.

The binomial distribution is one such distribution. The basic philosophy underpinning the distribution is the same as for the normal distribution; we will have a mathematical equation which will describe a distribution which will be a good match for many real world problems involving discrete variables. Let us begin with a simple problem.

Let us say that you operate a fleet and each year half of the fleet is involved in some kind of accident. One particular branch has three vehicles and you want to calculate the probability of one of the vehicles being in an accident. Why you would want to do this is rather obscure but it will act as a suitable example for us in the meantime.

The basics of our problem are that the probability of a vehicle being in an accident is 0.5; half of all vehicles are usually involved in accidents. There are three vehicles and we want to know the probability of one vehicle, only, having an accident.

We know from our earlier work on probability that the probability of three vehicles having an accident would be $(0.5)(0.5)(0.5)$, i.e. P(1st and 2nd and 3rd having accidents) is 0.125. But what is the probability of one vehicle, only, being in an accident? We cannot simply say that it is P(1st in an accident and 2nd not and 3rd not) as we do not know that the first will be in an accident. It could well be the second or the third vehicle which has the accident. In other words we have a number of possible ways in which we could have one accident.

1st is involved 2nd is not involved 3rd is not involved
1st is not involved 2nd is involved 3rd is not involved
1st is not involved 2nd is not involved 3rd is involved

There are three ways in which one of the three vehicles could be involved in an accident, but we cannot forget that there may be no accidents at all, or two vehicles may be involved, etc. In the tree in Fig 8.13 we have drawn all the possibilities.

Fig 8.13

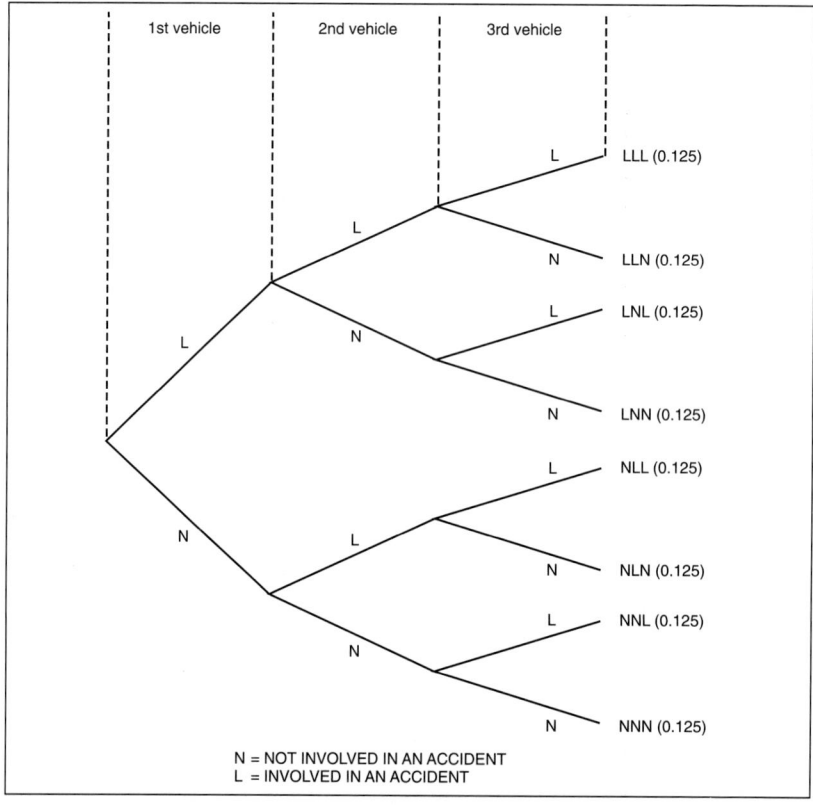

The Chances of One Vehicle Being Involved in an Accident

Of the eight possible ways our accident record may end up we can identify the three which involve only one accident.

LNN

NLN

NNL

The chance of one vehicle being in an accident is therefore ⅜ or 0.375. We could also have arrived at this figure by adding up the 0.125s at the tips of the tree in Fig 8.13 which involved only one accident.

You can imagine that this process would be very cumbersome if we had 25 vehicles and wanted to calculate the chance of 5 being in accidents. This is where the theoretical binomial distribution comes in.

If we can say that:

* we can only have two outcomes, e.g. success/failure, accident/no accident, fire/no fire

* the individual trials are independent, i.e. whether one vehicle is involved in an accident does not alter the probability of the second being involved in one, etc

* the probabilities do not change from trial to trial, i.e. the likelihood of fire does not increase over time, etc

then we can make use of the theoretical, binomial probability distribution.

You will recall from the discussion on the normal distribution that it was described by two parameters, the mean and the standard deviation. The binomial distribution is explained by n and p, where n is the number of trials, i.e. the number of cars, number of defective parts, etc, and p is the probability of success, i.e. the probability of having a specific number of defective parts, etc. Just as with the normal distribution we will be able to consult standard tables to obtain relevant probabilities. Before doing this, let us examine the two parameters. You will recall that the parameters of a theoretical distribution act in the same way as your own height, weight, chest size, arm length act in selecting an off-the-peg suit. You choose that suit which most closely matches your own measurements.

In the example we started with we had n = 3 and p = 0.5. This gave us eight possible ways in which we could have one vehicle involved in an accident. The eight possibilities are shown at the tips of tree in Fig 8.13. If we draw a histogram of these ways we would end up with the drawing in Fig 8.14. We had one way in which we could have no accidents, three ways we could have one accident, three ways we could have two accidents and one in which we could have three accidents.

We can see from the drawing that the probability of one vehicle being in an accident is 0.375. This is the figure we calculated earlier. As the value of n increases, the number of vehicles increases, then the shape of the distribution will change. As n gets larger the distribution becomes more peaked. For example if we now have five vehicles we find that there are 32 possible ways we could end up at the end of a year. You could draw the tree for this yourself and see if you agree. Of these 32 ways there are five which involve only one vehicle in an accident. The histogram is in Fig 8.15.

Fig 8.14

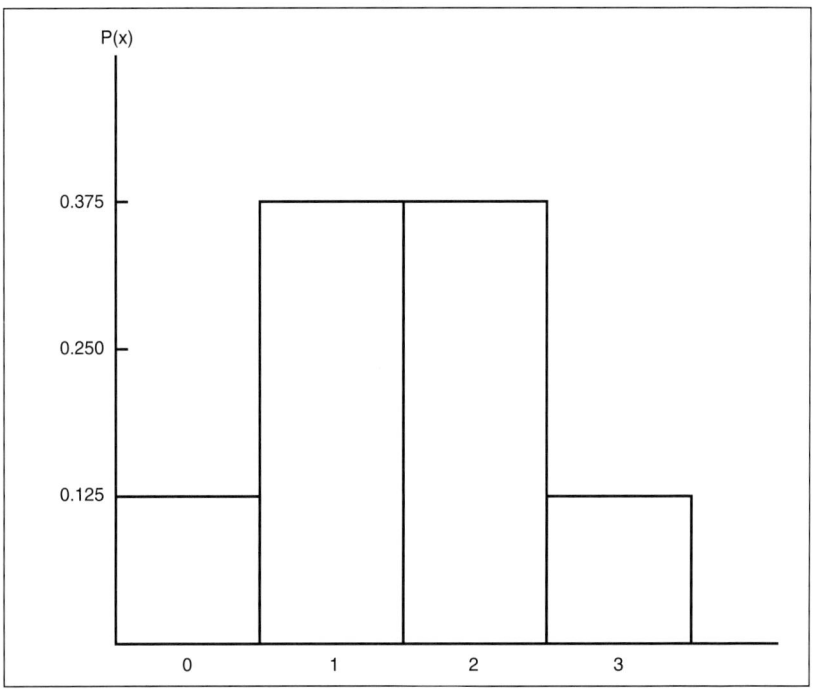

A Histogram Showing the Probability of Accidents

The probability of one of the five vehicles being in an accident is now 0.156. The parameter, n, has altered the shape of the distribution. As the number of trials, in this case the number of vehicles, increases then the distribution becomes more and more symmetrical, in fact it eventually assumes the characteristic bell shape of the normal distribution. However at the moment we can see that the parameter, n, has some effect on the distribution.

The other parameter is p, the probability of the event. In our examples so far we have kept this probability at 0.5. Let us see what effect a change to 0.1 would have.

If you go back to the drawing in Fig 8.13 you will see that each of the eight combinations had the same likelihood of occurring. This is due of course to the fact that the likelihood of a vehicle being involved in an accident was the same as not being involved in an accident. Let us change the probability to 0.1. It is now much less likely to have a vehicle in an accident. What effect will this have on the shape of the distribution?

Fig 8.15

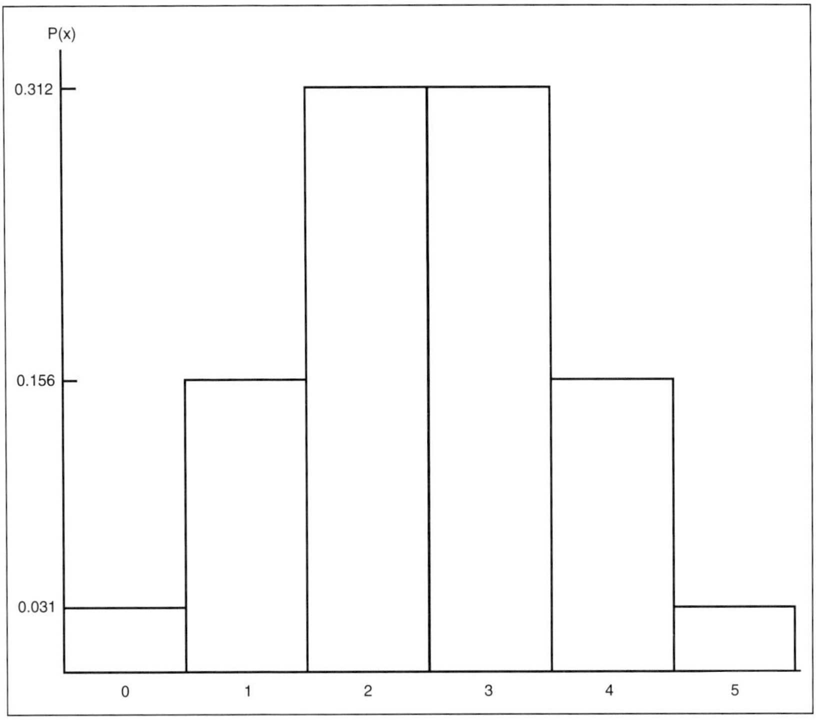

Probability Distribution of Accidents with 5 Vehicles

Well, we can list the eight possible outcomes and show their relative likelihoods:

L	=	0.1
N	=	0.9
LLL	=	0.001
LLN	=	0.009
LNL	=	0.009
LNN	=	0.081
NLL	=	0.009
NLN	=	0.081
NNL	=	0.081
NNN	=	0.729

The eight probabilities sum to one just as they did in Fig 8.13 but they are not all equal. The likelihood of one vehicle being in an accident is now:

$$
\begin{aligned}
LNN &= 0.081 \\
NLN &= 0.081 \\
NNL &= 0.081 \\
\hline
&\ \ 0.243
\end{aligned}
$$

This compares to a probability of 0.375 which we found when the probability of an accident was 0.5. We can draw the histogram of this new distribution and see what has happened to the shape of it.

Fig 8.16

			P		
n	r	0.05	0.1	0.25	0.5
3	0	857	729	422	125
	1	135	243	422	375
	2	007	027	141	375
	3	*	001	016	125
5	0	774	590	237	031
	1	204	328	396	156
	2	021	073	264	312
	3	001	008	088	312
	4	*	*	015	156
	5	*	*	001	031

n = number of trials, e.g. number of vehicles
r = number of events, e.g. number of accidents
P = the probability

In Fig 8.17 we can see that the shape is now quite skewed. The change in probability means that the likelihood of no accidents is fairly high and the chance of all vehicles being in accidents is very low. Notice that the change in the probability simply alters the shape of the distribution. A low probability of accident will give the positive skew in Fig 8.17 whereas a high probability of accident will give a negative skew, i.e. the peak would be to the right of the distribution.

What we need then are tables which will help us to find probabilities. An extract of one such table is shown in Fig 8.16.

To find a probability you locate the value of n, the value of r, and the probability. And so we would find the probability of having one accident from three vehicles where the probability is 0.5 by looking down the n column to 3, and then moving along the row corresponding to an r value of 1 to reach the column with a probability of 0.5. When we do this we find the probability to be 0.375. Use the table to find the probability of having one vehicle involved in an accident. You have three vehicles and the probability is 0.1 of a vehicle being in an accident. The figure should be the same as we found earlier, 0.243.

Fig 8.17

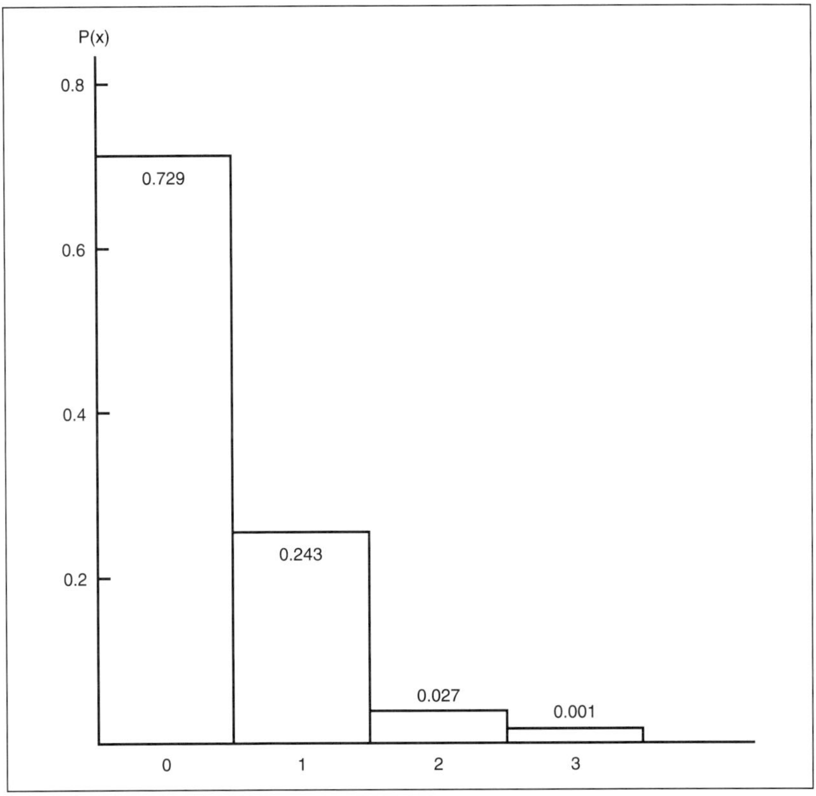

Accidents – The Change in Probability Skews the Shape

9

COMMUNICATING RISK

9.1   INTRODUCTION

We start from the position that communicating risk is difficult and different from many other communications tasks. We have looked at human behaviour and risk; we have examined a number of detailed risk identification and analysis techniques; we have looked at the role of statistical risk analysis and spent some time on probabilities. All of this work is not, however, an end in itself. The whole reason for studying these concepts is the hope that our eventual analysis of risk may be carried out more effectively. But what will happen to the findings of your risk analysis? Even assuming that all the techniques we have touched on in this text are applied expertly to each problem, what will happen then?

Clearly, the results of your analysis have to be acted upon and this will mean that they are communicated in some way. Just as the techniques in this text are not an end in themselves, so the analysis of risk is not an end in itself. There may be occasions when you yourself may take some action on the results of your analysis but there will also be many times when the results of your work will have to be communicated to others.

In this chapter we will look at a few general principles about communicating risk, move on to some detail on reports and then conclude with something on making oral presentations.

9.2   COMMUNICATING RISK INFORMATION

We said earlier that communicating risk information is a difficult task. Why should this be so ? There are three reasons we could suggest, although there will be many more that could be suggested.

The first is that generally, people do not find it comfortable or easy to think about unfortunate things in the future. We are much happier contemplating desirable things. We happily think about winning the lottery, going on holiday, etc. However, when it comes to the possibility of a loss, for example, or some other un-looked for or unfortunate event, we are much less comfortable. It might be that we are simply uncomfortable speculating about what might happen to us in an adverse kind of manner or that we do not think unfortunate events will actually happen to us – fires, accidents, etc always happen to someone else. Whatever the reason it is not something that most people take to naturally. Anyone who has ever been in the role of having to have colleagues think about disaster planning or business continuity in the event of a major incident will recognise the phenomenon. The second reason is the whole notion of dealing with uncertainty. Uncertainty is not something that forms part of the normal, formal education of most people and so when they come to it in later life it is perhaps not unexpected that they find the issue hard. The world of risk management is of course one in which uncertainty takes central stage and there are many people who prefer certainty, or at least the pretence of certainty, to uncertainty. The third is to do with the quantification of risk and the fact that some people are not too comfortable when it comes to handling statistical or quantitative data. Inevitably the measurement of risk will involve some number work, in certain cases some quite sophisticated numbers. We cannot expect that all those who read our reports or listen to us will have a firm grasp of whatever techniques we have used or will necessarily understand or need to understand the calculations that lie behind our assessment of risk.

These points must be borne in mind as we approach the topic of communicating risk. Our careful identification and measurement of risk will count for nothing if we fail at the last hurdle in communicating the results in a manner that can be understood by people. Before moving on to look at report writing we will pause to look at some alternative communication techniques that might be built into any report.

The first diagram in Fig 9.1 is a simple graphical representation of the two main characteristics of risk measurement, frequency and severity. Rather than write at length about variations in frequency and severity across different categories of risk, it is a simple matter to bring it all together in one picture. "One in the eye is always worth ten in the ear" is a very good maxim to have in mind. This diagram shows at a glance the key dimensions of risk and allows the reader to be directed to the main areas where energy needs to be expended. The example is simple but you can see how this would translate to many practical situations.

Fig 9.1

Frequency		
	(High)	● Domestic Fires
Severity		
(High)		(Low)
Nuclear Risks ●	(Low)	

A Simple Graphical Representation of Risk Measurement, Frequency and Severity

The second diagram, Fig 9.2, is the same kind of information but this time without the diagram. This indicates aspects or features of a risk, namely frequency, severity, predictability, and impact, with a qualitative description of what these features mean for the organisation. Types of events can then be slotted in against these descriptions to show what it would mean for the company or organisation. It clearly indicates those risks that will have a potentially catastrophic impact should they occur and separates them from predictable events, which because of their very predictability will have an insignificant impact.

The final point we make here before moving on to look at reports is one about the impact we want our results to have. In most cases we will be dealing with very busy people who do not have the time to pour over long reports and to draw out the relevance for them. The point has to be made simply and quickly. One useful technique in this respect is to think about risk equivalencies or risk relativities. Let us illustrate this with a few simple examples:

The first £x of turnover is needed to pay for motor fleet losses

Our theft losses equate to £x on the average price of every widget we sell

Total loss costs equal X% of trading profit

Someone was injured in our workplaces every X minutes

There is no particular magic about any of these statements but they do try to bring things home in a quick and simple manner. They are intended to make an impression and talk in a language that busy managers, particularly finance managers, will recognise.

Fig 9.2

L O W	FREQUENCY	–	HIGH
	SEVERITY	–	LOW
	PREDICTABILITY	–	HIGH
	IMPACT	–	INSIGNIFICANT
M I D	FREQUENCY	–	MEDIUM
	SEVERITY	–	MODERATE
	PREDICTABILITY	–	IRREGULAR
	IMPACT	–	SERIOUS
T O P	FREQUENCY	–	RARE
	SEVERITY	–	CATASTROPHIC
	PREDICTABILITY	–	POOR
	IMPACT	–	POSSIBLY RUINOUS

Risk Aspects: Frequency, Severity, Predictability and Impact

9.3   REPORTS

Risk analysis reports are extremely important but will only be one form of report which may be produced by the risk management department. Other reports which the department may produce include:

- the annual risk management report. This may be distributed widely within the company or may be for senior management consumption only.

- reports may be generated on major items of capital expenditure; you may wish to install a new security system, sprinkler system or build some fire defences. These items of expenditure will have to be justified and your justification included in a brief report.

- an annual report on losses within the company may be prepared. This could be separate from the annual report which has a far wider scope, and would concentrate on reporting the range of incidents which occurred. It may also point out or highlight lessons to be learned.

- the result of important decisions may be communicated in the form of a report. For example, the Safety Committee may have made some decision which will affect the duties of safety representatives and so a report may be prepared and distributed.

The list could go on and on. Whatever the report is about it must clearly reflect your intentions; whether it is a report intended to persuade people to your point of view, or to justify expenditure or simply to report facts, the report must perform the function you intended for it. In this course book we are primarily concerned with risk analysis but the comments we will make about report writing will hold true for many different forms of report.

We will concentrate on three aspects of report writing:

- preparation
- format
- writing

9.3.1 Preparation for Report Writing

Very few people will be able to sit down and write a good report without any preparation. Those who do, probably end up producing a report that looks 'quickly done'. Preparation is essential. It may be a bit frustrating to be preparing and apparently not actually writing anything but time spent in preparation is a wise investment.

A number of points should be borne in mind when preparing for report writing.

9.3.2 Know Your Reader

You must stand a far better chance of your report having the desired effect if you know who your reader is likely to be. Remember that all your reader knows will be contained on the printed pages of your report. You will not be there to amplify points, to give examples, to answer questions. The reader will read your report and form his opinion almost exclusively on the strength of it.

Viewed this way it is clear that a knowledge of the reader is essential if you hope to win him or her to your point of view. At least three aspects should be remembered.

a)   Language style. The wrong style of language could be a disaster. Writing a 'chatty' report to someone who prefers a far more formal approach can be just as bad as writing a terribly formal report to someone who responds to brief, chatty reports.

The choice is almost between a formal, impersonal style or a conversational, personal approach. Clearly there are many stages between these two extremes and the idea is to gauge where your reader is on that continuum.

As a general rule we could say that reports going up the way, to higher levels, tend to be more formal and impersonal than reports travelling along or downward. In addition, reports concentrating on financial matters tend to be less conversational than others. Obviously, a report about some critical incident or serious loss would not be written in an amusing, personal style of language.

Here are two different examples of ways in which the same thing could be reported. The first is much more formal than the second:

"The current problem, highlighted by the Finance Committee Convener, associated with time delays in small claims settlement could be resolved by allowing each subsidiary to create a fund out of which losses would be met, without reference to the centralised claims function."

"John Cumming has raised the problem of delays when subsidiary companies have to have small claims settled by the insurance department. How about letting each subsidiary settle their own claims up to £500 and reporting settlements to the insurance department twice a year?"

b)   Reader bias. The second point to bear in mind when thinking about the potential reader is to gauge whether or not he or she has any particular bias.

Your reader may be well known for disliking modern technology; he may be highly profit motivated, or safety conscious. It is important to gauge these things before framing the report.

It would be unfortunate if you were trying to acquire funds for the purchase of a computerised record keeping system and prepared a report assuming the reader was enthusiastic about computers, when in fact he or she was quite antagonistic towards modern technology. Knowing that he or she disliked computers would certainly condition how you should frame the report.

c)   Familiarity with the subject matter. Try also to ascertain how much your reader knows of the subject matter. You can avoid wasting space, and consequently time, if you find out how much he or she already knows about the issue under consideration. For example, if you are preparing a report on the possible purchase of a sprinkler system and find that the person who ultimately will make the decision is a mechanical engineer, then this will influence the report.

If on the other hand the decision maker was strictly a finance person then some of the technical terms and functions may have to be worded differently.

Try also to find out how much the reader knows about the background to the report. There is no point in including a lengthy introduction, painting the full background, if the reader is well acquainted with all of this. These points, and indeed many which will follow, may seem common sense. They are just that, but it is interesting to note the number of times that common sense seems to take a back seat. It does no harm to have these things brought to the forefront of our thinking.

9.3.3   Purpose

The second point to remember under the general heading of preparation is to establish the purpose of the report. The last thing you want is for a person to receive the report, read it and then say, "why did I get this report, what am I expected to do now, what was that all about?"

It is useful, at the very outset, to have a statement of the purpose of the report. You can keep this for your own use or can include it later at some point in the report. Having a purpose statement does help to focus attention on the business in hand and the job of preparing a statement of purpose can, itself, be a useful discipline.

The presence of a purpose statement should help avoid some of the reactions we mentioned above. In addition it may be possible to refer to previous correspondence or reports, previous meetings, the decisions at other meetings, etc. All of these should locate the purpose of the report in the mind of the reader and avoid confusion.

9.3.4   The Parameters of the Report

It is just as important to establish what the report does not cover as to establish what is covered. The purpose statement will give the broad purpose but the more particular parameters must also be defined.

For example, the purpose may be to prepare a report on industrial injury claims within the company. This may be the purpose but in addition you may define certain parameters, such as industrial injury claims made during the last financial year, industrial injury claims which were also the subject of civil action, etc. The purpose is the broad brush and the parameters more closely define the remit of the report.

It might then be useful to state in the report, possibly close to the purpose statement, that the report does not include the following, or that the report is limited to the following.

9.3.5   Management Support

For those reports where you are trying to persuade someone or some committee to your point of view then it is important that you have support. This touches on the very difficult area of 'corporate politics'. There is no denying that every organisation has its own form of politics. You cannot learn how to identify this, or deal with it, from a text book. It is very much something which you learn by experience, often hard experience.

Where you want to persuade someone to your point of view, or sell an idea or obtain permission for some action, then you will have to work out who is important in the decision making process. You would not want the report to be the first notice they had of your intentions.

In other words you may have to do some prior lobbying or selling.

9.3.6   Timing

Remember that someone has to read your report, or at least you hope they will read it. If this is the case then timing is important. Try not to send the report to someone when you know they are busy, when they are out of office, during heavy holiday periods, or at the run up to year ends or other crucial dates in the corporate calendar.

Timing could be crucial in obtaining the desired response to your report and so think carefully about it when preparing the report.

9.3.7   Format of the Report

Let us turn now to the report itself and consider the various formats it could take. All the preparation has been done and you are now ready to begin writing the report, but firstly you must work out what format or structure the report is to have.

A fairly straightforward format would be:

- title
- introduction
- body of the report
- summary
- conclusions and recommendations.

This is a simple structure and will not satisfy the needs of every kind of report but it is reasonably representative of what you might expect to find in many reports. We can look at each part in turn.

a)   Title. This would be a one page cover to the report and the title would explain the general purpose of the report. Often it is necessary to have an explanatory sub-title in addition to the main title, and so we have:

INDUSTRIAL INJURY CLAIMS

An evaluation of the cost of Industrial Injury Claims

Or,

GROUP INSURANCE COST

An analysis of the cost of insurance, for all group companies

In addition to the title you would also want to include your own department or name and the date the report is submitted.

b) Introduction. The introduction to a report can be fairly brief and should cover topics such as:

- the purpose
- the method
- the scope and parameters
- the definition of any technical terms used.

We have touched on most of these topics before, when we were discussing the preparatory work necessary. The list of definitions is important. In the case of a report on industrial injury claims you can imagine using words such as "claim", "absence", "injury", etc. Each of these words has a lay meaning and a more technical meaning, and so you will want to define each one clearly so that there is no ambiguity.

c) Body of the report. We are going to look at the actual writing of the report later but there are some general points we could make about the body of the report at this stage. This is the heart of the report and it is obviously important that it captures the real purpose of the whole report.

Each report will of course be quite different but there are possibly some general points which could apply across a wide range of reports:

- try and lead the reader to your conclusion. This is particularly the case if the report is intended to persuade someone to your point of view or is asking for permission to use funds, etc. You must try to frame the body of the report so that statements which are supportive of your case are made. Leading the reader to your conclusion is not easy but with a little practice you can develop the ability to leave the reader believing that there is little alternative to your recommendation.

- support your major statements. It is very easy to get carried away with the first point and to produce statements which cannot be supported. You can imagine a report which is attempting to persuade management to install a new security system at a particular plant. You want to lead the reader to the conclusion that money should be spent on buying the system for that plant.

If you get carried away with this desire you might make statements like, "this particular plant has the worst theft record in the group" or "more thefts take place at this plant than any other". These statements may well be accurate and could well convince the reader of your case. You will however need to support these statements with findings of some kind or another. Perhaps an appendix could be included which shows a comparison of theft losses for all plants. You cannot make such sweeping statements without providing supporting evidence.

- leave calculations to an appendix. It is often very difficult to maintain the impetus of the body of a report if it is continually interrupted by calculations. Statistics which support findings or conclusions, financial calculations, and any other forms of numbers can be assigned to an appendix without damaging the integrity of the report.

At the end of the day it is probable that only a few people will read through any calculations and those who do want to do this can still do so by consulting the appendix.

In the main we could generalize and say that most people are not terribly numerate. The average reader may well appreciate being relieved of the necessity to 'wade' through some 'heavy' calculations on the way to a conclusion.

- explain the significance and implications of your findings. Where important points are made then you should take time to explain their significance. This is not to imply that the reader could not work it out for him or herself but it is a useful reinforcement.

You could have come to the conclusion that the majority of claims from employees involve skin complaints. The report could then briefly outline the implications or significance of this finding:

"As the bulk of employee claims involve skin complaints it is essential that an immediate investigation takes place to establish:

i)   the nature of all chemicals and other substances handled by employees;
ii) the system of work for handling chemicals and hazardous substances;
iii) the current safety equipment;
iv) the extent to which current safety equipment is used and the extent to which employees are encouraged to use safety gear."

These implications of the major finding could have been worked out by any competent reader, but if the report highlights them then they are reinforced in the mind of the reader and there can be no ambiguity about what should now be done.

- calculate the cost of any recommendations. Following on from the previous point it is essential that all proposals are costed. There is little point in suggesting that a particular kind of glove be purchased or new washhand basins installed, etc, if costs are not given. Costs of all proposals should be included and properly stated. By properly stated we mean that they should be couched in terms that those involved in the finance of the company will appreciate.

Risk Management departments must submit their costings in just the same way as any other corporate function applies for funding. There is no point in relying on emotion or mystery alone.

- predict objections. Almost every report will be read by at least one person who objects to the findings or proposals suggested. (If only one person objects you are probably lucky.) It often seems as if people get a report and then feel that they must find at least one objection.

Try to anticipate these objections. For example, you may be suggesting that the company cancels all accidental damage cover on motor vehicles. You could reasonably anticipate that people will object on the grounds of the possible costs of such an idea. Either people will say that a large number of expensive incidents in the year could occur or that the company will be inundated with small 'scrapes and dents'. Try to anticipate these objections, for example, "some may suggest that a number of large, expensive incidents may occur during any one year and wipe out any cost savings by way of premium reductions. Our historical data does not support this view however. Over the last eighteen years we have never had more than three incidents per annum and on current day values the aggregate cost of claims has never exceeded £14,500. This is well within the expected savings."

Another point of view is that we may be inundated with a number of small claims on the basis that the "company will meet the bill". "This could have been a valid objection had it not been for the fact that we have been carrying a £1,000 accidental damage excess for the past five years and have experienced no increase in small claims over that period."

By anticipating these objections you may take some of the heat out of subsequent discussion. You may also prove to others that you have given sufficient thought to the issues.

- try to avoid your proposals being rejected. Everyone wants their proposals accepted but outright acceptance may not be too likely. What you want to do is to avoid an outright 'no'. For example, in the above example of cancelling the accidental damage cover you may think that the answer is either yes or no. You want to avoid the 'no' and so you may include an alternative to a straight 'yes' which is not 'no'.

For example you may suggest that if it is decided not to cancel the cover, that an alternative may be either to reduce the accidental damage cover to catastrophe cover or postpone a decision and monitor the claims for a year.

Either way the report does not end up on the shelf. It is likely that at least one of the alternatives will be selected, and this still keeps the issue alive.

d) Summary. A brief but concise summary should be placed at a suitable point in the report. Remember that many people may only read the summary and so it should cover all the essential points and make mention of the main conclusions.

e)   Conclusions and Recommendations. This is the 'bottom' line of the report. Many people will read the introduction, the summary, and skip over the body of the report to get to the conclusions.

State the main conclusions clearly and list all recommendations, leaving no ambiguity in the mind of the reader.

These five points all referred to the format of the actual report itself. We now turn our attention to the business of actually writing the report.

9.3.8   Writing the Report

It is very difficult to know what to say about writing the report without going back to the basic rules we learned at school. There are possibly one or two points which should be remembered.

a)   Avoid using jargon. Plain English is usually good enough for most reports. We have all read reports where people had to,

"operate within fixed cost envelopes"
"access funds from an ever decreasing reserve"
"prioritise capital projects"
"rank products profit-wise"

These may look good to you but are probably not highly regarded by others. One area where jargon is rampant is that of the computer and those who have begun using the computer often have a zeal for it which is reflected in their language.

The request to, "purchase a Winchester in order to bump up the RAM to 20 megabytes in order to dispense with the double density floppies, now that the new generation DB package is operational" will most probably leave people rather cold ... acceptance-wise!

b)   Use simple words and phrases. There is a great temptation when writing a report to get out the *Roget's Thesaurus* and use a 'fancy' word when a simple word would do.

This usually impresses nobody but yourself.

c)   Avoid padding out the report with unnecessary words and phrases. The quality of a report is often in inverse proportion to its quantity. As someone once said, "verbosity often conceals a paucity of ideas".

There are certain phrases and words which creep into many reports and are really not necessary.

"At this point in time the value of the premiums in monetary terms is continuing to maintain a steady increase. The reason for this may be due to the fact that the number of claims has not followed a downward trend."

Try and reduce the above paragraph. We could easily put a line through:

- at this point in time
- the value of
- in monetary terms
- continuing to maintain a steady
- the reason for this
- due to the fact
- not followed a downward trend.

By editing out these unnecessary phrases we could end up with:

"Premiums have continued to increase due to a corresponding rise in claims."

It is a useful discipline to read over a report you wrote a number of weeks or years ago and see how you would re-write it today.

d)   Use short paragraphs. You may often have picked up a report and it looked like one long paragraph from start to finish. People like to read short sharp paragraphs.

They can only retain a certain amount in their mind at one time and while reading a long paragraph will almost certainly lose track of what it was about.

Split long paragraphs in order to make the report easier to read. You can make use of headings, numbering, underlining, etc. All of these ideas help to split up a page and help the reader.

These are very general points about report writing itself and you should try to look over a number of reports in your department, looking for useful help and being critical where appropriate.

9.4   ORAL PRESENTATIONS

The final topic we will look at is the business of making oral presentations. Much of what we have said about preparing to write the report will apply to the preparatory work necessary for making an oral presentation.

One or two specific points could be made:

i)   Try and have a look at the room in which the presentation is to be made beforehand. This will ensure that there is somewhere to place your notes, the seating is as you would like it, and any visual aid equipment is ready for use.

ii)   Speak slowly and distinctly. There is little point in preparing an excellent report and then muff your way through it to the extent that no one understands a word.

iii) Use visual aids if you can. Listening to the one voice for any length of time can be monotonous and it is quite valuable to have slides or a flip chart to use. People can then, at least, have the diversion of looking at something.

Make sure however that the visual aid can be seen. There is nothing more annoying to an audience than a slide being put up and taken away before it can be read. In addition you must ensure that the print on any slide is of a size that it can be read, and of course you should not stand in front of the screen. Try to avoid the temptation of letting the technology run away with the presentation. Many will have been at presentations when the use of technology to prepare the 'all singing all dancing' presentation has left the audience cold and not able to see behind the glitz.

iv)   Try to look at the audience as much as possible. It is very easy for people in a group, especially a large group, to feel left out and eventually disinterested in the proceedings. Try to look at the people. It used to be the case that public speakers were advised to fix their eye on something at the back of the room so that they would not be distracted. This may help the speaker but doesn't do much for the audience.

v) If you have to read notes, try to make sure that your notes are in order. Try also to avoid it sounding as if you are reading notes. You can certainly add to this list from your own experience of listening to oral presentations.

To conclude, let us say that communicating the result of your risk analysis is often the end result of all the work and as such assumes quite an importance. Do not spend hours on a risk analysis project and spoil all chances of having your findings recognized by rushing at communicating the results.

General Index to Risk Analysis